widening horizons

by mining the wealth of creative thinkers

to seize the empowering
potentials of the digital age
with artists as precursors and basic income as the means

vivan storlund

To Malin, Erik and Stina with the hope that you, during your lifetime, will live in a world where the economy serves the good life for everyone, that we, Keynes' grandchildren have not yet been able to experience.

CONTENTS

PREFACE

We live in exciting times with a new era — the digital era — taking shape in astonishing new forms. Artificial intelligence and machine learning algorithms combined with the vast growth of available data bring the whole world to our fingertips. The sharing economy generated by the creative commons and open source offer a forceful alternative to the neoliberal economic culture. New forms of production bring us closer to a zero marginal cost society. And the internet of money could release us from the impasse in which the present economic system keeps us. To put it in the words of the Bitcoin champion, Andreas Antonopolous, things that were unthinkable have in today's digital age become thinkable. About the Internet of Money Antonopolous says "[i]t's coming faster than you can imagine. It's deeper than you can fathom. It's more sophisticated than you can immediately understand. ... It is a gift to the entire world".[1]

One outstanding example of what can be achieved with open source is Linux that has exceeded Microsoft Windows in market share in the server industry. Phil Champagne observes that Linux has so far demonstrated that the greater good and self-interest can work in concert. And an interesting feature of the digital age is that this openness ensures a high level of integrity not achievable in proprietary software. It ensures an autonomy for the players as opposed to the business world, where it is the reputation of the company responsible for the software that determines what it is supposed to do (Champagne, 2014: 26, Kindle location 412).

This is a time of great opportunities that are there to be seized. With these dynamic processes many societal structures that were tailored for the industrial society have exceeded their best before date. Whether they were best is a matter to be discussed at length in this book. To hold fast to

---

[1] The Internet of Money, Volume Two, Kindle location 171

obsolete structures is not only a nuisance, it can be very harmful. The new order that is in the making in the information and communication society is full of empowering potentials. It is at the grassroots level that innovations take place. To make these potentials available to everybody, we need to get rid of the shackles of old institutions and thought structures.

We are in the midst of a pulling game, with two teams pulling in opposite directions. The forceful changes that the digital age has brought about is met with an equally strong resistance from those who do not stand to gain from these developments. It is a process of change and drags on change. A central question is therefore, when will we reach critical mass that will allow the creative and empowering forces now in motion to win the day.

A central message of this book is that to catch up with societal change we need to redefine what we mean by work. We need to substitute the present perception of work that was tailored for the industrial society with a recognition of the nature of activities in which people are engaged. The status of artists is here central as their work does not fit the industrial rationale with its notion of work as employment. Yet, artists' contribution is central in many respects that will be spelled out at length in these pages. We thus urgently need to recognise the work that is factually done, to give it the value it is due and to compensate it in some form or other. One means is a universal basic income. As a basic income should be unconditional, it would offer a fertile ground for a much-needed bottom-up reorganisation of society. Maslow's need hierarchy gives interesting hints at where people's energies might be directed, once basic needs such as food and safety, security of body and other essential resources are catered for (Maslow 1943).

Basic income would allow people to move higher up in the need hierarchy. It would free space for things such as personal development. It would also boost creativity — immaterial production — that in fact already since some time now, has overtaken physical production as a driving economic force.

This book is based on 14 articles, conference papers and studies exploring societal change and accompanied challenges and potentials during the period 2001 to 2017. They deepen the issues I raised in my doctoral thesis *To each one's due at the borderline of work – Toward a theoretical framework for economic, social and cultural rights* (2002). The papers = chapters can be read independently of each other but taken together they offer the bigger picture of what should be done to remove obstacles that often constitute violations of economic, social and cultural rights and also impede the potentials of the digital age. For those papers that have been published I wish to thank the publishers for the right to use them here, acknowledged at the respective chapter.

There are many persons that have passed my way as discussion partners along my research path, to whom I wish to address my sincerest thanks. I can here only single out a few: in the field of human rights, ambassador emerita Anja-Riitta Ketokoski-Rexed and in the world of work professor emeritus Reinhold Fahlbeck. In civil society matters my thanks go to Aaro Harju, General Secretary of the Citizens' Forum. The artistic field opened up to me through my contacts in Malta among whom I wish to express my gratitude to the late professor of philosophy Peter Serracino Inglott as well as to the cultural 'super activist' actor, playwright, film-maker Narcy Calamatta. In Malta I wrote one of the two most challenging papers, *Artistic work a precursor of work in ICT society*. Through the artist association Suna I partook in running a gallery, Galleria Espoonsilta in Finland, that gave me first-hand experience of the often burdensome circumstances in which artists create their art. On the basic income score, the activities of the Basic Income Earth Network – BIEN in Finland, Europe and the Netherlands have been essential. Having moved to the Netherlands I wish to express my gratitude to Adriaan Planken, former chair of the Dutch Vereniging Basisinkomen, both for animated discussions and for introducing me, as a newcomer, to a number of activities and persons. In the Netherlands I wrote the second most challenging paper *Humanism versus neoliberalism*. I'm grateful to Leon J.J. Segers and Johan Horeman for helping me through the painstaking task of trying to make some sense of the economy. Furthermore, I wish to thank professor emerita Pirjo Kukkonen who inspired me to join international semiotics conferences where I presented the last three papers. And my warm thanks go to friends and family for animated discussions over the years around the topics raised in this book.

The great potentials that the internet offers and the amazing power of algorithms from which we profit on a daily basis, made me want to make it part of my publishing process. So, I opted for self-publishing. Without Jelle Schutte's and Robin Ketelaars' technical expertise this would not have been possible, so for this my warmest thanks. I also wish to express my appreciation for all the good advice I've got from people who share their knowledge and experience on the internet. Among them I want to mention Mark Dawson, Jane Friedman and Dave Chesson. Thanks! For me as an independent researcher, it is great to be part of the digital community.

Amsterdam, August 2018
Vivan Storlund

INTRODUCTION

The future of work is an issue that is being raised with increasing frequency. Working life has undergone profound changes due to a declining industry in developed economies, flexibilisation of working life, globalisation as well as information and communication technologies, with algorithms as an ultimate 'job-killer'. Here two random picks: Carl Benedikt Frey's and Michael A. Osborn's research from 2013 indicate that around 47 per cent of the 702 occupations they studied in the US are in the high risk category of disappearing.[2] In 2017, Janna Q. Anderson proposes that in the next few decades work in most conventional settings will be to nearly 100 percent accomplished by either 1) algorithm-driven software/machines that already accomplish a great deal of work, or 2) human-and-algorithm-based partnership.[3] According to some research, one profession that can relax a bit about their future is archaeologists. So how are we to go about these changes? Shall we talk, as some people do, of the emergence of a class of useless people? This is a utilitarian view that only sees people as cogs in an economic machinery. According to labour legislation, again, work equals employment. This is indeed a very narrow perception of work that disregards the profound changes and the great variety of forms in which work is performed. This legal deficiency has resulted in a growing precariat.

A redefinition of work is urgently required to take account of the variety of forms in which work is performed, as well as the different nature of activities (work) that people pursue. If we focus on people's activities in

---

[2] Frey, Carl Benedikt and Osborne, Michael A., The Future Of Employment: How Susceptible Are Jobs To Computerisation? September 17,2013 https://www.oxfordmartin.ox.ac.uk/downloads/academic/The_Future_of_Employment.pdf, accessed 4.2.2018

[3] Precarious times for traditional human 'employment' and the economy https://medium.com/@jannaq/the-,robot-takeover-is-already-here-5aa55e1d136a

their own right and accord them a value, talk about unemployment becomes meaningless as people ordinarily do something. Artists are a profession that never has fitted the employment model. Although art and culture has always contributed to both spiritual and material wealth, and increasingly so with a dynamic creative sector, artists who create outside an employment relationship or without a grant, will not profit economically from their contribution. A profound paradigmatic change is therefore required to disentangle human activities from the conceptual stronghold of current legislation and practices. This is what this book is about.

A paradigmatic change requires reconsiderations at several levels. At a theoretical level I will depart from theories of social justice that offer a conceptual apparatus for analysing present trends and their effects on people and the activities in which they are engaged. At a legal level economic, social and cultural rights provide the legal standards against which work is considered, with artists as a case study of a profession that has longstanding experience of not fitting into the labour law model. Conditioned by both our theoretical landscape and legislation, administrative practices contribute their share to present day impasses and need to be reformed, thus a third level.

This is a daunting reform agenda to which I wish that this book would bring a contribution. Because as Aristotle has fittingly put it: "Investigation of reality is in a way difficult, in a way easy. An indication of this is that no one can attain it in a wholly satisfactory way, and that no one misses it completely: each of us say something about nature, and although as individual we advance the subject little if at all, from all of us taken together something sizeable results — and as the proverb has it, who can miss a barn-door." (Aristotle, cited in Barnes, 1985:17)

There is an urgent need to map out and steer the profound societal changes we have been surrounded by during the past few decades, and still are. To put the concerns of this book in a comprehensive perspective, I want to cite Yuval Noah Harari who in his book *Sapiens, A Brief History of Humankind*, in an enchanting way shows how we base our reality on myths. Since large-scale cooperation is based on myths, he says, the way people cooperate can be changed by changing the myths — by telling different stories. Harari mentions one instance when the myth changed almost overnight — the French revolution. Thus, in 1789, people switched from believing in the myth of the divine right of kings to believing in the myth of the sovereignty of the people. Homo sapiens has been able to revise its behaviour rapidly in accordance with changing needs, Harari observes (2011: 36).

With the motto of the French revolution, liberty, equality, fraternity, myth had it that the human entered centre-stage. But this has long been a myth rather than reality. Instead we are constantly faced with a drama where ordinary people's conditions of life have been challenged by the state, the church or the economy with variations in emphasis over time. And as myth has it, there is a neutral empire that spells out the truth = the academic community. One of the myths that we live by in the theoretical world is that that there are scientific truths that we need to abide by. How these 'truths' have changed over time provides the storyline of this book, the red line being 'it all boils down to perception'. This book is made up of articles and conference papers that I have written to deepen aspects I investigated in my doctoral thesis *To each one's due at the borderline of work. Toward a theoretical framework for economic, social and cultural rights* (2002).[4]

The incentive for my research was the deep structural changes that set in after the oil crisis in the 1970s, and how these changes have altered the societal rationale from one of the industrial society to today's information and communication society, the ICT society. In opposition to the view of objective scientific truths, I join those who see our theoretical landscapes as human-made expressions of values. Many scholars make the pertinent

[4] http://ethesis.helsinki.fi/julkaisut/oik/julki/vk/storlund/

point that it is not only an academic or theoretical matter to react to present changes. On the contrary, postmodernism has very much to do with our own plans of life, our lifestyle and the ways we interact with others in society, as well as with our choice of political agenda.

Thanks to information and communication technologies civil society offers unprecedented opportunities for people to assume a role as active players on a large scale. Many scholars also see civil society as the societal sector where new solutions will be found in a fractured world, to borrow the theme of World Economic Forum in Davos in 2018. Today humanity is, at least in the affluent part of the world, at a juncture where there is ample scope for human aspirations, creativity and artistic creation that conveys a human perspective on life. Such human energies are, however, often constrained partly because of legacies of old times, partly by new restraints such as today's one-dimensional focus on money and competition. Here we have the paradox that never before has the work of an individual been more central in the value creating process. But independently of qualifications, people are increasingly submitted to the mercy of a changed working life that generates a growing precariat. This development, scholars emphasise, is not due to any 'inherent necessity'. It is an expression of a process of a changing relationship between capital and labour.

Layout of the book

This book is based on 14 articles exploring societal change and accompanied challenges and potentials during the period 2001 to 2017. All papers revolve around the question how we at a level of perception deal with:
- the individualising trend that has been part of societal change
- the diversification of working life and the growing volume of precarious work
- the role of art and civil society

- the conceptual changes that are required to make sense of these changes, as well as
- giving affected persons their proper space and appreciation.

By 2007 I had reached the point in my investigations where I saw a basic income as an appropriate remedy for the problems I had identified. This implied for me a tipping point from problem orientation to solution. Another tipping point occurred when I realised that neuroscience and semiotics offered missing links in my search up till 2015 for an understanding of how and why things are the way they are. As all papers = chapters revolve around the same core there is repetition on a number of points. However, it is my intention that all chapters can be read independently as the book cover several areas, the main ones being working life, art, civil society and basic income and theoretical questions associated with them. The chapters also picture my search for an understanding of the things I investigate at the time of writing, reflecting also the change of focus from human rights to semiotics and neuroscience. I will start with the three most recent papers:

1. Uncovering a new societal reality — could basic income be a stabilising driver? (2015). This paper offers a synthesis of major societal changes and how a basic income could act as a stabilising driver, steering the development in a human-centred direction.[5]

5 Published in Finnish in an shortened version - Olisiko perustulosta muuttuvan työelämän vakauttajaksi?, in Vihreä Tuuma, the net journal of the Green think-tank Ajatuspaja Vision, 5.3.2015 http://www.vihreatuuma.fi/artikkeli/olisiko-perustulosta-muuttuvan-tyoelaman-vakauttajaksi, and presented in a working group at the congress of the International Semiotics Institute, Kaunas, Lithuania in 2016

2. Translating between paradigms (2016). Here I rely on neuroscience and semiotics as disciplines that could throw some light on many questions that had puzzled me along my research path. An intriguing phenomenon that neuroscience reveals is that the brain's left hemisphere's 'way of being' that decontextualizes, is abstract and provides instrumental feedback, is more culturally contagious than the right hemisphere that relate to us as humans of flesh and blood. It is suggested that slowly but surely, the left hemisphere's perspective will shape our culture in such a way that the culture begins to respond to it as the dominant one. The way the neoliberal economic culture has occupied and overtaken many human-centred activities is a case in point.[6]

3. Humanism versus neoliberalism (2017). This paper deepens the analysis of the way the neoliberal world-view has invaded the human sphere, bringing the analysis to a more concrete level. The way the neoliberal economic tradition has come to dominate over human aspects and a good life is blatantly exposed in today's Greece, the cradle of western civilisation. This is illustrated through the way the troika, the European Central Bank, ECB, the European Commission, EC, and the International Monetary Fund, IMF, have made Greece a 'morality tale' for economic behaviour.[7]

The storyline that has brought me to these last three texts will unfold in the rest of the book. Having, in a legal context, made a 180-degree change of perception from what the law says (legal positivism) to the implications of ill-functioning legal systems that raise questions of human

[6] Presented in a working group at the congress of the International Semiotics Institute, Kaunas, Lithuania in 2016

[7] Presented in a working group at the congress of the International Semiotics Institute, Kaunas, Lithuania in 2016

rights and justice, I felt that I was faced with a formidable research task. In addition to insisting on human rights I also convey my concerns that the rule of law or the *Rechtsstaat* should be there for everybody and not only for those holding power. I have likened this research agenda to an elephant that you cannot eat in one go, but that you have to consume bit by bit. This is what the ensuing articles do, making their way to the last three papers.

Working life the point of departure

4. Reflexive labour law (2001). Working life is the sphere of life in which people often in a concrete way feel the effects of changing societal conditions. A first matter to acknowledge when addressing present day challenges is to recognise that what has been considered as standard work, is no longer sufficient as a standard. Account must be taken of the multi-facetted categories of work that for all too long has been called atypical. Precarious work is the appropriate term.[8]

5. Art the key to a transition from HR to HB - from human resources to human beings (2004). Artistic work assists in displaying the changing makeup of information and communication society. Within a span of a few decades, people have been expected to transmute from passive men and women by the assembly line, subdued to cost-effectiveness in time and movement, to a person who is expected to be one's own architect of fortune, a policy aspiration now often articulated. These aspirations reflect a

[8] Presented at a seminar Reflexive Labour Law: Next Step, 13-14.12.2001, associated with the book Reflexive Labour Law, Kluwer 1994, Ralf Rogowski, Ton Wilthagen (eds.)

decisive change of emphasis in social and political organisation, that has not yet been properly reflected in legislation and legal practices.[9]

6. Time to give artists their due - A matter of perception (2004/2006). What would our recollection of history be, if we did not have the work of artists conveying to us past times and cultures? Throughout time, most artists have had to struggle for their material survival while doing what they had to do — create. There has not been much improvement in this regard notwithstanding the human rights standards introduced during the past century, particularly economic, social and cultural rights. Artistic work is work, and it has a value, independently of whether it generates money or not.[10]

7. Artistic work — a precursor of work in ICT society (2005). How should labour and social security legislation be redesigned to accord legal protection to persons working in so called atypical work formats on a par with the legal protection accorded those we term typical? This question involves international labour standards and human rights. Equally, it raises questions of fundamental prerequisites of a legal order, such as predictability, legal certainty, equality before the law, etcetera. Questions have to be put differently when art and culture is involved than when the primary function of a job is to secure one's material subsistence. It requires looking at work from a perspective that is perhaps as far removed

---

[9] In A journey of Exploration: Composing Europe, European Identity Cultural Caravan April 4th -11th 2004 (Eds.) Miha Pogacnik -, InnoVatio Verlag, Bonn 2004, p. 180-195

[10] In Mediterranean Seascapes, Proceedings of an International Conference, Navigation du Savoir Project, Valletta, Malta 2004, (Ed.) Simon Mercieca, Malta University Publishers Ltd. 2006, p. 309-318

as can be from the ideal-type underpinning labour law — a male blue-collar worker. Artists can be seen as precursors of work in ICT society.[11]

8. Recognising artists' rights: A new challenge to the human rights paradigm (2006). Artistic work is a strange bird in our legal culture, particularly so in labour law that is permeated by the logic of industrial production. We therefore have difficulties in envisaging the kind of protection that labour law should accord artists as well as other persons, whose work differs from the standard on which labour law is based. To recognise artistic and cultural work and to introduce appropriate provisions for such work is a compelling need in order to catch up with societal change.[12]

The bigger picture of human rights and basic income

9. Civil society – Conditions for an active citizenship (2006). What conditions are required to allow people to act as active citizens? This is something that changes over time, where different kinds of structural and legal as well as cultural restraints condition people's abilities to take an active part in civil life. To get a perspective on the challenges facing us today, it is instructive to see how enlightenment philosophers have addressed these questions. For them the rule of law, free markets, democracy and freedom of association where seen as means to overcome obstacles deriving from old power centres. All these issues that we now take for granted

---

[11] In Liber Amicorum Reinhold Fahlbeck, (Eds.) Birgitta Nyström, Annamaria Westregård, Hans-Heinrich Vogel, Juristförlaget I Lund, Lund 2005, p. 543-572

[12] In Mediterranean Journal of Human Rights, Volume 10 Number 1 2006, Faculty of Laws, University of Malta, p. 161-183

involved in their time great controversy, particularly so freedom of association. Against this background focus lies on today's challenges.[13]

10. Conditions for democracy — economic, social and cultural rights in focus (2007). How well does democracy materialise today? How have changes in working life and social security affected people's ability to go about their life? What are the conditions for work in civil society? We need to consider what values are involved in the work done, and devise means of financing it, so that people are allowed to pursue the work of their own choice. A universal basic income could be a first step to remedy much of the problems that people outside the conventional working life encounter. It would correct some of the most blatant injustices and nuisances.[14]

11. A global basic income — compensation and investment (2009). A global problem requires global solutions. While taxpayers' money is used to save financial institutions from a crisis caused by reckless behaviour, innocent people lose their jobs, homes, pensions, or in other ways the control of their lives. On a worldwide scale, the satisfaction of everybody's basic needs in the form of a global basic income, could have tremendous preventive effects on measures that people may resort to in desperation, such as child labour, prostitution, drug trafficking, organ trade and trafficking, as well as migration that often results in human trafficking. Such preventive effects should also be accounted for in a cost — benefit calculus.[15]

---

[13] Conditions for an active citizenship - A problem inventory. A conceptual study for the project Conditions for an active citizenship, Experiences of civil activities at Pappilantie, Espoo, 2006, unpublished

[14] Unpublished

[15] Unpublished

12. Basic Income: How it Fits the Policy Framework for Green Jobs (2011). When green is the qualifying criterion for work rather than profit or economic growth, the world of work and the economic scenario in which it has to operate assumes a different dimension. Work in the intersection between employment and entrepreneurship can be characterised as 'meaningful', as there is some value attached to it that the pursuer considers worth striving for, as opposed to a bread-winning job. How work in this sector should be compensated is a big challenge, to which a basic income could be a solution. A basic income would serve the environment in multiple ways as it facilitates people's individual work that often is small-scale and thereby mostly local and light. A basic income would assist in levelling the very uneven playing field we face on many fronts.[16]

13. Basic income and the value of work (2012). Hardly any piece of the jigsaw puzzle that the industrial society was made of fits today's reality. New bits and pieces need to be gathered to display the bigger picture of today's information and communication society — its challenges as well as the opportunities it offers. A basic income could

- counterbalance injustices and undo knots in institutional structures that have passed their best before date;
- reduce the price people have had to pay for reckless behaviour in the financial and business world;
- favour entrepreneurial activities that are more focussed on people's needs than big business does;
- favour artistic work, contributing thereby to a greatly expanding sector that do people good and does not burden mother earth;
- reduce our ecological footprints;

[16] Chapter 6 in Green Jobs from a Small State Perspective. Case studies from Malta. Saviour Rizzo (ed) Green European Foundation – Fondazzoni Ceratonia, 2011[16] 2011, p. 55-64.

- generate a virtuous circle with spin off effects for people as well as local and national economies.[17]

14. Human rights update — from sovereignty to coexistence (2003 /2015). In this paper we travel centuries in time and, as a logical consequence of the new human rights paradigm, we make a 180 degree change of perception from an undifferentiated departure in state sovereignty to the human being as a point of departure. Also, the role of the researcher has changed from an allegedly disinterested neutral observer of facts that can be scientifically verified, to one that mediates between theory and practice. I call this constellation a 'we paradigm'.

---

[17] Paper presented in working group at the Basic Income Earth Network (Bien) Congress, München 14-16 September 2012 Pathways to a Basic Income, HOW: The Big Picture – Social and Political Dimensions http://www.bien2012.org/sites/default/files/paper_150_en.pdf

CHAPTER 1

MAPPING OUT A NEW SOCIETAL REALITY

2016 - International Semiotics Institute Congress
23–26.6. Kaunas, Lithuania

Information and communication technology and globalisation have been major drivers for profound changes surrounding us, that can be epitomised through the title of Jeremy Rifkin's book The Zero Marginal Cost Society, The Internet of Things, the Collaborative Commons, and the Eclipse of Capitalism (2014). This is a paradigm shift — big time — full of both threats and potentials. So, the question is: How shall we go about these changes?

The question I want to explore is what role basic income could play in strengthening positive traits and counterbalancing dangerous ones in present developments. Could basic income steer development toward more just societies? In a paradigm shift the intellectual categories that we have used to understand what surround us are no longer appropriate. A collective effort is therefore required to grasp the new reality. Here guidance from Aristotle for my quest for cooperation on this score. To investigate reality is, he said, in a way difficult, in a way easy. No one can attain it in a wholly satisfactory way, and no one misses it completely. We all have our understanding and although we as individual persons don't advance the subject matter very much, from all of us taken together something sizeable results — and as the proverb has it, who can miss a barn-door (Cited in Barnes, 1985: 17). Here is my take on challenges and opportunities and the role a basic income could play.

Where we stand today

I will here draw on some scholars who have captured the bigger picture by mapping out present day changes and pointing to the challenges they pose as well as the opportunities they offer. They are Manuel Castells, Jeremy Rifkin, Guy Standing and Richard Florida. There is an urgent need for a new approach to understanding the kind of economy, culture and society in which we live, Manuel Castells says in the preface to the 2010 edition of The Rise of the Network Society (1996). Crises have been piling up in the first decade of the 21st century he notes listing financial crisis, upheaval in business and labour markets and a growing global criminal economy. Furthermore, he notes that large parts of the population are socially and culturally excluded from global networks that accumulate knowledge, wealth and power. There is religious fundamentalism and violence of different kinds. Yet another set of problems that Castells mentions is the environmental crisis and the incapacity of political institutions based on the nation-state to handle global problems and local demands. "[T]hese are all expressions of a process of multidimensional, structural change that takes place in the midst of agony and uncertainty." "These are indeed troubled times", Castells concludes.

Jeremy Rifkin foresees a struggle between the economy as we know it, and the collaborative commons that is now emerging. He predicts that the struggle between these competing paradigms is going to be protracted and hard fought. The capitalist system has peaked and begun its slow decline. Instead we have the collaborative commons that brings us ever closer to a near zero marginal cost society. "The once unchallenged prowess of capitalism is diminishing, making way for an entirely new way of organizing economic life in an age characterized by abundance rather than scarcity." Rifkin concludes: "A new economic model is emerging in the twilight of the capitalist era that is better suited to organize a society in which more and more goods and services are nearly free." (2014: 9)

Guy Standing, whose focus lies on working life and the emergence of the precariat, says: "Across the world, there is an energy building around the precariat. It is organizing, and struggling to define a new forward march." (Standing 2011: 6) And he warns: "There is a danger that, unless the precariat is understood, its emergence could lead society towards a politics of inferno. This is not a prediction. It is a disturbing possibility." (2011: 9)

Among these scholars Richard Florida is the one with the least complicated message. As an urban theorist he has mapped out the greatly expanding creative sector and its relation to urban economic development. The focus in his research is on the central players in this process that he singles out as a new class, the creative class. The creative class should therefore be added to the collaborative commons as a major driving force during the past decades. But Florida also warns of the social divide that is caused by the decline in industry. We have a fundamental task ahead of us to overcome the class-divide that weakens the social fabric and threatens economic well-being. Florida's message is that new forms of social cohesion needs to be constructed in a world defined by increasing diversity and beset by growing fragmentation.[18]

An interesting aspect that these scholars bring forth is that we all partake in this new setting. Castells notes that this is not a purely academic debate. Cooperation is needed to jointly steer an increasingly dangerous world. We need to realise the diversity and complexity of our world, the contradictory dynamics between global markets and local identities, and the tension between a common technological paradigm and divers institutional uses of technology (Identity preface 2010).

---

[18] The Rise of the Creative Class And How It's transforming Work, Leisure, Community and Everyday Life, 2002: 318.

Working life is the sector of society in which we ordinary folks most directly feel the effects of these changes. In his book *The End of Work* Jeremy Rifkin drew, in 1995, our attention to how new technology would do away with jobs, and that this will pose enormous challenges both for society at large and us as individuals. Rifkin saw as the single most pressing issue the need to redefine the role of the individual in a near workerless society. "The wholesale substitution of machines for workers is going to force every nation to rethink the role of human beings in the social process. Redefining opportunities and responsibilities for millions of people in a society absent of mass formal employment is likely to be the single most pressing social issue of the coming century." (1995: xv)

In addition to the effects of technology, we also have the effects of flexibilisation of working life and globalisation. Guy Standing paints a chilling picture of the effects of changes in working life in three books, *Work after Globalisation* (2009), *The Precariat: The New* Dangerous Class (2011) and *A Precariat Charter, From denizens to citizens* (2014). In working life, people are bit by bit stripped of both income and rights. People have been reduced from citizens to denizens, which means that they have lost cultural, civil, social and political rights that have been built up over generations (2011: 6). This makes the precariat a dangerous class, Standing notes. "A group that sees no future of security and identity will feel fear and frustration that could lead to it lashing out at identifiable or imagined causes of its lot. ... Tensions within the precariat are setting people against each other, preventing them from recognising that the social and economic structure is producing their common set of vulnerabilities." (2011: 40)

It is confusing, it is dangerous but there are great potentials

Rifkin's message in 1995 was a need to redefine opportunities and responsibilities for millions of people in a society absent of mass formal employment (1995: xv). In 2014 he is able to report stunning developments of the collaborative commons and the internet of things that hold great potentials as a substitution for conventional work and the economy as we know it. This will, however, be a great challenge for the prevailing power structures. They will have to let go of the steering and controlling power they now exercise and allow the self-organising processes now in motion to develop and mature. An interesting aspect of the internet of things is that it is boosting productivity to the point where the marginal cost of producing many goods and services is close to zero, making them practically free. In economic theory terms this means that scarcity is giving way to an economy of abundance. Corporate profits are beginning to dry up and property rights are weakening (2014:11).

The challenging question is how the waning capitalism is to be accommodated with the collaborative commons? In practice, the collaborative commons stand for a participatory system where people become prosumers. Rifkin foresees that "[w]ithin the next two to three decades, prosumers in vast continental and global networks will be producing and sharing green energy as well as physical goods and services, and learning in online virtual classrooms at near zero marginal cost, bringing the economy into an era of nearly free goods and services." (2014: 4) Rifkin has hit the nerve of this development when observing that "we find ourselves in uncharted territory and are on a steep learning curve to figure out how to best build out the new smart society." (2014: 15)

The challenge: to find a modus vivendi

We need to find a way to accommodate the old and new economic cultures. As Standing's accounts so well show, we are far from such an accommodation at present. Economic players, employers as well as public organisations, from bodies such as the European Union to local authorities, need to find a modus vivendi to make current transitions as smooth and constructive as possible. The workfare policy that is increasingly pursued by the EU and national authorities is blatantly at odds with the internal logic of present developments. The new modus vivendi that we need could be so easily achieved if we changed our perception of work. Standing has made an important distinction between labour and work that makes it easier to see the phenomena facing us. With close to zero marginal cost at which we can produce many things, we are almost in a position where we could adapt the ancient Greek perception of work, instead of our view of work as employment. "Every age has had it stupidities about what is work and what is not. The twentieth century was the most stupid of all", Standing says and his advice is that "we should return to the insights of the ancient Greeks, who had a better conceptualisation of work." Work was what the citizen and his family did around the home; it was reproductive activity, it involved building civic friendship, philia and also play that was central for recuperation and a balance of life. Here we do of course have to remember that women did not have civil rights and that labour was performed by slaves, banausoi and metics (2011: 144, 2014: 11).

Labour, as we know it today, was not done by citizens. Ironically enough, it is mainly this kind of labour opportunities that we now put so much effort into creating, while a lot of obstacles are placed on activities that correspond to work in the ancient Greek sense, focussed on people's wellbeing. Creative work and work in civil society are often misperceived and also easily hindered because of our labour-focussed perception of work. At the same time, it is in these sectors that the new economy is growing, with affinities to the ancient Greek perception of work.

Parallel with the decline in industrial production in developed economies there has been an explosive growth in creative work, making this sector one of the fastest growing sectors of the economy. However, much of the value created through artistic work is done outside the narrow perception of labour, which in practice means employment. An effect of this is that artists are often not properly compensated for their work. Work in civil society, again, is often undervalued and can even be obstructed because of the selection and control that is associated with funding civic activities. This is ironic considering the nature of work in civil society that Rifkin fittingly characterises in the following way: It is "the realm in which fiduciary arrangements give way to community bonds, and where the giving of one's time to others takes the place of artificially imposed market relationships based on selling oneself and one's services to others." (Rifkin 1995: 239) Now that the market and government spheres are diminishing in importance Rifkin urges us to seriously explore the possibility of resurrecting and transforming civil society and making it a vehicle for the creation of a vibrant post-market era (1995: 240).

One of the most pressing questions we face is how to accommodate the collaborative commons and capitalism in order to avoid a further decline in people's conditions in working life and outside of it. As long as business runs as usual there will be continued precarisation. As saturated markets are a major problem, slimming the organisations will be a way to meet out profit, with increasing precarisation as a consequence. How long can this development continue — and at what cost? A growing precariat will mean that an increasing number of people are compelled to rely on social support of some kind. This will place them in a situation of dependency, which in reality changes a person's status from citizen to denizen, as pictured by

Standing. This is a double penalisation; first people become victims of employers' search for profit, and then they will be deprived of civil rights when they seek compensation in the form of social security.

In civil society there is another threat to democratic standards that is at odds with the *raison d'être* of civil society. This is the selection and control associated with the project economy on which many organisations have to rely in order to be able to carry out their functions. This authoritarian attitude and control mentality infringe on the autonomy of players in civil society. This is detrimental as civil society is the sector in which people join in self-organising processes, reflecting people's interests, needs and care for others. This reflexivity is a fairly good indicator that the activities meet their goals. It is from here that a new rationality should emerge.

How basic income could steer the development

The secured income that a basic income would provide would offer people the personal autonomy that is required for human rights, particularly economic, social and cultural rights to materialise (Storlund 2002). It also implies power for people to say no, which is a vital precondition for freedom as elaborated by Karl Widerquist (2006). Autonomy, in both these senses, is central for the self-organising process through which people can voice and act upon their needs and interests. This is what we need to steer developments in a human direction. The Internet and globalisation have generated unprecedented opportunities for people to join forces around a joint cause. Now people's voices are heard from blood-stained squares in the Arab spring and beyond to movements such as EuroMayDay and Occupy Wall Street. These are some of the social movements that on the one hand react against oppressive rule, and on the other hand against an oppressive economy as well as the failure of governments and the trade union movement to defend people's rights against economic malpractices.

Manuel Castells has drawn attention to how the role of the individual has changed as part of these profound changes. In the 2010 preface to his book *The Construction of Identity* he describes people's new identity as a project identity (2010, Kindle version location 468). People build a new identity that redefines their position in society, and by doing so they seek to transform the overall social structure. Castells illustrates these changes with feminism and environmentalism that he sees as representing the most profound changes. He exemplifies the decisive step that is required in a change of identity with feminism "when feminism moves out to the trenches of resistance of women's identity and women's rights, to challenge patriarchalism, thus the patriarchal family, and thus the entire structure of production, reproduction, sexuality, and personality on which societies have been historically based." (2010 location 981)

This broader human mobilisation that Castells refers to has been going on for some time. Richard Florida was on to something similar when working on his book *The* Creative Class (2002). "Though most experts continued to point to technology as the driving force of broad social change, I became convinced that the truly fundamental changes of our time had to do with subtler alterations in the way we live and work — gradually accumulating shifts in our workplaces, leisure activities, communities and everyday lives. ... it became increasingly evident to me that the emerging Creative Economy was a dynamic and turbulent system — exciting and liberating in some ways, divisive and stressful in others." (2002: x, xi) Florida's conclusion is that "[a] new social class, in short, has risen to a position of dominance in the last two decades, and this shift has fundamentally transformed our economy and society — and continues to do so." (2002: 82)

A human-centred economy

The challenges posed by a close to workerless society is at the same time one of the most promising aspects of present changes. This makes work in civil society pivotal where people and planet are placed before profit, as Rifkin notes, citing John Elkinton, a great authority on corporate responsibility and sustainable development. Civil society is also to Rifkin the sphere to which we should direct our attention as well as our aspirations. Here activities are performed that the public sector or the formal economy are unwilling or incapable of performing. Civil society often acts as an advocate on behalf of groups and constituencies whose interests are being ignored by the marketplace or compromised in political processes. Notwithstanding, there is a widespread ignorance of the work done in civil society. It has also been underrated despite the fact that the economic turnover of activities in civil society is considerable. Neither have researchers paid much attention to civil society, which adds to the general ignorance. Nonetheless, the non-profit sphere is already the fastest growing employment sector in many advanced economies. A Johns Hopkins study of 42 countries revealed that, contrary to the view of many economists, approximately 50 per cent of the aggregate revenue of the non-profit sector operating on the commons already comes from fees for services, while government support accounts for only 36 per cent of the revenues and private philanthropy for only 14 per cent (Rifkin 2014: 268).

With the growth of the collaborative commons, civil society has become an even more dynamic sphere. Rifkin points to social entrepreneurship as an emerging category where the profit and non-profit spheres are creating new business arrangements in a commercial space made up of both the market economy and the collaborative commons (Rifkin 2014: 264). The commons is of course nothing new, as Rifkin also points out. It predates both the capitalist market and representative government, being the oldest form of institutionalised, self-managed activity in the world

(2014 : 472). The contemporary commons encompass the whole range of life with billions of people engaged in deeply social activities. Rifkin's list is long. The commons is made up of literally millions of self-managed, mostly democratically run organisations, including charities, religious bodies, arts and cultural groups, foundations, amateur sports clubs, producer and consumer cooperatives, credit unions, health-care organisations, advocacy groups, condominium associations and a near endless list of other formal and informal institutions that generate the social capital of the society (2014: 16).

New opportunities have emerged that need to be facilitated through an adaptation of attitudes and structures. One example from the US is Benefit corporations that offer entrepreneurs a form of legal protection against outside investors who might force them to give up their social or environmental commitments in return for new financing. Such corporations are now regulated as legal entities in 18 states in the US (Rifkin 2014: 262–263). In addition, there are a variety of other forms of funding, such as crowd funding.

A basic income could assist in steering development in a human and social direction

Pilot projects with basic income that have been carried out in Canada, the US, Namibia, India and other places all show that a basic income has an empowering effect on people in vulnerable positions. In a close to workerless society the populist idea — or economic theory? — that people would not work if they got money for free seems fairly meaningless. Instead, if we look at all the cooperation that is going on in the social economy — an under-researched field in economic theory — we see that people do a lot of hard work although they do not get paid for it. But as people need some kind of income to live on, basic income would serve that purpose. How a basic income should be financed in a zero marginal cost society should be a most inspiring question to explore.

CHAPTER 2

TRANSLATING BETWEEN PARADIGMS

2016 - International Semiotics Institute Congress,
23–26.16 Kaunas, Lithuania

The paradigm conditions our perception. The steering power of a paradigm is caught in a nutshell by David E. Cooper: "1,500 years divide Plotinus' chapter on beauty from Hume's essay on taste (1757), but it might as well be 15,000, so different are the contexts assumed and the problems addressed." Before the enlightenment focus was placed on the value of art and beauty as contributing to human life, whereas by the 18th century focus had become placed on the status of judgments of aesthetic values such as 'This design is beautiful'.[19] The difference between these two paradigms and their consequences are decisive and their effects is something we have struggled to overcome for quite some time.

So, the question is, how are we to recuperate the lost dimension of art and beauty as contributing to human life? The insight that art and beauty have these characteristics goes way back to ancient wisdoms and equally so to ancient Greek philosophy. A recognition of the significance of art and beauty resurfaced during the renaissance and early enlightenment to be lost again when natural sciences became the canon postulating what should be seen as knowledge and truth. In present times recognition of the impact of art and beauty has fortunately re-emerged and is by now a well-established fact in disciplines such as medicine and neuroscience. Today neuroscience plays a pivotal role in rearranging established truths

[19] Cooper, David, E. Ed, *Aesthetics* 1997.

by bringing forth human sentiments. Along with semiotics, neuroscience can give a more accurate picture of people's reality, bridging thereby the gap Cooper pointed to between the two theoretical traditions. Neuroscience offers the kind of facts (knowledge) that natural sciences require whereas semiotics through its reflection on reality (interpretation) can act as a translator between the two paradigms.

What neuroscience can tell us

In Divided Brain, Divided World. Why The Best Part of us Struggles to be Heard, Jonathan Rowson and Iain McGilchrist have, in the form of a dialogue, analysed how the different brain halves condition our perception and how perception changes over time. The authors hope that their discussion will offer intellectual resources for people's anxiety, or hope for some insight into "why we might be blinkered enough to destroy our own planet". And here arts and humanities are given their proper due. "If you have ever had the feeling that the world is deeply out of kilter in a way that you can't quite articulate", Rowson says in the preface, "suspect that the growing neglect of arts and humanities is even more tragic than most people believe." McGilchrist's book The Master and his Emissary, provides the background for the dialogue. There McGilchrist analyses the profound significance of the radically different 'world views' that our brain's left and right hemispheres represent. In Rowson's words, it is a hidden story of western culture, told by McGilchrist, about how the abstract, instrumental, articulate and assured left hemisphere has gradually usurped the more contextual right brain hemisphere (Rowson, McGilchrist 2013: 4–5). In his existential semiotics, Eero Tarasti illuminates such a process as 'post-colonial semiosis': "Any message can become part of the colonializing act of signification, and it often proves futile to try to change this situation by emphasizing the inherent value of the colonized." The fault does not lie in the content of the sign, Tarasti points out, "but in the way in which another sign system grasps, frames, defines, and finally deprives it of use by the larger 'Great Society'". (see Tarasti 2000:137).

Setting the scene, Jonathan Rowson, Director of The Social Brain Centre at the Royal Society for the encouragement of Arts, Manufactures and Commerce, RSA, notes that a completely false view has prevailed that the right brain hemisphere is somehow airy-fairy and unreliable adding only some emotional colour to the perceptions of the 'intelligent' left brain hemisphere. But in reality it is the right hemisphere that sees more, that is more in touch with reality, and is more intellectually sophisticated. Incidentally, Rowson notes, there is evidence that those of highest intelligence, whatever their discipline, may rely more on the right brain hemisphere (Rowson, McGilchrist, 2013: 17).

I will explore the road from Plotinus to findings in neuroscience today, in search of explanations to the challenges facing us, that is, how we are to recuperate the lost dimensions of art and beauty. A quantum leap is what my brain insists upon, which in physics terms signifies an abrupt transition of a system. To put it differently, we need to reach a tipping point or critical mass to make a human dimension involving meaning, art and beauty count on equal terms with the paradigm of the scientific left side brain hemisphere, in order for people "to become heard", to put it in McGilchrist's words.

This is how Rowson pictures the significant differences in the two hemispheres: For instance, the left hemisphere tends to de-contextualise issues while the right contextualises, the left tends to abstract while the right makes vivid and concrete, the left seeks instrumental feedback while the right prefers affectively nuanced responses. The right hemisphere appears to be much more receptive to evidence that challenges its own position. Both of these 'hows' are important and necessary, Rowson says, noting that the evidence for these differences is meticulously unpacked in McGilchrist's book in a cautious but extensive inductive argument (2013: 8).

McGilchrist explicates that as to its structure, the brain has not changed in any significant way in the last 500 years or so. It is rather the function that has changed. Nowadays we tend to interpret the world, ourselves and our experience using only one part of the brain, and we rely on that part more and more. "It is like a form of blindness. At other eras of human history and in other cultures people were aware of much that it seems we have forgotten". It is not a question of us having 'outgrown' because of our intelligence or sophistication, as we fondly think. We may be the least perceptive, most dangerous people that have ever lived, and at the same time we have more power, for good or ill, says McGilchrist (Rowson, McGilchrist, 2013: 20).

If we bother to take account of people's existential dimension, we make use of both brain hemispheres. In other words, the human dimension should be considered on a par with the quantifiable dimension. Instead of the present tendency to squeeze a complex reality into a 'one size fits all' scientific format we need to draw on whatever discipline that best reflects people's reality. Here existential semiotics holds great potentials in bringing together different strands. This strand will however not be pursued further here. RSA's Social Brain project, again, has since 2009 sought to make theories of human nature more accurate through research, more explicit through public dissemination, and more empowering through practical engagement.

The notion that we are rational individuals who respond to information by making decisions consciously, consistently and independently is, at best, a very partial account of who we are. A wide body of scientific knowledge is now telling us what many have long intuitively sensed — humans are a fundamentally social species, formed through and for social interaction, and most of our behaviour is habitual (Rowson, McGilchrist, 2013: 3). McGilchrist points out that what is at stake is obviously two competing sets of values — enshrined in two different perspectives on the world subtended by the two brain hemispheres. I can't deny that I prefer the values of the right hemisphere, he says, although I need to pay due respect to those of the left hemisphere.

But, McGilchrist says, it's not just a matter of my opinion. What the brain shows — what it adds to the argument — is that, indisputably, one view of the world sees more, and is truer to that what is. This can be demonstrated and proved to be the case. That it also happens to be the view of the hemisphere, which is more capable of empathy, more in favour of consensuality and co-operation, just happens to be a bonus. McGilchrist notes that the fact that it is not just neuroscientists, neurologists, psychiatrists and psychologists, who have been struck by his hypothesis, but also philosophers, theologians, cultural historians and critics, artists and composers, suggests to him that his interpretation has intuitive validity (2013: 27).

McGilchrist puts the challenging question whether there is a un-resoluble conflict between the two world-views. It would be quite extraordinary if the differences he refers to, which are the same distinctions that artists and philosophers have for centuries pointed to as un-resoluble conflicts in the human mind or spirit, were not associated with the division between the hemispheres. The evidence from brain science, that that is precisely what they are, is extensive, coherent and compelling (2013: 28). Contrary to the received view, the intuitive and holistic has its representation, not just as instincts at the lowest level of the brain, but in complex thinking at the highest, in the right frontal cortex (2013: 30).

Paradigmatic translation exercise

The profound changes that we are undergoing impacts not only on our material conditions but also on our personal perceptions, aspirations and actions. Industrial production that had offered working men and women their livelihood during a considerable part of the 19th and 20th centuries, has to an equally considerable degree been substituted by service, art and creative activities today. At a symbolic level this can be seen in art taking over old industrial premises. In addition to enriching people's lives, art and culture have the additional virtue that they nurture people in immaterial ways in contrast to industrial production that in its consumer-function often is harmful to the environment.

We are thereby faced with a paradigmatic translation exercise. What theoretical groundwork is required to make art and beauty relevant as a personal experience? In other words, how are we to make a transition from a perspective on art that is concerned with statements of its nature to its impact on people's lives? This question is not limited to any specific discipline but encompasses the whole theoretical field. My focus is on what repercussions this theoretical divide has for law, making the recognition of artistic work as work a test case for the perception of substantive aspects such as people's aspirations toward beauty and the good life. The challenge we face today is thus to have perception reflect the changed environment in which we live. This concerns above all the power strata of society that need to become aware of and act upon these new settings. In addition to legal structures it involves business and administrative practices, as well. A major question facing us is how knowledge is formed and what it is perceived as representing.

How knowledge is formed

As a working life researcher, I have been amused and intrigued by the choreography of collective bargaining. The setting remains the same over years and decades. What is called bargaining is in fact two monologues pursued from two different points of departure without ever turning into a genuine dialogue. Instead the bargaining ends in a give and take compromise. The unions' point of departure is that employees should be entitled to fair compensation and protection. This actualises economic, social and sometimes also cultural rights. The employers' side relies on economically related facts actualising classical rights and liberties. The effect of these differences can in a caricatured way be illustrated by rulings of the US Supreme Court in the early 20th century. The court was faced with a number of cases in which it assessed the constitutionality of protective statutes. The reasoning could go like this: "[T]he right of the employee to quit for any reason he saw fit was the same as the right of the employer to discharge for any reason... In all such particulars the employer and the employee have equality of right, and any legislation that disturbs that equality is an arbitrary interference with the liberty of contract which no government can legally justify in a free land."[20]

Here we see the de-contextualisation that the brain's left hemisphere produces. Although governments in free lands have adopted protective statutes and many of them have, on paper at least, adopted international and regional economic, social and cultural rights standards, this dichotomy still persists (Storlund 2002). The increasing precarisation in working life during the past decades clearly reveals that there is no proper bridging between the two hemispheres, one representing substance the other form. So let's explore the setting. Elisa P. Reis has together with Mick Moore edited a book *Elite Perceptions of Poverty and Inequality* (International Studies in Poverty Research 2005) where they investigated the elites' political culture, their deeper beliefs and values about questions of poverty and inequality.[21] The authors were in search of answers to questions such as: What sort of explanations do they offer to justify or condemn persistent poverty and inequality? Who do they tend to blame for

[20] Justice Harlan, in Adair v. United States, 208 UL 161, 1908, cited in Hale, Robert, *Freedom through Law*, 1952: 390.

[21] I here rely on a paper *Elite Perceptions of Poverty and Inequality* that Elisa P. Reis presented at the UNU-Wider Conference on The Role of Elites in Economic Development in Helsinki, Finland 2009.

the fate of the poor? What do they think should and / or could be done? The authors base themselves on Abraham de Swaan's pioneering book *In Care of the State*, where he has traced the historical origins of health, education and welfare policies in Europe and the USA, whereas it is the situation in Brazil that Reis and Moore have studied.

With reference to de Swaan, Reis asserts that social policy depends on the formation of a 'social consciousness' that can be defined as a set of perceptions conducive to the adoption of measures to reduce poverty. Reis points out that social consciousness is not synonymous to good will, philanthropy, charity or similar notions. Instead it implies that the problem of poverty is perceived as one that creates negative externalities, that it is the elites' business and that it can be realistically tackled. This entails (a) a belief in social interdependence, (b) a sense of responsibility, and (c) an assessment that it is possible to change the status quo, and that it is worth doing something (Reis 2009: 18).

Reis' investigations into the Brazilian elites revealed that they believe that anti-poverty measures are viable. The elites listed as viable measures, among others, investments in education and health and also land distribution to improve the lot of the poor. Notwithstanding, the sense of social responsibility appears to be the fragile element in engaging elites in social policy (Reis 2009: 19). When asked who should provide the resources to expand educational opportunities, the answer is invariably 'the government'. To the question whether they would agree to pay more taxes for this purpose the answer was: "Of course not, we already pay too many taxes". This message, repeated again and again, is summed up by one respondent. "Even a very poor child, if she gets a good education and works hard, she will certainly improve her living conditions and will have the chance to overcome poverty. If education is provided, inequality will gradually be reduced because everybody will have better wages, better job positions ... No there is no need to increase taxation, if the government is really committed it is possible to provide better education. It is a question of political will." (Reis 2009: 13–14)

Yet again, we see a de-contextualisation exercise. Reis observes that the elites live in a world apart from the rest of the population. This is something that Ross Jackson brings forcefully to the fore in his book *Occupy World Street, A global roadmap for radical economic and political reform* (R. Jackson 2012). There Jackson identifies drivers of destruction emanating from the brain's left-side worldview of separation that considers Nature as a collection of resources to be exploited but with no intrinsic value in itself; and humans as separate both from Nature and other humans. Jackson points out that this way of thinking has created a society that is destroying its natural capital, the source of all life; it has created increasing inequality, it has created a speculative financial system driven by greed that is destabilising and out of control. Jackson proceeds to examine the human decision making that allow these disasters to happen, i.e., the political power structures that define the human factor that is driving the drivers (R. Jackson 2012: 120–121). Political power is not exercised directly by the super rich, but rather by their allies who run the largest American corporations. This corporate power is grounded in a number of US Supreme Court decisions dating back to the early 19th century that in essence gave corporations many of the same constitutional rights as persons — so-called corporate personhood. Of utmost importance is the right to make political contributions. This enables the business elite to acquire loyal allies in Congress through campaign contributions and other forms of political support (R. Jackson 2012: 146).

"An unintended 'Frankenstein's monster' has been created. The difference between individual personhood and corporate personhood is critical", Jackson asserts. Profit-seeking corporations have no feelings, no emotions or social dimensions, like humans have. In fact, Jackson notes, a large corporation acts very much like a human being suffering from 'dissocial personality disorder' involving characteristics such as "disregard for social norms, rules and obligations; callous unconcern for the feelings of others; incapacity to experience guilt and to profit from experience, particularly punishment, a proneness to blame others, or to offer plausible rationalisations for the behaviour that has brought the patient into conflict with society". What has happened over the past decades is that political power in the US has been transferred to a sociopathic 'corporatocracy' — a term coined by John Perkins in his book *Confessions of an Economic Hit Man* (2004). The result is entirely predictable and should not surprise anyone: widespread human suffering in the general population while the ruling elite acquires an increasing proportion of the national wealth year after year (R. Jackson 2012: 147).

How can the elite behave like this? An explanation that Jackson sees is that corporate CEOs - while not themselves sociopaths — accept the responsibility of running sociopathic corporations because they are firmly addicted to a lifestyle filled with the rush of power and influence that is as difficult to break as a heroin addiction. Many corporate executives are totally removed from and insensitive to the problems of ordinary folks at home and abroad. They spend money without limits, move only in influential circles, live in guarded compounds and travel from one five-star hotel to another, often by private plane. If addiction is the case, then perhaps they just don't care what happens to the rest of humanity and the environment as long as they can remain in charge and maintain their lifestyle (R. Jackson 2012:156).

The power of the paradigm

The paradigm that 'gives space' for the above accounted scenarios represents that of the age of capital, which came to fruition with the introduction of freedom of trade in the latter part of the 19th century. This represented a paradigmatic quantum leap that in working life signified a change from status to contract, making employers and workers 'formally' equal contracting partners, as implied in the US Supreme Court ruling referred to above. McGilchrist asserts that if he is right that we are living in the west in a culture dominated by the take on the world of the left hemisphere, his question is how did this come about? "Surely, you may say, it's because it has proved itself more successful than any of the alternatives. Well, that all depends on what you mean by success. It is, I repeat, a culture that is very good at using the world, as if it were just a heap of resource to further our plans. But are our plans necessarily wise?" asks McGilchrist. He sees several reasons for the success of the left hemisphere. First, it makes you powerful, and power is very seductive, as R. Jackson illustrated. Second, it offers very simple explanations, that are in their own terms convincing. This is because what doesn't fit the plan is simply declared to be meaningless. "For example, to declare talk of 'consciousness' a delusion or a linguistic error has the virtue of simplicity. It may not, however, satisfy the more sceptical among us, those who are not in thrall to our left hemisphere's way of thinking." (Rowson – McGilchrist, 2013:20)

McGilchrist maintains that if what does not fit the model is just discarded, we will never learn, never sophisticate our model of reality, and our understanding will come to a standstill where it is. The left hemisphere is also, he suggests, the Berlusconi of the brain — a political heavyweight that controls the media. It does the speaking and constructs the arguments in its own favour. And finally, since the industrial revolution, we have constructed a world around us externally that is the image of the world the left brain hemisphere has made internally. "Appeals to the natural world, to the history of a culture, to art, to the body, and to spirituality, ... have been cut off, undercut and ironised out of existence, and when we look out of the window — we see more of the world we had created in our minds extended in concrete all around us." (Rowson - McGilchrist 2013: 20)

Diagnosis

There is an interesting blend between what we see and what we think. Fredrik Lång has lucidly illuminated this in his book about image and thought, on the genesis of categorical perception, (Bild och tanke). There Lång shows how different theoretical traditions either restrain or liberate thought. The book starts with an aphorism. "Many years ago I wrote an aphorism that went like this. On the despair of comprehension. During the 20th century artists, in despair, destroyed their ideal of beauty. Nowadays the idyllic can only be seen as naivety. I do understand, but what am I to do with my despair?" "What induced me to these thoughts was puzzlement rather than despair", Lång says. "I was puzzled by the question: Where was the ideal of beauty lost, inherent in visual art from Leonardo to Cezanne, after Cezanne? Or the other way around: Why did it become a necessity to do as Duchamp did, to smash these ideals?" (translated here), (Lång 1999: 7)

As Lång illustrates in his book, there is an intimate relationship between a certain historical phase and the worldview generated through our thought structures. Perhaps is it not surprising that Duchamp did what he did, smashed the ideals of beauty, as anything metaphysical was banned from the theoretical landscape, leaving people in 'puzzlement and despair'. Perhaps are we therefore now at a threshold similar to that of Petrarch, that Lång pictures in his book. Lång observes that St. Augustine and Petrarch stand at the outer posts of one thousand years of obliteration and silence. With St. Augustine the quest for knowledge and curiosity was cut off. But Petrarch lived at a time when nature had captured the imagination of people, directing interest and curiosity in other directions than the divine order. St. Augustine and Petrarch reflect on the same questions. They try to find the place of worldly and divine love in life, the role of truth and man's assignment. Whereas the response to divine love finally excludes all other considerations in St. Augustine's case, it is the worldly love that wins the battle over Petrarch's soul. Petrarch finds himself in a very delicate position: In his thoughts he accepts the Augustinian virtues, but in practice he breaks with all of them (Lång 1999: 132).

During Petrarch's time people's attitudes toward nature had changed to such a degree that nothing could prevent curiosity about the secrets of nature. Lång observes about Petrarch that, fitting as it is for a person standing on the threshold to a new epoch, endowed with a sensibility great enough to differentiate contradictory impulses, Petrarch wants to live up to the requirements of the old truth, but he cannot resist the new ones. Notwithstanding the revealed Augustinian truth, he constantly sees the evident, empirical or sensual truth, one that gives pleasure to the eye, delight to the senses and pride to the heart, which he can no longer resist. Baffled he notes, citing Ovidius: "I agree that this would be better, but I do what is worse." (translated here) (Lång 1999:133)

We are today at a similar threshold to that of Petrarch in the 14th century. He took a decisive step in the transition from scholasticism to the renaissance. By reviving the tradition of antiquity, he sought a union of elegance and power with virtue. One who studied language and rhetoric in the tradition of the great orators of antiquity did so for a moral purpose to persuade men and women to the good life. Petrarch says in a dictum that could stand as the slogan of renaissance humanism, "it is better to will the good than to know the truth." (translated here) (Lång 1999: 158)

Paradigmatic roadmap

So let's relate Plotinus thinking to the paradigmatic findings of neuroscience. Plotinus was a follower of Plato, born in Egypt (204–270 AD). For Plotinus, (Enneads, I.6) there is an intimate connection between the beautiful and the good. It is Plotinus (not Plato) who inspired the renaissance's elevated conception of art as a medium for communicating an invisible and intelligible world to us. Plotinus stands behind the still powerful tradition of locating aesthetic value in the form of artworks or natural objects, as opposed to the form of matter or content. Here is Cooper's advice: "[I]t is to Plotinus that those people should look for whom the experience of beauty purifies and edifies, educating the understanding of our moral being and of the intelligible order upon which we depend." (D. E. Cooper [1997] 2000: 55–56)

Reflecting on the nature of beauty Plotinus elucidates (1) "Beauty is mostly in sight, but it is to be found too in things we hear, in combinations of worlds and also in music, and in all music ... And there is the beauty of virtue". (Cooper [1997] 2000: 56–57) In addition to beauties in the realm of sense there are "images and shadows which, so to speak, sally out and come into matter and adorn it and excite us when they appear." And in point 4 Plotinus makes a decisive paradigmatic point about the beauties beyond. "(4.) But about the beauties beyond, which it is no more the part of sense to see, but the soul sees them and speaks of them without instruments — we must go up to them and contemplate them and leave sense to stay down below. Just as in the case of the beauties of sense it is impossible for those who have not seen them or grasped their beauty – those born blind, for instance, - to speak about them, in the same way only those can speak about the beauty of ways of life who have accepted the beauty of ways of life and kinds of knowledge and everything else of the sort; and people cannot speak about the splendor of virtue who have never even imagined how fair is the face of justice and moral order." (Cooper [1997] 2000: 59–60)

Here, we can say, it is the hemisphere of the left brain half that is at a loss. So, what did subsequently happen? Why did not the paradigm represented by Plotinus persist when it resurfaced during the renaissance? Pirjo Kukkonen has in her PhD From Art to Science" (Från konst till vetenskap) contributed to this intriguing subject by investigating at a linguistic level how the notion of art was transformed into science during a period of 400 years from 1477 to 1976.[22] Her aim was to discern the word science as a cultural phenomenon through a qualitative study of semantic fields, with the purpose of throwing light on a set of concepts (begreppskomplex) as they appear in the history of ideas (Kukkonen, 1989: 2). Inspired by Socrates, Kukkonen's original intention was to investigate the word knowledge, but as so often happens, the material started to live its own life and out came the word science as the lead player, a word that in former times had signified both 'knowledge', and 'skill', 'magic' and 'vetskap' before it got its modern meaning science.

Art again signified in former times also 'ability', 'skill, and 'fine arts' but also 'knowledge' and 'science', meanings that were soon out-manoeuvred by science and research. Kukkonen traces how these different meanings relate to each other during the period she studied. During the 18th century the meaning of art and science starts to be separated whereby art is assigned the meaning of artistic art and science is assigned its scientific meaning. At the end of the 19th century these two words are given clearly distinct meanings: art has gained an own meaning signifying skill whereas science has assumed the meaning knowledge. Thereby the centuries old connection between art and science is broken, states (Kukkonen 1989: 141).

This was the theoretical landscape I encountered when I started doing research in the 1970s and I felt the same kind of despair as Fredrik Lång did, at the total dominance of a worldview where any discipline in order to be viable had to squeeze its substance into a format borrowed from natural sciences. In my discipline, law, Hans Kelsen's *Reine Rechtslehre* (Pure Theory of Law) constituted a pinnacle. And I was not alone among

---

[22] in learned texts and literature since 1477 when the University of Uppsala was established. The main research data is the Swedish Academy Dictionary excerpt material, since its inception 1526, with analyses of press material in the 19th century up to 1976.

lawyers with my frustration. Looking back at his legal studies in the period when a Kelsenian tradition was at its peak Lars D. Eriksson recalls: During my studies in the late 1950s and early 1960s, Finnish legal dogmatics was largely a technical field of knowledge. One was supposed to know the systematisation of the legal order and the rules and methods of interpretation. Much more than that was not required. Different methods of interpretation that in principle could have made law become alive, where not discussed. The methods were considered as given and there were no problems associated with them. And Eriksson notes that for a young soul with a genuine interest in philosophy and politics, the whole situation appeared rather hopeless. "I did not intend to get a training as an engineer." (translated here) (Eriksson 1997: 57).

The clearest scientific significance assigned art can be seen in combinations such as konstlära (1811) and konstvetenskap (1859). The latter combination shows how art after having been a central word or a general concept to indicate science (knowledge) in the modern Swedish language now forms only a part of science, a systematic and theoretical presentation of aesthetic activities, that is to say, a methodological system (Kukkonen 1989 : 141). This is thus how we arrived at the separate 'universes' that Cooper pointed at at the opening of this chapter. It is the hidden story about how the left brain hemisphere gradually usurped the more contextual, humane, systemic, holistic but relatively tentative and inarticulate right hemisphere, transforming thereby western culture in an abstract, instrumental, articulate and assured direction (Rowson 2013: 4–5). It is thus from here that we need to recapture lost clusters.

The monopolising process of a paradigm change, how domination comes about is an interesting question of colonisation as Tarasti described above. "'If I am right, that the story of the Western world is one of increasing left hemisphere domination, we would not expect insight to be the key note. Instead, we would expect a sort of insouciant optimism, the sleepwalker whistling a happy tune as he ambles towards the abyss." With this citation Rawson and McGilchrist open their report *Divided Brain, Divided World. Why The Best Part of us Struggles to be Heard.* Rowson's and McGilchrist's message is a deep conviction that we need to become more reflexive about human nature and that we need to address the major adaptive challenges of our time. In their own work they strive to link theory to practice in ways that would make a distinctive and enduring contribution to social innovation (Rowson 2013, Preface).

A profound rethinking is required, Rawson and McGilchirst insist. If we are going to make 'behaviour change' about more than the technocratic application of behavioural insights to mostly minor problems, we need to work hard to think about the influence of deep structures and root causes, including planetary boundaries, political systems, social networks, inequality, the structure of the macro economy, and, in this case, the structure of the brain. If we don't link up behaviour change to deep and systemic influences, we will be stuck with superficial tinkering rather than meaningful social innovation, Rowson says in the introduction to the report (Rowson, McGilchrist 2013: 6).

An intriguing phenomenon Rowson brings to the fore, is that the left hemisphere's 'way of being' is more culturally contagious than the 'way of being' of the right hemisphere. It is suggested that, slowly but surely, the left hemisphere's perspective shapes our culture in such a way that the culture begins to respond to it as the dominant one. Your thesis matters, Rowson tells McGilchrist, because there is a very real danger that we may reach what you call 'a hall of mirrors' in which the explicit, instrumental, defined, confident, abstract voice (not unlike the current voice of the materialistic orthodoxy in neuroscience or the neoliberal voice placing unqualified faith in markets) becomes the only one we appreciate, while the relatively implicit, intrinsic, fluid, visceral perspective of the right hemisphere begins to sound diminished and irrelevant (Rowson, McGilchrist 2013: 8). McGilchrist clarifies that this is not about 'thinking versus feeling'. It is –about two kinds of thinking. And, contrary to popular belief, it is the right hemisphere's, not the left hemisphere's, thinking that is more accurate, more down to earth –'truer' to what is (Rowson, McGilchrist 2013: 9).

McGilchrist mentions the financial crash as an example. It was fuelled by a belief that human behaviour can be confidently predicted by algorithms, whereas in fact we not only don't know – but in principle we can never know – enough for this sort of prediction to be valid. We lost track of what these figures represented in the real world. Financial institutions disregarded the importance of trust, and instead traded in a war of all-against-all, inducing an atmosphere of paranoia, deception and chicanery. All these are features of the way the left hemisphere conceives the world, not the way the whole brain would have seen it (Rowson, McGilchrist 2013: 9).

Ross Jackson recounts in his book *Occupy World Street* the shocking message a widely respected spiritual leader, Andrew Harvey, got from a leading member of the corporatocracy – the CEO of a major agribusiness corporation, of which here an extract: "Let me tell you what you are up against. You are up against people like me. I know exactly what my company is doing and what devastation it is causing to thousands of lives. I should know; I'm running it and I do not care. I have decided I want a grand gold-plated lifestyle and the perks and jets and houses that go with it and I will do anything – bend the law, have people 'removed', bribe local government officials, you name it – to get what I want. I know too, that none of my shareholders care a rat's ass what I do or how I do it, providing I keep them swimming in cash." (R. Jackson 2012: 157)

Each brain hemisphere has a quite consistent, but radically different, 'take' on the world, McGilchrist says. This means that, at the core of our thinking about ourselves, the world and our relationship with it, there are two incompatible but necessary views that we need to try to combine. And things go badly wrong when we do not (Rowson, McGilchrist, 2013: 12). So it's as if we live simultaneously in two different worlds, but we don't realise how radically different they are, nor do we sense that they are competing, Rowson suggests, which McGilchrist confirms. Exactly! (Rowson, McGilchrist, 2013: 14). It is like comparing a world in all its richness with a useful map of that world, which leaves almost everything out, except the strategic essentials. We have become like people who have mistaken the map for the thing itself.

McGilchrist points to the two meanings for the word seeing. In almost every language, seeing is a metaphor both for perception and for understanding. What I mean by it, he says, is that the two hemispheres differ in their awareness, therefore both in what they literally perceive, and, more broadly, in what they then make of it. They construct the world from their own perceptions. Because of its narrow focus and emphasis on getting certainty, the left hemisphere sees only bits and pieces, fragments which it attempts to put together to form a whole. The left hemisphere alone encodes tools and machines. In the living world, again, context is everything, but this is neglected by the left hemisphere. Thus, the left hemisphere prefers the explicit, without understanding that rendering things explicit, and isolating them under the spotlight of attention, denatures and ultimately kills them, just as explaining a joke or a poetic metaphor robs it of its meaning and power. The view through the lab window distorts the meaning of everything most precious to us – the natural world, sexual love, art and spirituality all fare badly when treated in this detached and de-contextualised way, says McGilchrist (Rowson, McGilchrist: 2013: 16–17).

The left hemisphere focuses on detail at the expense of the bigger picture, and on procedures at the expense of their meaning. This loss of proportion and preference for the forms of things over any real-world content, lend themselves to a 'tick box' mentality, which is also an aspect of its risk-averse nature. Since its purpose is control in the service of grasp or manipulation, rather than understanding of the world, it is anxious and even paranoid if it senses loss of control. This makes it prone to bureaucracy, and indeed one could see the bureaucratic mind as an epitome of the left hemisphere's take on the world, prioritising not just control but procedures that are explicit and that favour abstraction, anonymity, organisability and predictability over what is individual, unique, embodied and flexible. In the process justice gets reinterpreted simply as equality. If I seem to have a lot to say in favour of the right hemisphere in the book, McGilchrist observes, it is because there was a balance here that needed to be redressed – and still does (Rowson, McGilchrist 2013: 17).

The left hemisphere does not understand things, it is the right hemisphere that is the basis of understanding. This has an impact on the way we live now: because the left hemisphere is better than the right hemisphere at manipulating both figures and words, but less good than it at understanding their meaning (or in fact meaning in any sense). Information becomes more important for it than knowledge, and knowledge than wisdom, which is implicit, paradoxical, and discoverable only by experience. Similarly, skills and judgment, embodied, implicit and born of experience, seem merely unreliable versions of a procedure, and have to be 'operationalised' by algorithms that a machine could follow. This produces a standard product that is guaranteed to rule out any form of excellence (Rowson, McGilchrist 2013: 17–18). Systems become designed to maximise utility, that is to say the efficiency that one would require of a machine: quantity, speed, and reliability of production. "The problem here is that while this may apply to making plastic spoons, it does not apply to any human relationship, such as that with a teacher, a doctor, a policeman, a clergyman, a judge, or a social worker, all of whom will do a worse job by doing more, more quickly and to a standard template. Reasonableness, a highly sophisticated quality that used to be thought a goal of education, as well as a hallmark of civilisation, becomes replaced by mere rationality, and there is a resounding failure of common sense." (Rowson, McGilchrist 2013: 18)

Root causes

The introduction of freedom of trade in the latter part of the 19th century can be seen as a paradigmatic quantum leap that set the scene for the development from which we now need another quantum leap. One of the cornerstones in this liberal scheme was freedom of contract. Everyone was free to conclude such contracts as one pleased, and this was accompanied by a strict adherence to the fulfilment of contractual obligations. In the law of contract of the time, there was no room given social equity aspects. Labour contracts where thus treated under the same conditions as a contract between merchants or manufacturers. In the United States where the liberal scheme existed in about its purest form, legislation aimed at protecting workers against coercive measures by the employer, were for a long time viewed as unwarranted deprivations of liberty and property, and disturbances of equality of rights, as pictured above. This view equally applied to workers rights to belong to a union (Storlund 2002: 106).

The left hemisphere must conceive of society as an aggregate of individuals, seen as equal, but inert, units. The right hemisphere alone can understand that individuals are unique and reciprocally bound in a network, based on a host of things that could never be rationalised, creating something much greater than the sum of its parts, a society; and that that society has no meaning apart from them, but neither do they apart from it. The left hemisphere's 'mis-take' on this tends towards a mechanistic idea of society that does not take into account emergent properties of a system, or complex reciprocal and fundamentally unpredictable interactions. It leads to a loss of social cohesion, and an emphasis on a mass of rules, regulations, and mechanisms of accountability, which are supposed to substitute for trust. This has huge financial and social costs, as well as costs in terms of the further erosion of trust and morale (Rowson, McGilchrist 2013: 18–19).

This dominance of the worldview representing natural sciences and the left brain hemisphere has evidently not gone without protest. Sociology, theories of justice and semiotics are among those disciplines that 'wage a war' against the natural sciences emphasis on the brain's left hemisphere, in order to recuperate the clusters that have been lost. Ferdinand Tönnies has been a leading thinker differentiating the one-dimensional view on the world that emanated from natural science, in the distinction between *Gemeinschaft* and *Gesellschaft* Other central thinkers are John Rawls and Depak Chopra. For decades now, Rawls' magnum opus *A theory of justice* has been a precursor for a paradigm change from a positivist analytical tradition to one that encompasses meaning and substance. Depak Chopra, again, has enriched the outlook on the world by combining ancient wisdoms and neuroscience. We can thus seek guidance both from past times and also from other cultures. Rowson and McGilchrist point to far eastern cultures that attend to the world in ways typical of both the left and right hemispheres, and they draw on strategies of both hemispheres more or less equally. This is nice confirmatory evidence as we in the west are heavily skewed toward the attentive viewpoint and strategies of the left hemisphere alone (Rowson, McGilchrist 2013: 24). Instead of the 'one size fit all' mentality that a paradigm that engages the brain's left hemisphere represents, we need to contextualise and see when and for what purpose a human or formal paradigm should apply.

CHAPTER 3

HUMANISM VERSUS NEOLIBERALISM - TWO DISCOURSES THAT NEVER MEET

2017 - International Semiotics Institute Congress 26-30.6.2017 Kaunas, Lithuania [23]

"And so it was that politicians used to quibbling over a few million euros to be spent on pensioners, health or education gave their governments carte blance to transfer hundreds of billions to bankers hitherto awash with liquidity." Yanis Varoufakis (2016:154–155)

I propose to address the question of humanism, humanity and a good life through the question what obstructs these values. Obstacles are manifold but I will narrow my focus to how perception can constitute a formidable obstacle. Compared to many obstacles that are material in nature, perception has to do with the 'immaterial reality' we create through our thought structures. It has to do with how we look at different states of affairs and what is legitimized when a theoretical orientation has been taken on board by those exercising factual power. Neoliberalism is a case in point. The political traces of this theoretical orientation can be seen as a frontal attack on humanism, humanity and a good life. This paper set out to explore the relation and tension between humanism and neoliberalism. To me the magnitude of the economic exploration exploded in my face,

[23] Program title What obstructs humanism, humanity and a good life? - Humanism versus neoliberalism .

although it has been part of my investigations since the 1990s. In this paper I have made only fragmentary references to humanism and the good life, while the part of this paper that I have been struggling with and given space is neoliberal economics. Why? Because the way we approach the economy will be decisive for the space given to human and social concerns. This paper is a follow up of my paper *Translating between paradigms*, presented at the International Semiotics Institute's (ISI) congress in 2016. The agenda in these two papers is the same, to lay bare the power of a paradigm, how it steers perception.[24]

In 2016 I took departure in how art and beauty have been perceived, focussing on the different world-views represented by the brain's left and right hemispheres. I there relied on Jonathan Rowson's and Iain McGilchrist's analysis of what neuroscience can tell us, based on their publication *Divided Brain, Divided World. Why the Best Part of us Struggles to be Heard?* In the preface Rowson says: "If you have ever had the feeling that the world is deeply out of kilter in a way that you can't quite articulate, suspect that the growing neglect of arts and humanities is even more tragic than most people believe." (Rowson, McGilchrist (2003) This pessimistic view is sadly repeated when bringing neoliberalism into the picture, and contrasting it to humanism and a good life, which is the level at which I will dwell here.

In the very sinister picture that today's economic scenery displays, Maynard Keynes offers us light at the end of the tunnel when he in 1930

[24] In the previous paper I illustrated the need to translate between paradigms through the following observation made by David E. Cooper: "1,500 years divide Plotinus' chapter on beauty from Hume's essay on taste (1757), but it might as well be 15,000, so different are the contexts assumed and the problems addressed." Before the enlightenment focus was placed on the value of art and beauty as contributing to human life, whereas by the 18th century focus had became placed on the status of judgments of aesthetic values such as 'This design is beautiful'. Cooper, David, E. Ed, Aesthetics 1997.

looked into the future in his paper *Economic Possibilities for our Grandchildren* (1930). He there expresses the view that we in 100 years will be free from many distasteful and unjust practices affecting the distribution of wealth (Essays in Persuasion, 1932). Unfortunately, we have not moved beyond distasteful and unjust practices, but the profound changes we are going through will hopefully bring along alternatives.

In new situations we find ourselves in uncharted territories. To navigate in these territories is a constant balancing act, to see the trees for the forest and vice versa. The way the neoliberal economic tradition has come to dominate over human aspects and a good life is blatantly exposed in today's Greece, the cradle of the western civilisation that by the troika, the European Central Bank, ECB, the European Commission, EC, and the International Monetary Fund, IMF has been made a 'morality tale' for economic behaviour. Greece will below serve as an illustration.

Where we stand

Social and political theorists have for some time lamented the exhaustion and marginalisation of political imagination (Dean, Capitalism and Citizenship 2003: x). Postmodernist thinkers, for their part, consider that we are at a loss because we have lost the 'grand narratives'. It is felt that direction, purpose and meaning is lost, inducing in its stead a state of fear. "What is going on?", asks Beverly Southgate, "Is fear an appropriate response – or should we rather be celebrating greater freedom?"[25] Each paradigmatic shift requires its own road map. But how long does it take before we have mapped out new constellations and their implications? Many scholars, Southgate among them, make the pertinent point that to react to present changes is not only an academic or theoretical matter. On the contrary, postmodernism has very much to do with practicalities, "with the

[25] Southgate, Postmodernism in History (2003: ix).

ways we choose to live as individuals, with the ways we interact with others in society, and with our choice of political agenda. And it has to do not least with our aspirations for the future." (Southgate 2003: ix) Southgate notes that it is a question of coming to terms with the theoretical heritage of modernism, that "inspires both optimism and gloom. On the positive side, it provides enormous and potentially liberating advantages, but more negatively it shackles with its inbuilt constraints." (2003: 116)

I suggest that we have entered an age of personhood, where we should be able to celebrate greater freedom. To make use of the potentials that surrounds us we do, however, need to update our conceptual schemes to reflect present day conditions and values, and also to remove mental and institutional shackles deriving from both old times and present ones. Thus 'updated' we are better placed to insist on human values in the present setting where neoliberal economics encroaches on human values. Yanis Varoufakis, again, has in a talk characterised our time as the time of finance and that is certainly true, too. It is thus on the axis humans versus finance that we need to look for root causes and suggest remedies to recapture and secure human values.

Thanks to information and communication technologies civil society offers unprecedented opportunities for people to assume a role as active players on a large scale. The means available through new technology has made identity a primary organising principle, as Manuel Castells notes in his analysis of the changes that have led to the raise of the network society (1999: 35). Today humanity is, at least in the affluent part of the world, at a juncture where there is or should be ample scope for human aspirations, creativity and artistic creation that conveys a human perspective on life. Such human energies are, however, often constrained, partly because of legacies of old times, partly because of the restraints that neoliberal economic policies impose. Castells notes that never before has the work of an individual been more central in the value creating process. But independently of qualifications, the worker is, as never before, submitted to the mercy of the organisation as it now operates, with 'slimmed' individuals, contracted out in flexible networks. Castells emphasises that this development is not due to any 'inherent necessity'. This trend is not an expression of any structural logic, inherent in the informational paradigm. It is an expression of a process of a changing relationship between capital and labour (Castells 1999: 286). And not only that! Robotization and algorithms present unprecedented challenges that requires humans to be part of the equation.

Two discourses that never meet

The conflict inherent in the humanistic versus neoliberal orientation is best seen and most concretely felt at a personal level in working life. Whereas the focus of the social welfare state is to secure the position of working men and women in as well as outside of employment, the neoliberal orientation focuses on costs of production and profits, on speculation, and increasingly also on private service production that has led to growing economic disparities with money accumulating for a small minority with increasing poverty and insecurity in its wake for most people.

The 20th century income distribution has irretrievably broken down. This is the verdict of Guy Standing, who has followed the growth of the precariat, a story that runs parallel to neoliberal economic policies and practices. This verdict he presents in his book *The Corruption of Capitalism: Why rentiers thrive and work does not pay?* (2016) It is more than money, Standing maintains. It also involves what could be called 'social income', and furthermore it involves the predictability of the income. These are, as Standing notes, aspects that statistics fail to recognise. "For example, guaranteed access to state benefits is worth more than access to benefits of equivalent amount that depend on means testing, behaviour testing or the discretion of bureaucratic officials. Income security has a value in itself". (Standing 2016: Kindle location 178)

This is, indeed, a constellation that nurtures uncertainty and fear. Although we can look back at a century with a democratic form of government, the question is, have we transformed form into substance? What democracy entails is one such strand. Carol C. Gould observes in her book *Rethinking democracy* that the concept of freedom has to be understood more broadly than it is in traditional theories of democracy. Whereas freedom is often understood as the absence of external constraint or as free choice, Gould argues that it should be interpreted as the activity of self-development, requiring not only the absence of external constraint but also the availability of social and material conditions necessary for the achievement of purposes and plans. The concept of equality needs, likewise, to be extended beyond the way it is perceived in liberal democratic theory, so that it, in addition to political and legal equality, would encompass equality in social and economic life, as well.[26] These observations date back to the late 1980s and no fundamental change has occurred since then in the direction Gould indicated. On the contrary, the onslaught of neoliberalism has largely put a halt to such trends at a political level.

The onslaught of neoliberalism

The neoliberal theoretical tradition dates back to the 1930s but it was with Ronald Reagan and Margaret Thatcher that this orientation entered politics with force in the 1970s. It represented a sea change to the way societies had been developed after world-war II, in a Keynesian tradition with social welfare as a policy aim. It would appear that it is in this transition from a Keynesian to a neoliberal economic tradition that politicians have lost imagination, making neoliberalism and its offspring new public management the sole alternative. And interestingly enough, it is through their own actions - privatisation and flexibilisation - that politicians have

[26] Gould, Carol C, Rethinking democracy (1988: 19)

brought about this change, handing over power to the economic sector. As James Robertson puts it, this makes the public economic crisis a self-inflicted one. To see what this entails, we need to look beyond the neoliberal rhetoric.

Ross Jackson points out that the real role of economics as a political tool is disguised – hidden from view of a public that is led to believe that economics is an objective science, whose consequences they must passively accept. For example, some modern economists like to claim that the currently dominant 'free market' economic system is the natural end result of an evolutionary process. Nothing could be further from the truth. It is a man-made, politically determined system designed to benefit a particular segment of society, and it can be changed, Jackson asserts (R. Jackson, 2012:52). "The political power of the business community has been increasing steadily for two hundred years to the point that we can no longer separate politics from business, ... The combination of powerful business interest, political allies and popular support makes it almost impossible to stop the growth bubble from bursting either when the ecosystem can no longer take the pressure, or more likely when the reality of the coming period of energy decent hits the financial markets", Jackson observes in 2012 (2012: 74–75).

Leon J.J. Segers stresses that this tendency to separate economy from the society as a whole and to define it as a Law of Nature, has to be exposed as false and unjust. The economy is really a part of the social order, so standards have to originate in and be based on society itself (Segers, 2012:12). True, Segers notes, people are subjected to economic laws but the playing fields of those economic laws are determined by politics. In that respect also prices can be manipulated or changed by political decisions. Equally so, a lot of arrangements in our social organisation have been made that are decisive for prices and price-relations. Democracy needs the availability of social and material conditions necessary for the achievement of purposes and plans as Gould puts it, Segers says, and proposes a universal basic income as an important tool for levelling the playing field.[27]

How it started

Privatisation is a cornerstone in neoliberal policies, which Rodney Lord has illustrated in an article Privatization - the boom goes on. Depicting the scenery of the early 1990s, Lord labels the global movement towards economic liberalisation and privatisation as one of the biggest business opportunities of this century. He notes that in the past three years governments worldwide have sold assets worth close to $ 100 billion. This has created big investment opportunities. It has also meant that governments have given access to private business in areas, from which they have previously been barred. This new outlet for private business has also had its spill over effects on services, with increased demands for investment banks, tax accountants, pension consultants, insurance brokers, public relations companies and many other services for which they had little use in the state sector. This means new big markets, for which multinationals are the ideal players. Lord notes: "Often multinationals are best placed to exploit these opportunities.... Multinational companies with their global reach can follow the trail of liberal economics as it leads on from market to market and use their financial muscle to take advantage of new opportunities as they arise."

Lord further observes that this refocusing of economic aims and enormous transfer of economic power between different sectors creates a multitude of opportunities for business. Even the least far-reaching changes from the point of view of the public sector can revolutionise the

---

[27] These are comments made to my text by Leon J.J. Segers, as will be the case in the following, where no literary reference is made.

shape of an industry and create billions of dollars of new business for private sector firms. In principle, the author notes, privatisation should be good investment opportunities. Given political stability, an efficient private sector company operating in a competitive market place should be able to extract "significantly more profitability from a state enterprise than its public sector owners who are subject to all kinds of political pressure (for instance to maintain employment) " (Lord 1991:6).

This was thus the setting in the early 1990s. By the mid 2010s the effects of privatisation are well documented. So, Ross Jackson, who has proposed a radical change to the present economic system in his book Occupy World Street, A global roadmap for radical economic and political reform (2012) comments: "Indeed, if the objective of someone was to drive our civilization to ruin, nothing could do it more effectively than the invention of the currently dominant economic system – neoliberalism." (2012: 51) What has ensued since the 1980s, is like a thriller. Who are the perpetrators? How did they go about it? Who will stand to pay for the damages caused? As Jackson notes: "Understanding the economic system is the key to understanding what is happening to our civilisation at this time." (2012: 51)

The economic scenario is an extremely complex one, and I will here merely point to some dominant features that can throw some light on the way neoliberalism has encroached on human values.[28] Public Private Partnership has been one contributing factor to present economic trends. Through this PPP, the state has guaranteed the market whereas the private sector has provided the money having thereby secured long term profits (Johan Horeman). Another effect of the liberalisation of markets is that the labour supply tripled, which in the advanced economies is seen

---

[28] I'm grateful for comments and advice I have received from Johan Horeman and Leon J.J. Segers to the text, recognised here in brackets.

in raising unemployment and a growing precariat because of the flexibilisation of labour standards. This has led to increasing economic insecurity. So, what are the governments' responses? Governments compensated for this "by allowing an orgy of consumption based on rising household debts, as well as subsidies such as tax credits that propped up workers' earnings" (Standing 2016 Kindle location 553).

Segers points to the initial failure to regulate money volumes/quantity and he sees this as one reason why the US money developed into a policy of "easy money" during the Reagan reign. This thus led to neoliberalism being introduced without any control- or steering mechanisms in place, and it was further stimulated by the easy money policy and the ongoing demolition of the regulation of the financial system. This money market ideology was considered as just another market, supported by the large global conglomerates whereas their entourage, financial boundaries and limits to their reach were felt as obstacles to further expansion. This left society as a whole unprotected against the use and abuse of money on a global scale (Segers 2012: 5–6). The "easy money"- policy led to increased public debt. When the Faustian bargaining came to its predictable end in 2008, governments, financial communities and banks orchestrated a response summarised in a single word: 'austerity' (Standing 2016: 23). And here Standing's view on austerity: "The austerity strategy is based on falsehoods intended to create a smokescreen behind which to pursue the political objective of shrinking public social spending. The first falsehood is that the crash was caused by ordinary people 'living beyond their means', requiring them to cut back to 'balance the budget'." "A second falsehood is that cutting public debt will revive growth, along with employment and income. In fact, austerity has a dampening effect, as even the IMF has warned." (Standing, 2016: 23)

A tentative balance sheet

In 2013 The Transnational Institute, TNI published an investigation into the privatisation wave observing that government debts in crisis countries have predictably soared: the highest ratios of debt to the gross domestic product, GDP in the third quarter of 2012 were recorded in Greece (153 per cent), Italy (127 per cent), Portugal (120 per cent) and Ireland (117 per cent). The results, like those in the southern hemisphere, have punished the poorest the hardest, while the richest Europeans – including the banking elite that caused the financial crisis – have emerged unscathed or even richer than before (TNI 2013:3). It is pointed out that their working paper gives a broad but still incomplete overview of what can best be described as a great 'fire sale' of public services and national assets across Europe. Coupled with deregulation and austerity measures, it is proving a disaster for citizens whereas private companies have been clear winners as they have been able to scoop up public assets in a crisis at low prices and banks involved in reckless lending have been paid back at citizens' expense (TNI 2013:3). So, their conclusion is that the European Commission far from solving the crisis is using it to entrench the same failed neoliberal policies (TNI 2013:3). To this, Horeman observes that the mistake was made already in the seventies through the EU system of government procurement.

In 2016, The Transnational Institute's report *The Bail Out Business* reveals that up to October 2016, € 213 billion of taxpayers' money – equivalent to the GDP of Finland and Luxembourg – has been permanently lost as a result of the various rescue packages. In addition to this sizeable and growing number, bail out packages have a further hidden cost: the massive fees charged by financial experts for giving advice to governments and EU institutions about how to rescue the banks (TNI 2016:4 Executive Summary). This is thus the other side of the story Rodney Lord told, foreseeing the great business opportunities in the 1990s. How can this state of affairs be justified in a democratic society? In the neoliberal paradigm, as opposed to the Keynesian one, there is no meeting point between economic and human aspects. And as the theoretical doctrines have it, economic facts hold a truth-value. So, a tentative answer is that economic matters have been given priority over human aspects, such as democracy, human rights and justice. This illustrates the steering power of the paradigm. But this is not the whole story. It is also a question of how different systems are constructed, and obviously also a question of power politics.

In its report in 2013, The Transnational Institute shows that the euro crisis has been incorrectly blamed on government spending, and that the subsequent imposition of cuts and increased borrowing has resulted in growing national debts and rising unemployment. This is the narrative we have been offered by the politicians. Government spending, yes, but for what purpose? Robertson points out that a major reason for the national debts is the bailout of banks with taxpayers' money because of the banks' reckless handling of money matters. And what aggravates the situation is that the debt includes interest on the money borrowed from the banks that have been bailed out (Robertson 2012:93). Insane, isn't it? Yes, according to Robertson, among others: "If the way we now manage our national money supply had not grown up bit by bit, century by century; if it had not become thoughtlessly accepted as the status quo; and if we were now starting from scratch to arrange how money should be supplied to a democratic society – nobody in their right mind would dream of setting it up as it is now." (Robertson, 2012: 97)

The only reason why these total debts and the interest payments on them may have to stay at these absurdly high levels is our self-inflicted dependence on the commercial banks to provide our money supply as interest-bearing debt. Once we have got rid of that burden, a good deal more than the present annual interest cost (of £ 43bn in Britain) will become available for other public purposes (Robertson 2012: 99).

A twist in perception

Here we see how the dominant paradigm steers our perception, determining what is good or bad, acceptable or unacceptable. To put the paradigm in perspective, it is instructive to recall that a decisive change of perception concerning the role of the economy has occurred over time. It was out of ethical and moral philosophy that political economy emerged as an academic subject exploring what those political and economic principles should be, and how they should be put into practice. Predecessors were Plato's Republic and Aristotle's Ethics and Politics in Greece in the 5th and 4th centuries BC. Adam Smith was the Professor of Moral Philosophy in Glasgow and published The Theory of Moral Sentiments in 1759 – seven years before he published The Wealth of Nations that earned him the title of 'father of economics'. Not to forget John Stuart Mill's Principles of Political Economy (1848). His professed aim was "to unite the greatest individual liberty of action, with a common ownership in the raw material of the globe", to combine economic democracy with the end of economic growth. "It is more relevant today than ever.", observes Robertson (2012: 71).

In his insightful text Economic *Possibilities for our Grandchildren* that John Maynard Keynes wrote in 1930, he envisaged a function for economics rid of the then prevailing perceptions: "We shall be able to rid ourselves of many of the pseudo-moral principles which have hag-ridden us for two hundred years, by which we have exalted some of the most distasteful of human qualities into the position of the highest virtues. We shall be able to afford to dare to assess the money-motive at its true value. The love of money as a possession - as distinguished from the love of money as a means to the enjoyments and realities of life - will be recognised for what it is, a somewhat disgusting morbidity, one of those semi-criminal, semi-pathological propensities which one hands over with a shudder to the specialists in mental disease." (Robertson, 2012: 90)

How we got here

Keynes came to the conclusion that demand and supply of goods and services would not automatically result in price equilibrium, because of time-lags and poverty gaps. It would not be possible to automatically achieve price equilibrium and at the same time achieve full employment. Consequently, it was necessary for governments to step in, in order to achieve a perceived 'optimal economic production of prosperity'. In doing so the government was actively steering demand and supply. As Keynes' analyses had been proven correct, especially during and after world war II, governments were, in the post war period, given a new important mission: to monitor the macro-economic equilibrium and keep it balanced (Segers, 2012: 2). But then came the time when more government spending was no longer perceived as 'productive' but rather as waste; not so much as job creation but rather as causing tax burden and increasing national debts. As a result the so-called Keynesian ideology was no longer considered opportune and was being questioned instead (Segers, 2012: 5).

The Dutch scene may here illustrate the development as depicted by Horeman. He notes that during the 1970s politicians still thought in national terms, and politics was still focussed on the national domain. The investment and wage policies of the Dutch were confronted by increasing imports; debts were rising, unemployment did not decrease. It was another pricing method used by the Japanese that made Asian products more attractive. Later the export of jobs started in the USA by outsourcing production to China.

Affluence is, yet, another reason for the changing economic rationale that Segers points to. In Keynes' times society was poor. This meant scarcity of products at the same time as there was an unused capacity expressed in the form of unemployment. Rich people had what they needed whereas poor people had no money, thus no purchasing power. So, the government had to intervene and spend (via public investments) in order to bring more money to people so that they could satisfy their needs. In our days we have far more production (capacity) that we (people that have the money) can use. There is a plea for new public investments (such as glass-fiber and education) to "create work", but automatization (robotization) diminishes it. The costs of labour (incl. taxes and social security) are relatively seen far too high, Segers observes, and labour is priced out of the market (the economic system, as it now works, drives it out). Segers sees a basic income as a solution to this problem as it would lower the price of labour, drastically and make men free to work with things they like. Segers points out that as labour is no longer equal to income, the income from work needs only to be a supplement to the unconditional basic income.

Break down of the Bretton Woods

Breaking up the gold standard behind the Bretton Woods system paved the way for the neoliberal orientation. Gold was first replaced by baskets of currencies. Saving banks, mortgage banks, commercial banks, investment banks, insurance sectors were originally separated to secure the financial system. But now barriers between different banks were dismantled for which the International Monetary Fund, IMF, and the World Bank were advocates, and still are. This was also the case with the Organisation of Economic Co-operation and Development, OECD. The Bretton Woods system was a negotiated monetary order intended to govern monetary relations among independent nation-states. The chief features of the Bretton Woods system were an obligation for each country to fix the currencies to the gold standard, as well as the ability of the IMF to bridge temporary imbalances of payments. The Bretton Woods system contained shock absorbers for economies badly hit. Yanis Varoufakis observes that it was thanks to the design of the Bretton Woods system that inequality between and within nations shrank in the 1950's and 1960's. As a result, "the poor had, as the phrase goes, never had it so good, courtesy of a leviathan keenly aware that its self-interest was best served by an enlightened equilibration of world capitalism, involving controls of finance, limits to all sorts of profiteering and the active redistribution to the have-nots." (Varoufakis, 2016: 81)

Keynes had envisaged an International Monetary Fund (IMF) of quite another calibre. So according to "Keynes's IMF, recognizing that one nation's deficit is another's surplus, would levy a tax on a nation's account if its imports and exports diverged too much. The idea was to penalize both types of imbalances (excessive surpluses as well as excessive deficits; the Germanys of the world as well as the Greeks) and in the process build up a war chest of bancors at the IMF so that, when some crisis hit, deficit nations in trouble could be propped up and prevented from falling into a black hole of debt and recession that might spread throughout the Bretton Woods system." (Varoufakis, 2016: 26) This proposal was too democratic to win the day. This is how Varoufakis characterises Keynes proposal projecting it through the eyes of Harry Dexter White, a leading US figure in the Bretton Woods negotiations: "For White the die had already been cast: Europe was to be dollarized and the dollar would be the world currency. The bancor was a great idea in a multilateral world but a joke in one where the dollar had already been crowned king and queen. Moreover, the idea that the IMF's governing committee, with the Europeans in the majority, would tax America's surpluses seemed to him too ludicrous for words. America owned its surpluses and would recycle them herself, without petitioning a group of bankrupt Europeans for their permission to do so." (Varoufakis, 2016: 26–27)

The Bretton woods system (1944 –1971) that had fixed the world currency-rates via the Dollar to the value of gold, had worked for ±20 years. It grew shaky because of the development of the world economy. The world trade development was so fast and strong that all rules came too late and too slow. The US ended the exchangeability of the dollar in gold to a fixed price and so the dollar became the world coin, but without any international agreement or rule. The US made their own rules on this matter. The world money-lobby was so strong that after 1971 also in the nineties some very important rules on monetary behaviour were abandoned e.g. The Glass Steagel Act. All these were ingredients for the Banking Crisis in 2008 as the anarchistic increase in the money supply on a world scale burst. Some banks went bust as the money shrank again but by far the majority of the lost money had to be paid by ordinary people via an austerity policy (Segers).

Horeman explicates: The balancing effect of the IMF and Bretton Woods was working well until the USA started overspending dollars and other countries started claiming gold in return. That happened in the sixties and seventies. But inside the economies there were still barriers between saving and between investing smartly used by capitalist businesses that used loans to create profits at a higher level than was possible with only shareholder's equity. Besides, inflation was considered a problem. Too much money was floating around, spending was going up, interest rates were low and profits were high. People's savings were going down the drain and under Reagan the tight money supply was introduced to stimulate interest rates, and compensate lower profits with lower taxes. But it was more complex than that, Horeman notes. To this, Siegers adds: Although the world economy in Keynes times was very different from the system now, there was already then the threat of world disequilibrium. Keynes wanted it to be corrected, a currency system led by a Bancor authority. Such a financial crisis is not abnormal on a world scale, Segers notes. We had Argentina -, the Asian – and some other financial crises. The cause is always the same, that there is no monetary authority on a world scale, no Bancor; so the money system is a uncoordinated chaos. Seger's assessment is that since the 2008 crisis many bankers want more regulation but a logical and fair regime is still far away and there is no political consensus on the matter. The current 'system' favours greatly the US dollar and the Americans want to keep it as it is now.

Varoufakis points out that in the 1980s and 1990s, time had overrun the Bretton Woods system and Europe's social democrats and America's Democrats had abandoned the idea that capitalism had to be civilized by driving a hard bargain with the captains of industry, supporting organised labour and containing bankers' natural instincts. So, Varoufakis says, they lost sight of the fact that inequality destabilises financial markets and reinforces capitalism's tendency to fall on its face (Varoufakis 2016: 210). The tumultuous way in which the international and global economy developed since the 1980s resulted in a lot of mere bubbles, which as such went unnoticed by statistics. Economists and politicians perceived this development as a confirmation of the validity of the neoliberal 'theory', Segers notes. He points out that big business took over the direction of the economic development on a global scale whereas politics only facilitated this movement. "The economic forces that were set free by the dynamics of the globalisation itself were so huge that they covered up all theory and all question marks that were placed by the theorists. On top of that, the collapse of the Sovjet system in 1989, resulted in another impulse for international business developments." (Segers, 2012: 7) This had the effect that society as a whole was left unprotected against the use and abuse of money on a global scale (Segers 2012: 5).

Horeman assesses the Dutch scene as follows: In the Netherlands the money of the pension funds were made available for the money game to create endless growth of pensions almost without paying pension contributions. Unemployment became part of the state's social security because unemployment was very low and the risk considered less. It was an exchange for the control that was taken away from the social partners that has continued to backfire for many years now. It created the opportunity for the state to take severe control over the unemployed leading to workfare and cuts in social security, which in turn has fuelled the idea of a basic income.

The drama that ensued after the break-down of the Bretton Woods system has been mercilessly accounted by Yanis Varoufakis in his book *And The Weak Suffer What They Must?, Europe, Austerity and the Threat to Global Stability* (2016). As a scholar, an economist, and game theorist, Varoufakis had researched and analysed the way the EU went about the economic crisis of 2008 and the bail-out of banks. In the process of writing that book, his role changed from researcher and writer to actor as finance minister of Greece. Thereby he is able to give both a theoretical – outside - and a practical - inside - perspective on the economic system in operation. A decisive change that occurred with the break down of the Bretton Woods system, followed by privatisation and liberalisation, was the process in which private banks began to create money in the form of derivatives. "Financialization, as we now call this process, was the critical by-product of maintaining and enhancing US dominance on the back of increasing trade imbalances and in the interest of financing America's ever-expanding ... deficits." This process turned "finance into the driver and industry into its servant."" (Varoufakis, 2016:89) "It was as if Europe had turned its own Balkanization into an objective, into an art form.", Varoufakis avows. " What would have otherwise been relatively benign recessions ended up dividing Europeans and ruling over them, deepening divisions in living standards and causing different life prospects in different parts of the union. This was the consequence of attempting to keep currencies locked into one another before establishing any mechanism for recycling the surpluses of those who produced them by investing part of those surpluses into countries and regions in serious deficit (Varoufakis, 2016: 143).

Collaborators

Although Reagan and Thatcher had brought neoliberalism on to the political agenda, much of what ensued was initiated in more democratic quarters. Here Varoufakis' exposé: "What possessed the Clinton administration to dismantle the New Deal's last remaining constraints on Wall Street? After all, it was not Reaganites or neocons but bona fide democrats like Robert Rubin, Larry Summers and Tim Geitner who in the 1990s took apart the Glass-Steagall Act that had imposed legal constraints on finance, thus unleashing turbocharged financialization on an unsuspecting planet." (Varoufakis, 2016: 210) To this scenery Varoufakis offers the following explanation: "With paper profits mounting, European social democrats and American Democrats in government were lured into a Faustian bargain with the bankers of Wall Street, the City of London, Frankfurt and Paris, who were only too pleased to let reformist politicians take a small cut of their loot as long as the politicians consented to the complete deregulation of financial markets." (Varoufakis 2016: 210–211)

"In this brave new world of financialisaton, of bankers creating new 'products' that soon after their birth behave like privately minted money, the world of finance and banking decoupled from planet Earth in ways that the world came painfully to grasp in late 2008. A worldwide spending and investment spree was powered by private money created within the private banks and financial institutions – Lehman Brothers, Goldman Sachs, AIG and the like – whose activities became increasingly distant from those which common folk, including German manufactures, understood as banking." (Varoufakis 2016: 132)

And so, when in 2008 the vast pyramid of financial capital came crashing down, the government would, Varoufakis observes, "allow one bank, Lehman, to fail as a morality tale for the rest of the bankers and as a signal to the American people that their public officials were not entirely under the bank's spell." Meanwhile they were preparing to bail out all other financial institutions if Lehman's insolvency got out of hand. "The result was the largest ever transfer of private losses from banks' books onto the public debt ledger..." (*Varoufakis* 2016: 154) This development did, howsoever, not go without opposition. Horeman points out that there were social democratic governments creating social capitalistic responses but they were counteracted by right wing governments, like the German, and the money markets, which created the financial break down. In the Netherlands the Social Democrat Bos in a government with the Christian Democrats and Christian Unionists funded potentially bankrupt banks and stimulated the economy with 20 billion euros. There was also a 200 billion guarantee available for business refinancing. But even with the aid of government and the troubles their activities caused society, the banks were mainly caring for themselves. Less mortgages, less financing of businesses, no interbank loans, no transfer of low ECB interest to clients. They obstructed the economy.

The government led by the (neo)liberal party VVD aimed at changing national financial politics by reducing economic support, by a policy of austerity and by privatisation. Where the social democrats reduced the impact of the financial crisis, the (neo) liberals of VVD intensified the crisis. It took the Netherlands 8 years to get at the level of the 2008 economy. Most countries did it in a few years, Horeman asserts. In Europe and the EU the risky investments of the wealthy financial institutes were transferred from business to business loans into state backed loans, meaning that the people was made responsible for risks engaged by the elite when things looked sunny. This prevented bankruptcy, while the crisis was used to enforce reduction of social benefits and to freeze pensions. The state loans were used to pay off the obligation to the financing institutes. Thus, Horeman's account of the situation in the Netherlands.

In Europe it was Greece that was given the task to offer the morality tale. In Varoufakis' words:" The Greek loan thus came with strings attached – strings designed to cause visible pain to the weakest Greeks. The conditionalities, as the strings were called, boiled down to the dismantling of basic social welfare provisions, to be supervised by officials representing the European Central Bank, the European Commission and the International Monetary Fund." Thus, the troika – the triumvirate of ECB, the EC and the IMF – was born. "It comprised a small group of bailiffs, disguised as technocrats, who acquired powers that Europe's governments cannot dream of. With every visitation of the troika, the dream of shared European prosperity was dealt another blow." (Varoufakis, 2016:160)

Defenceless?

Varoufakis says that Europe's social democrats did not have the mental tools or moral values with which to combat the bankers or to subject the collapsing system to critical scrutiny (2016: 211). Because of the rules through which the euro was introduced, there are no such levelling mechanisms as Keynes had wished for for the IMF, nor is it designed like the US system, which contains shock absorbers for locations facing economic hardship. Instead the so-called Maastricht criteria specifies common rules governing the total amount of public debt and the maximum budget deficit the member state was allowed, which is 3 per cent. For such a deficit the Commission issues warnings and the deficit can eventually lead to sanctions (Varoufakis 2016: 219).

Member countries should fund their own deficits without counting on the new central bank providing shock absorbers, which is one form of solidarity (see Varoufakis, 2016:120). Varoufakis saw himself defeated when trying to get a 'human' deal for Greece from the troika. His answer was to resign from the post of finance minister instead of agreeing to the troika's dictate. The EU system has been created under pressure from the German

CSU finance minister in Maastricht in 1992, as well as later. Behind the system there are ministers Waigel and Schäuble drawing on the Bavarian experience that other 'Bundesländer' are profiting from their success. They wanted to prevent this on a European scale and pulled strings to do so. Austerity was the result (Horeman). Varoufakis' verdict: "The eurozone's architecture was incapable of sustaining the shock waves of the 2008 earthquake. Since then it has been in deep crisis reinforced largely by the European Union's denial that there is anything the matter with its currency's rules, as opposed to their enforcement." (Varoufakis, 2016:138)

Human rights and the EU

Within the European Union the root problem is the Maastricht criteria that need to be contrasted to the values that should govern the EU. So, it is in place to contrast the handling of the economic crisis with the values declared in the Charter of Fundamental Rights of the European Union (2010/C 83/02) .This is how the charter opens: "Preamble. The peoples of Europe, in creating an ever closer union among them, are resolved to share a peaceful future based on common values. Conscious of its spiritual and moral heritage, the Union is founded on the indivisible, universal values of human dignity, freedom, equality and solidarity; it is based on the principles of democracy and the rule of law. It places the individual at the heart of its activities, by establishing the citizenship of the Union and by creating an area of freedom, security and justice."

What discrepancy is there not between these standards and the way the troika has gone about member countries faced with severe debt problems that often was of others' making? It goes beyond the scope here to go into the frustrating manoeuvres that Greece and other countries had to face. Fortunately, the process is well documented by Yanis Varoufakis in his book *And The Weak Suffer What They Must?* (2016). This book gives a unique insight into the fight between democracy and decency on the Greek side and the sinister practices of the troika on the other. After five months Varoufakis resigned as he was not ready to sign a bail-out dictate by the troika that he, based on democratic arguments as well as economic analysis, considered unsustainable.

So, the crucial question of this chapter Humanism versus neoliberalism is: What is the weight of human rights standards faced with the economic dictates? Is there more to it than just power politics? When to this is added a public debt that is caused by taxpayers bailing out banks, we truly find ourselves in a Kafka-like landscape. As long as there was a level playing field between major players in society a fair accommodation could be achieved, as was the case in the post world war II era. This balance is now lacking, although there is presently an impressive mobilisation occurring in different quarters against neoliberal policies and practices.

As the Charter of Fundamental Rights of the European Union shows, there is no lack of standards to defend humanism and a good life. Human rights standards represent the legal expression of humanity. These rights are now under attack from the neoliberal rationale and the challenge is to have human and cultural values weighed on equal terms with economic ones. How to go about it? We are faced with the same setting, as Keynes' was when he during the great depression of 1929 wrote about the grand-children's economic prospects. "The prevailing world depression, the enormous anomaly of unemployment in a world full of wants, the disastrous mistakes we have made, blind us to what is going on under the surface to the true interpretation of the trend of things ... What can we reasonably expect the level of our economic life to be a hundred years hence? What are the economic possibilities for our grandchildren?" On this question Robertson comments: "We are now getting on towards the hundred years since Keynes wrote those words. But beware! We are now running out of time. "Avarice and usury" are carrying us all too fast toward self-destruction. Can we wean ourselves off them in time to survive their consequences? That is an open question now. In principle, if enough of us decide that the way the money system now works must be changed in order to reduce the conflict between present money values and universal values such as "democracy, the rule of law and human rights", we should be able to do so." (Robertson 2012: 90, 77)

In short, Robertson asserts, we have to accept that there is no way to make the present misconceived arrangement for creating the money supply work satisfactorily. The monetary reform Robertson proposes will avoid, he says, further costly and fruitless, national and international consultations on how to square that circle. The model he proposes will liberate us to develop a more democratic, decentralised money system serving the majority of citizens, not just a favoured minority that benefits from the subsidised profits of the financial sector (Robertson 2012: 123). And Robertson is certainly not alone in arguing that the money system should be changed.

New purposes and principles

There is thus ample evidence that the neoliberal system does not work and there is a long line of economists and other scholars who convey messages of an urgent need for change. Humanism, democracy, justice, human rights are the motivating forces for the changes they propose. In addition, they represent the view that economics is not a purely theoretical matter, but has to do with how we live and act. This in contrast to the view that economics is an objective science, which Robertson disdains: "Ironically, many potentially good students now, looking for a field of learning that will enable them to do something useful and valuable with their working lives, are put off economics by its pretensions to be an objective science, independent of morality and ethics." (Robertson 2012: 72) Here are suggestions from James Robertson, Yanis Varoufakis and Leon J.J. Segers.

In his book *Future Money – Breakdown or Breakthrough* (2012), James Robertson has developed new principles for the money system, of which here his summary: ”Public agencies serving the common interest should create the public money supply. People and businesses and other organisations should be rewarded untaxed for the contributions we make by our efforts and skills to the well-being of other people and for the value we add to the value of common resources. People and businesses and other organisations, including public service and other non-profit organisations, should be taxed on the value they take from common resources. The revenue from those taxes – after democratic decisions on what is needed to finance other public services – should be fairly shared among us all as a citizen's income. Those arrangements should be designed to free us from continually increasing dependence on centralised national and international money, and on big business and government to meet all our needs, and so enable us to reduce our use of conventional mainstream money.“ (Robertson 2012: 87)

Robertson observes that the reform he proposes will have serious consequences for the banks. ”Those must be recognised. But, as with most practical problems, it will be sensible to put the horse before the cart.“ (2012: 98) Robertson directed his aspirations to Greece. At the time he is writing the book (which he finished writing in January 2012), Robertson notes that the possibility is growing that Greece may be the first country to leave the eurozone. If it does so and brings back the drachma as its national currency, the Greek government should seriously consider adopting a reformed monetary regime on the lines he proposes in his book. ”The Greeks are a proud people. By making good use of the otherwise insoluble eurozone crisis, they could pioneer the new path into the future – for themselves, for other European countries and eventually for the rest of the world." (Robertson, 2012: 122)

Varoufakis' answer to Greece's anti-democratic experience was to launch a project for the democratisation of the European Union – *A New*

Deal for Europe. The European New Deal should include five precise goals and the means to achieve them under existing EU treaties, without any centralisation of power in Brussels or further loss of sovereignty:

- Large-scale green investment will be funded by a partnership between Europe's public investment banks (the European Investment Bank, KfW, and others) and central banks (on the basis of directing quantitative easing to investment project bonds) to channel up to 5 per cent of European total income into investments in green energy and sustainable technologies.
- An employment guarantee scheme to provide living-wage jobs in the public and non-profit sectors for every European in their home country, available on demand for all who want them. On condition that the scheme does not replace civil-service jobs, carry tenure, or replace existing benefits, it would establish an alternative to choosing between misery and emigration.
- An anti-poverty fund that provides for basic needs across Europe, which would also serve as the foundation of an eventual benefits union.
- A universal basic dividend to socialize a greater share of growing returns to capital.
- Immediate anti-eviction protection, in the form of a right-to-rent rule that permits homeowners facing foreclosure to remain in their homes at a fair rent set by local community boards. In the longer term, Europe must fund and guarantee decent housing for every European in their home country, restoring the model of social housing that has been dismantled across the continent. Both the employment scheme and the anti-poverty program should be based on a modern version of an old practice: public banking for public purpose, funded by a pragmatic but radical currency reform within the euro zone and the EU, as well as in non-EU European

countries. Specifically, all seignior age profits of central banks would be used for these purposes.[29]

Basic income - a way of compensating citizens

Robertson asserts that if the money system remains unreformed, its workings will continue to frustrate all the well-meant efforts of active citizens, NGOs (non-governmental organisations) and government agencies, to deal with our present ills and problems – including worldwide poverty, environmental destruction, social injustice, economic inefficiency, and political unrest and violence within and between nations. Again, that is why failure to reform the world's money system urgently and radically – that is to say, from its roots up – could bring on the self-destruction of our civilisation before the end of this century (Robertson 2012: 11–12).

Robertson sees 'quantitative easing' as an immediate response to create new money to be put into circulation directly into the real economy – for example via a citizen's income – and not in further bail-outs to banks and the financial sector. "Once the decision is made that it is the only responsible course of action and must be done urgently, it can be done almost immediately." (Robertson 2012: 123) Robertson sees thus a universal citizen's income as one of the main positive shifts in national public spending that would be payable to all citizens as a right. It will cover state pensions, child allowances, and many other existing social benefits, tax allowances, tax reliefs and tax credits. It will recognise that responsible citizens in a democratic society have a right to share a significant part of the public revenue from the value of common resources. It will enable people to become less dependent on welfare and work of big government, big

[29] Yaroufakis, a new deal to save Europe https://www.project-syndicate.org/commentary/new-deal-for-europe-by-yanis-varoufakis-2017-01

business, big finance and foreign trade, because all of those incur environmentally wasteful overhead costs. An important aspect associated with a basic income is also the changed nature of work. Segers, who also advocates a basic income makes the pertinent point that the increasing automation of production also necessitates some automation of the income distribution and consequently a conceptual de-linkage of labour and income (2012: 4).

Human activities instead of employment

Already in the 1930s, Keynes foresaw how automation would transform working life and this he considered to be a great challenge. "Yet there is no country and no people, I think, who can look forward to the age of leisure and of abundance without a dread. For we have been trained too long to strive and not to enjoy" (emphasis added). This is an interesting contrast to the way those who oppose a basic income anticipate people's behaviour. This could be summarised in one word, 'laziness', without further specification. Here Robertson differentiate the picture: "It may be objected that many irresponsible people at both ends of the social spectrum – richest and poorest – will take advantage of a Citizen's Income to make no useful contribution to society. It will be necessary to correct the danger of that possible effect, at the rich end of the spectrum by closing off the present opportunities for avoiding payment of due taxes, and at the poorer end by providing wide ranges of better social, economic and cultural opportunities for a socially useful life, and sharper deterrents against anti-social behaviour. In order to be effective, the necessary action – especially at the poorer end of the spectrum – will have to go forward against a much more genuine background of social and economic justice than exists today (Robertson, 2012:130).

Here humanism has a great vacuum to fill. This is the playing field of artistic creation and civil society that just wait to be freed from the shackles that austerity and other neoliberal inventions, such as workfare, pose. A basic income would be the means through which people who struggle to be able to pursue their chosen plan of life, artists among others, would be able to do so without all the constraints faced within the wage labour society. A citizen's income would also give us more power of control over how the money is spent and invested, and of deciding how we will work to meet our own local needs and priorities and those of our families and neighbours. Today we have to depend on remotely controlled big business, big finance and big government to make those decisions for us (Robertson, 2012: 132). This is also Segers' point: "In any case the introduction of a basic income will have the tendency to bring back a lot of risks into the heart of the regional society, where solidarity and transparency can result in people themselves being in the lead on their own destiny." (2012:14)

As a welcome contrast to the often hear argument against a basic income, "can we afford it?", Segers shows how a global universal basic income would have nurturing effects on the economy, levelling the playing field also at a global level. The most essential aspect, Segers stresses, is to bring balance in international economic relations, that is, in the real economy and real trade relations, by terminating the perversion of the international labour market due to international prosperity differences. And then Segers makes the somewhat surprising observation about the effects of a global basic income. "Introduction of a basic income is most important for the rich societies, as the impact on the world labour market is far bigger than it would be introducing it elsewhere. The first rationale of this big effect is that the social costs for society will disappear from labour costs, secondly, the wage-tax will disappear and thirdly all wages will get a "subsidy" that equals the basic income. So the total impact of reshuffling taxes in this way is really big (Segers 2012: 14).

Segers further observes that the implementation of a basic income in general would bring a wave of de-globalisation and it would reverse a lot of unsustainable developments that took place in the last decades / years. It would also cause a lot of global trades to return to a level that is much closer to sustainability. This is not only based on the cost calculation of the industry but on the costs of society as a whole. It would bring more and more diverse developments to the region and it would bring real political and democratic power back to the basic and a lot of transparency in society itself (Segers, 2012: 15).

Yuval Noah Harari sees universal basic income as a good start but adds to this a number of reservations, one of them being that it should be global – a good qualification!

Concluding balance sheet

This paper set out to explore the relation and tension between humanism and neoliberalism. As noted above, the magnitude of the economic exploration exploded in my face, although it has been part of my investigations since the 1990s. It has been a struggle to manage this vast field, an elephant! But I had to try. Why? Because the way we approach the economy will be decisive for the space given to human and social concerns. So here Aristotle assists in differentiating the economic scene. The good life, which Aristotle has designated as the ultimate purpose of government, requires a certain minimum supply of necessities. Property is one prerequisite, which he considers necessary in order to satisfy basic needs. Property is thus a means for the end of satisfying basic needs, and thereby there is also a natural limit to the acquisition of property. But, Aristotle notes, "there is another kind of property-getting, to which the term 'acquisition of goods' applies, and it is due to this that there is thought to be no limit to wealth or property."

Elaborating on the phenomenon of acquisition of goods, Aristotle establishes a distinction between property aimed at satisfying basic needs, and the acquisition of goods for its own sake. The kind which is household-management does have a limit, since it is the function of household-management to acquire goods. Both kinds of property overlap in that both are concerned with the same thing, property; but in their use of it they are dissimilar: in one case the end is sheer increase, in the other something different (Politics, I.iv, 1256b40, p 81). Segers brings us to today's reality: The most important function of a monetary system is to serve the real economy and to facilitate it, which means the economy has to be protected against gambling and speculation in the monetary world in any shape or form. It should be forbidden or be defined away. The circulating of money has to function as a medium of exchange, so "financial products" should only be basic ones (2012: 12–13).

Humanism and work

The end of work is increasingly occupying people's minds. In 1985 James Robertson drew attention to the opportunities involved in decreasing industrial work in his book Future work. Jobs, self-employment and leisure after the industrial age. There he observes that, at times of uncertainty like the present, different people perceive the future in different ways. There are at least three distinct views about the future of work. The keyword for the first is employment. The keyword for the second is leisure. The keyword for the third is ownwork. They are based on three distinct perceptions of the future of industrialised society. Robertson calls them Business As Usual, HE (Hyper-Expansionist) and SHE (Sane, Humane, Ecological). Business As Usual assumes that the society of the future will not be very different from late industrial society as it is today. HE and SHE are contrasting visions of a post-industrial society which, in either case, will be distinctly different from the society we have today. To this Robertson proposes as a third alternative that people choose their own way of work in areas of their own choice (1985: 3, 7–8).

10 years, later, in 1995, Jeremy Rifkin published his book *End of Work* where he pointed to a need to redefine opportunities and responsibilities for millions of people in a society absent of mass formal employment (1995: xv).[30] However, it took some time before discussions about robotization finally opened people's eyes on a larger scale to the profound changes there are in working life. A central ingredient in this discussion is what professions are going to be substituted by robots. Adding algorithms to this picture Yuval Noah Harari sees most professions replaceable by computers. Research indicates that archaeologists is a profession with a low probability to be replaced by computers.

Redefinition of work

Our perception of work is crucial for how we look at and administer a 'workerless' society. This is our chance to give space to and give appreciation for meaningful activities that people pursue – their own work. This is the humanist side of the picture that need to be emphasised to avoid that people fall into the perceptional trap of 'unnecessary people', as Harari provokingly suggests: In the 21st century we might witness the creation of a massive new unworking class: people devoid of any economic, political or even artistic value, who contribute nothing to the prosperity, power and glory of society. This 'useless class' will not merely be unemployed — it will be unemployable.[31] Harari expresses here a utilitarian view of the workerless society that at a political level leads to all kinds of misconceived 'remedies' such as the disciplining workfare and other 'well

---

30 https://www.youtube.com/watch?v=kJMYdG1SUnM

31 This reference is based on an excerpt from Harari's book *Homo Deus: A brief history of tomorrow* (Reprinted by permission of Harperan imprint of HarperCollins)"

intended' means of disciplining people who are innocent victims of profit ridden neoliberal policies. So, what are the remedies to the injustices to which these perceptional views lead? The three first articles in this book have given a snapshot of where we stand in 2017, at a time when a neoliberal world view is increasing encroaching on a human way of life. The rest of the book is my account, since 2001, of societal change and how we should respond to it with human rights and social justice as guiding principles.

CHAPTER 4

REFLEXIVE LABOUR LAW IN ICT SOCIETY

2001 - International workshop Reflexive Labour Law: The Next Step, Amsterdam 13-14.12.2001

Crossroads

The use of what we for a long time have called atypical work has, since the 1970s and 80s, increased from a few per cent to some 30 per cent or more, in most post-industrial countries. To consider a phenomenon of this scope as atypical is an indication that the theoretical tools we use are not reflective of factual conditions in today's information and communication society. An effect of this, again, is that a large part of the working population stands the risk of being deprived of the legal protection aimed at by labour law. At the turn of the millennium experts predicted that within a decade only half the German population of working age would be engaged in full-time long-term employment. The other half will either be unemployed or engaged in atypical work.[32] For other countries the trend is similar. If we want labour law to be reflexive, we need to take account of factual practices, and scrutinize where and how legal provisions need to be introduced in order to make so called atypical work a viable alternative, avoiding thereby the present trend of increasing social marginalisation.

I will address the challenges for labour and associated social security legislation, to reflect factual conditions by looking at the status of artists

[32] Heikka, Mikko, Jäähyväiset täystyöllisyydelle, 2000: 87.

and freelancers. These are two professional groups for whom neither theoretical, nor factual categories have been devised in labour and social security legislation. Artists are a particularly fruitful group to consider, as an assessment of their status in the labour market requires other criteria than those embedded in labour law. We cannot do justice to the nature of artists' work through the conventional theoretical tools used in labour law. Instead we need to recognise that artistic work is of another kind than an ordinary breadwinning job or entrepreneurship. This requires a decisive change of perception that will make it possible to see a number of activities that are not visible through present concepts used both in labour and social security legislation. Through an approach that considers the work that is factually done, rather than a legal definition of an activity (an employment relationship), it will equally be easier to see the great diversification of working and economic life that information and communication society has brought along.

Characteristics of information and communication society

One central aspect of work in information and communication society, ICT society, is that much work has become individualised, as opposed to the logic of mass production. This implies that an individual work input has become central in the value creating process. Nevertheless, as Castells points out, the worker is, as never before, submitted to the mercy of the organisation as it now operates, with 'slimmed' individuals, contracted out in flexible networks in information and communication society (Castells 1999: 286). In his penetrating analysis of the emergence of the network society, Castells notes that information technology holds the potential of increased productivity, a higher standard of living and increased employment, if only certain technical choices were made (1999: 280). The informational paradigm is a socially open one; it is a politically administered paradigm, the most important common elements of which are technical (1999: 238). The present development is thus the result of economic and political choices, through which business and governments have opted for an easy way out in the transformation toward the new informational economy. This stands in obvious contrast to the potentials inherent in the informational paradigm, Castells asserts (1999: 247).

However, this problem does not solely concern business and politics. The research community has its part to play, in providing theoretical tools for handling these new human and societal phenomena. As long as we lack appropriate theoretical schemes and tools, through which to capture the legal problems involved, present deficiencies are carried over in legislation, impeding thereby the potentials inherent in present developments, as the transformation of working life during the past decades clearly reveals. A central problem from a legal point of view is that different policies, such as cultural policies aimed at enhancing the position of artists, may be undermined by provisions in other administrative sectors, such as the regulation of working life and social security.

Reflexivity and flexibility

The changes that have occurred in working life require flexibility, for employers as well as for workers. Flexibility as such is not a problem, the problem is the implications of the way in which flexibility is now introduced. A decisive question is how rights and responsibilities associated with flexible work formats are distributed. In addition to the changing nature of economic life in ICT society, we also have a change of mentality whereby an increasing number of persons wish to work in a flexible manner. And there are professional groups like artists and freelancers whose work does not fit the labour law standard. The challenge is thus to make flexible work formats a viable alternative. This again requires different societal players to assume their responsibility. Reinhold Fahlbeck has summed up employers' responsibilities as follows: (a) social responsibility of employers, (b) objectivity of treatment of workers, including equal opportunity and non-discrimination, (c) transparency in matters regarding manpower and manpower handling, (d) proportionality, (e) predictability (or legal certainty) and (f) legal protection of employees, particularly employment security. "This is a rather formidable gamut of interests", Fahlbeck notes, that are all part of today's legal debate (Fahlbeck,1998:12).

Balancing flexibility and security

In adapting legislation and institutional arrangements to factual conditions, a reasonable requirement should be that people be able, as far as possible, to live from their own work. This is also an aim expressed in the European Union's employment guidelines (2001), where the notion that 'work should pay' is expressed. A first matter to acknowledge when addressing present day challenges is to recognise that what has been considered as standard work, that is, full-time, long-term employment is no longer sufficient as a standard. Account must also be taken of the multifacetted categories of work that still today are called atypical. There is a need to consider what kinds of adaptations are required in legislation and institutional arrangements, to make such free work formats a viable alternative. A balancing is here required between flexibility and security in the labour market, that Ton Wilthagen and Ralf Rogowski have formulated as "[a] policy strategy that attempts, synchronically and in a coordinated way, to enhance the flexibility of labour markets, the work organisation and labour relations on the one hand, and to enhance security - employment security and social security - notably for weaker groups in and outside the labour market on the other hand."[33] A Dutch scheme for artists, who cannot live on the income from their artistic work, illustrates in an interesting way how flexibility and security can be achieved (Wet Inkomensvoorziening Kunstenaars (Wik 1998). This scheme will be looked at below.

Post script: The WIK systemin has been discontinued. According to the experience of artists who relied on it, the system did not offer the flexibility and predictability I so enthusiastically read into it. This is thus a reservation for the enthusiasm that will be displayed in the rest of the text.

The problem illustrated

The economic depression of the early 1990s that followed in the wake of the speculation wave of the 1980s, resulted in high unemployment rates, in Finland close to 20 per cent. Despite a recovered and boosting economy since then, the risk of becoming unemployed has not decreased, on the contrary. In 1993 there were 813 000 instances of people getting unemployed in Finland, whereas the number had increased to 910 000, by 1999. This is an illustration of an increasing use of fixed-term employment, accompanied by reoccurring spells of unemployment. In contrast to the time of the depression people are now relatively soon employed again (Harju 2001: 20). For the person concerned this requires relying on unemployment compensation that, in turn, actualise another set of both practical and theoretical problems associated with access to social security. Problems associated with social security are exposed in a caricatured way in regard to artists, as artistic work does not automatically provide

[33] Cited in Wilthagen, Ton, 'Flexicurity' reflexivity in national and European systems of labour law and industrial relations p. 3.

an income to sustain a person's living. Attention must in such conditions be directed toward how different sectors of society interact. In the case of artists, attention must be directed to whether and how the practices of the authorities in the fields of labour and social security, as well as funding agencies and business, relate to the aims and policies of the cultural administration. As things now stand, policies and provisions aimed at enhancing the status of artists are easily undermined when artists are confronted, above all, with social security regulations and practices. Problems equally occur in transitions between 'conventional' work and other statuses (see Korver 2001).

It is important to scrutinise how labour law relates to broader regulatory frameworks. One way out of the impasses into which the concepts used in labour and social security legislation have led, is to relate them to the general principals of a legal order, such as legal certainty and predictability. Regulations and factual practices also need to be contrasted to a policy level.[34] Here again art and culture offer practical illustrations of the challenges we face. Culture and entertainment is one of the most expansive sectors in post-industrial societies. US international trade in culture and entertainment has grown from 95 billion dollars in 1980 to 387 billion dollars in 1998. The trend is similar in other countries.[35] A study made by the Finnish Arts Council reveals that in 1997 the cultural industry had a turnover that exceeded the official support for art and culture seven times. In other words, the cultural industry is a highly productive sector that produces a substantive return for the state (Hellman *2001: 28–29).* Notwithstanding this considerable growth in art and culture, there has not been any corresponding clarification of the status of artists, whose

---

[34] The theoretical groundwork for the analysis I suggest, has been prepared in my doctoral thesis *To each one's due at the borderline of work. Toward a theoretical framework for economic, social and cultural rights,* 2002.

[35] Hellman, Kulturindustrin som investeringsområde 2001: 28.

work input to a notable degree is performed as freelance work. And the number of artists is equally growing. During the period 1970 to 1995 there was a 127 per cent increase in the number of persons engaged in art and entertainment in Finland. The number of designers had increased with 101 per cent, musicians with 93 per cent, and the number of artists engaged in theatre, opera and visual arts had grown with 39 per cent (Karhunen 2002).

A major problem facing artists is that labour and social security legislation primarily is based on the notion of an employment relationship. There are no proper criteria for artists and freelancers that would give their case a consideration that is reflective of their work input. Thresholds and ceilings embedded in labour and social security legislation often have the effect of excluding artists and freelancers from the standards and protection at which both labour and social security legislation aim. Artists and freelancers share problems associated with thresholds and ceilings with all other so-called atypical workers (such as persons holding fixed-term or part-time employment). The problems are, however, revealed in a caricatured way in case of artists and freelancers.

This general problem is recognised in the EU employment guidelines 2001 that point, among others, to a need for modernising social protection, for promoting social inclusion, while ensuring that work pays, and that the long-term sustainability of social protection systems is secured.[36] One step toward achieving these aims is to take a critical look at the theoretical foundation on which present-day systems are based. Artists and freelancers offer in this respect a fresh approach to work in information and communication society.

---

[36] Council Decision of 19 January 2001 on Guidelines for Member States' employment policies for the year 2001 (2001/63/EC), cited in Korver, Ton, *Reflexive labour law and adaptability*, December 2001, unpublished.

Legal and theoretical issues involved

The nature of the relationship between the employer and the home-worker is "surrounded by a vagueness in practice and a vacuum in law such as are quite unknown in the realm of civil contracts."[37] This is how the legal position of one group of so-called atypical workers, home-workers, is characterised in a Council of Europe document dealing with the need to protect persons working at home. Most persons holding so-called atypical positions in the labour market share these problems with home-workers. Lack of labour standards is here not a problem. The standards established by the International Labour Organisation, ILO, are clear in this regard; that everybody should enjoy protection against abuse by the employer, and that everybody likewise should have access to social security. The problem resides in the way these standards are implemented at a national level, which has resulted in the kind of vacuum in law referred to above. By taking the approach that everybody should be entitled to the same standards, unnecessary energy is wasted in contemplating definitions and testing thresholds, which have followed in the wake of an increasing use of irregular work formats.

The fragmentation of working life has also generated a need to consider labour law and social security provisions conjointly. We need to take a comprehensive approach to the position of persons residing at the borderline of work, instead of a piecemeal approach to atypical work, which Mark Jeffery fittingly pictures as "plugging only some of the holes in a sinking boat." in an article *Part-time Work, 'Atypical Work' and attempts to regulate it* (1998: 212). An effect of the present trend is that those who are most vulnerable in the labour market bear the brunt of the present

[37] *Home work*, report 95, reference to Council of Europe document *The protection of persons working at home*, p. 53, Report prepared by the Study Group of the 1987-88 Co-ordinated Social Research Programme, Strasbourg 1989.

economic development. This is because employers transfer the cost of uncertainty in demand from the enterprise to the individual worker (Jeffery 1998: 210). The need is greater than ever to help disadvantaged workers retain and become reintegrated into the labour market and to alleviate poverty", Eddy Lee notes. He also points to the need for specific labour regulations to protect vulnerable groups in the labour market. All these are important for maintaining social cohesion, and staving off the political discontent that could thwart the process of globalisation, Lee notes.[38]

To introduce protection for those who today are the most vulnerable in the labour market is one, and a very important side of the coin. But there is also another one, the new potentials inherent in the changed nature of working life in information and communication society. Today there is ample space for people's own preferences and priorities. What is needed is to adapt legislation to these new conditions, to facilitate work that is more or less invisible in the wage-labour perspective, such as creative work of different kinds that does not lend itself to an eight to five format. This requires a differentiated approach to the question of flexibility, instead of the one-sided focus on employers' flexibility. "Does flexibility necessarily connote to unilateral control of one party?", Reinhold Fahlbeck asks. "Does, in the labour context, flexibility mean unilateral employer freedom to arrange matters as it sees fit? Or is the notion of flexibility neutral in this respect, lending itself not only to unilateral but also to multilateral avenues to flexibility?" Fahlbeck observes that there is probably no common agreement in this respect, partly because this question has hardly been discussed (1998: 12).

[38] Globalization and employment: Is anxiety justified? 1996: 496.

Personal autonomy a yardstick for social security

Social security legislation offers its own specific problems that equally require critical scrutiny and revision. To be dependent on unemployment compensation can constitute a severe infringement on a person's autonomy. This is largely due to the nature of social security regulation and the ideology residing behind it. Part of the problem is that social security provisions often are related to a person's status in the labour market (an employment relationship). In addition to, or perhaps rather as a consequence of this, thresholds and ceilings are increasingly introduced, conditioning thereby whether a person will get access to (income-related) social benefits or not. At a conceptual level, the biggest challenge in the field of social security is to loosen up the tendency of categorising people, and, as a consequence, evaluating them.

Here we have a long-standing tradition to make up with, an echo of the past, ever since poor laws were introduced in the 16th century. This is something Peter Englund pertinently draws our attention to in his account of the history of poverty. Since the 16th century, we have the oppressive apparatus of the state through which the idea is nurtured that people should be made happy, by force if necessary. This is a crazy idea that has remained with us and bothered us ever since then, Englund asserts (Englund 1991: 169). Teuvo Raiskio amply illustrates the forms that this evaluation has taken in Finnish society in an article *Oppressive evaluation at the borderline of work in post-war Finland* (2001). Raiskio points to how development generates a need to evaluate people. The more thresholds and ceilings there are in labour and social security regulation, the greater the need to evaluate. Lars D. Eriksson points to a need to critically scrutinize the validity of the premises on which social policy is based, with its corollary in the drafting of laws and their administration (*Socialrätten - I kris eller utveckling?* 1992: 241). Eriksson observes that we today face critical choices regarding social policy. Within the frame of social policy, heavy and labyrinthine institutions have evolved. On the one hand, these structures undermine existing social structures, and on the other, they more or less effectively 'normalise' people by force. So Eriksson asks whether the traditional social policy is any longer suited, as cultural and structural changes occur with an increasing speed, generating new distinctions between individuals and groups, creating in its wake new forms of inequality (1992: 238).

Among the many problems Eriksson identifies in social security legislation, he points to the nature and consequences of frame legislation; how this form of legal regulation threatens traditional principles of legal certainty. Legal certainty presupposes that citizens should be able to foresee the decisions with which they will be confronted. Furthermore, legal certainty presupposes that public authorities should be submitted to an effective control. Eriksson says that, as things now stand, the individual is about to disappear as a legal subject (1992: 248). He questions whether the basic principles governing a legal system are applicable in the fields covered by frame legislation. There appears to be a need to device altogether new legal principles for areas of law such as social security, Eriksson concludes (1992: 246).

A crucial problem associated with unemployment compensation is that it is designed for the labour law standard of full-time employment and a requirement that a person touching such compensation should be available for this so-called standard work. This requirement of availability has, at least in Finland, been interpreted as not allowing an unemployed person to pursue different kinds of activities if they are not 'sanctioned' by the authorities. This requirement stands in blatant contrast to general policy aspirations that a person should be active and strive to find means of sustaining one's living. Freelance work illustrates this problem. A freelancer must always be on the search for an income, which clashes with the requirement of 'availability'. The unemployment compensation schemes thus reveal an incompatibility between policy aspirations and the nature of much work that is factually done. This is one potential course of exclusion and marginalisation.

Eriksson notes that the linkage between income and social security has ceased to provide a viable basis in present-day society. He therefore advocates a new point of departure for social policy that would be founded on citizenship, not on salaried employment (1992: 259). Eriksson notes that all citizens should be guaranteed a minimum income that is not subject to means testing. An insurance system based on citizenship would accord citizens tangible rights, and in addition, an enlarged scope of manoeuvre that would have the effect of offering a certain degree of security (1992: 262) that today is lacking for many persons living at the borderline of work.

The Dutch basic support system for artists, the Wik, offers an interesting model in the direction Eriksson indicates. In 1999 the *Wet inkomensvoorziening Kunstenaars* became operative, providing an income support for artists whose work does not generate enough income to live by. This system is based on the recognition that artistic work does not necessarily generate an income to sustain an artist's living. By recognising this fact, artistic work is accorded a value on other premises than 'ordinary work'.[39] At a perceptional level, this recognition has the effect of giving contours to work performed in the intersection between employment, unemployment and entrepreneurship. Without the Wik system, many artists who qualify for the scheme would be classified as unemployed persons, when forced to rely on social welfare. The decisive issue for artists and many other 'atypical' workers involved in creative work or caring functions of different kinds is not that they do not work, but that they lack adequate compensation for the work they are doing.

---

[39] See Wik informatie, Kunstenaarswijzer, nr 29, herfst 2000: 18-20.

Flexibility illustrated

The Wik system provides a basic support for artists for four years, but this support can be used during a period of ten years. This offers flexibility for those making use of the system. It allows them to rely on the income provided by the Wik in periods when income is low, and to exit the system temporarily when an income is forthcoming from their work. The logic underpinning the Wik system is something that could be applied to the whole field of so called atypical work. The basic trust of the system is that the income from one's own work, and social security provisions complement each other. They are mutually supportive rather than excluding one another, which today largely is the case with social security in the form of unemployment compensation. Another merit of the Wik is that a person can gain an income up to 125 per cent of the basic support without losing the latter. This means that artists with a low income have the opportunity to improve a strained economy.

A personified working life

The problems relating to perception have their origin in the premises of labour law, and social security as an appendix to this, that take their departure in industrial production. As Castells pointed out, the work of an individual person has become central in value creating processes. There is thus a factual emphasis on identity that is not as yet sufficiently recognised and consequently neither reflected in the drafting of laws nor in legal practices. The Wik system is a welcome model that offers alternative ways of looking at working life. At a legal level it is precisely among persons with an individualised work that the shortcomings of legal regulation are revealed. By focussing on human beings, on identity, it will be easier to perceive factual situations. We also need to take a comprehensive view on society and address questions of a fair distribution in society.

Differentiation on a novel axis

What theoretical tools do we need to capture issues involved in a transformed working life? The challenge is to make legislation reflect factual conditions in such a way that the potentials of ICT society can be seized. We need to take departure in human beings rather than in an employment relationship, the traditional legal point of departure. Approached from a human perspective, questions of justice actualise, for which I rely on concepts elaborated in theories of social justice. In order to bring forth a human perspective I propose the notion of personal autonomy. By focussing on how a person's autonomy is affected by factual and legal practices, it is possible to identify arrangements that subdue rather than empower a person. Attention should here be extended beyond conventional working life, also to other activities aimed at securing a person's material existence, or to the pursuit of an important plan of life, such as artistic work.

Theories of social justice assist in differentiating the nature of various settings in a justice perspective. I will therefore briefly account some major prerequisites with which theories of justice elaborate that assist in indicating substantive aspects (how a person's autonomy is affected) in working life and social security. I here rely on the theories of John Rawls, *A Theory of Justice*, David Miller, *Social Justice*, and Wojciech Sadurski, *Giving desert its due - Social Justice and Legal Theory*, which all illustrate some aspects or open some venues for analysing working life and social security. Common to these theories is that they provide alternatives to a longstanding and well-established tradition of utilitarian thinking and legal positivism.

Social justice criteria

By focussing on human beings, on identity, it will be easier to perceive factual situations. It will allow us to see to what degree different constellations in working life allow for moral autonomy and responsibility. In her book The Ethics of an Artificial Person, Elizabeth Wolgast notes in regard to moral autonomy and responsibility that this requires us to make radical revisions, both in our ways of thinking and in our institutions. "[I]n evaluating institutions, we should consider not only their usefulness in producing wide social goods but also their moral effects on individuals in them, particularly the attitudes they encourage in the name of their defined functions. This dimension is neglected when institutions are founded and justified simply on broad, impersonal considerations of public benefit." (1992: 146) Atypical work is a case in point, that has been well documented i.e. by the ILO in regard to home-workers and part-time workers.[40] Through the criteria with which theories of social justice operate, it becomes possible to differentiate the nature of laws and societal institutions and practices on another axis than is the case in a legal positivist paradigm.

Autonomy as freedom: Rawls moves at the most general level among these three scholars. He singles out autonomy as freedom. Rawls notes that a society satisfying the principles of justice as fairness comes as close as a society can to being a voluntary scheme. This implies that people are free and equal, and that *they are ready to assent to arrangements that they perceive of as fair* (emphasis added). In such a scheme people are autonomous and the obligations they recognise are self-imposed (*A Theory of Justice* 1972: 13).

---

40 *ILO, Part-time work*, Report V(1), International Labour Conference 80th Session, 1993 and *Homework*, Report V (1), International Labour Conference, 82nd Session, 1995

Autonomy as 'to each one's due': Miller advances 'to each one's due' as the criteria that best captures the distributive principle. The distributive principle is basic to theories of justice, pointing to how benefits and burdens are shared throughout a society. This notion brings forth *the distinctiveness of persons and a concern for the individual* (emphasis added). At the same time it brings fort the central prerequisites of justice, that is, rights, desert and needs. The principle of rights guaranteeing security of expectation and freedom of choice; the principle of desert recognising the distinctive value of each person's actions and qualities and the principle of need that points to the prerequisites for individual plans of life (*Social Justice* 1979: 20, 27–28).

Autonomy as desert: Sadurski notes that, what justice as desert ultimately is about, is an attempt to make a person's situation dependent on one's own free choices. Through this focus, Sadurski's aspiration is to liberate, to the largest possible extent, people from the operation of uncontrollable forces in social distribution. "It is a protest against the reduction of social life to a game or to a lottery, and it is a defence of the relevance of morality to social allocation of desired goods" (*Giving Desert Its Due* 1985: 157).

By applying these social justice criteria we are able to get flexible cognition of the factual status of different agents in working life, particularly those who do not fit into the prevailing schemes and are therefore conveniently labelled atypical - an easy way out. Instead we need reflectivity and recognition. As a first step, I propose that we identify when and how harm is caused for identifiable groups and persons. From this point, the next step should be to consider how such harm could be remedied.

Harm a starting point instead of utility

A Benthamite utility formula is very much at play in economic life, equalling the greatest happiness of the greatest numbers, whereas atypical workers have been made to pay for the happiness of others. This has caused harm to many of them, because they may have forfeited a number of rights that labour law is aimed at securing, such as the right to equal pay for equal work, as well as different social security entitlements. In practice we see that economic, social and cultural rights are easy targets when confronted with property rights, as the latter are reflected in the employer prerogative. If we approach the reliance on atypical work from an autonomy perspective, we are freed from the bias in favour of property rights that thus is an implicit point of departure in labour law. In an autonomy perspective, we are instead able to see and assess the extent to which an employer causes harm to employees, by hiring them as atypical workers. A major incentive for an employer to use atypical work formats is to avoid the costs of employer obligations in relation to them. This leads to a situation whereby a person so employed may, bit by bit, be stripped of a number of entitlements provided by labour and social security legislation (because of the thresholds and ceilings such legislation contains). A harm is thereby caused that should be remedied in different ways.

If an assessment of a person's autonomy is made at each instance, where it is infringed upon, a different logic ensues. Sadurski notes that if there is full respect for each person's sphere of autonomy, then everybody will share the same benefits of autonomy and the same burden of self-restraint (1985: 104). If we take a harm done as a point of departure, the notion of desert actualises; a person deserves a compensation for a harm done. Through adequate compensation a person's autonomy, when infringed upon, can be restored in a manner that can be conceived of as fair. Here we can see how property rights embedded in the employer prerogative, have to be accommodated with an employee's right to a compensation for a harm done, something this person deserves, because of the inconvenience involved. In this constellation the conflict between 'conservative' and 'prosthetic' justice is resolved, that is, one that conserves rights and one that modifies rights in terms of an ideal standard (Miller 1979: 77).

The standard here is social justice, measured through the degree of autonomy the persons involved enjoy in a specific setting. When differentiating a context through social justice criteria, it will also be easier to perceive the great variety of work that is carried out, much of which is invisible because of the conceptual tools we today apply. Miller notes that the equal satisfaction of needs is the most important element in bringing about equality, and that the premise underlying distribution according to need, also underlies equality in the broader sense. Miller considers that the principle of need represents the most urgent part of the principle of equality (1979: 149). Thus, for work such as that of artists, questions of equality actualises, rather than rights or desert, that mainly actualise in the case of a breadwinning job.

Starting with perception

With the theoretical considerations above, I have wanted to point to the way in which perception conditions the way we approach different phenomena. If we recognise changes that have occurred in working life, and introduce support for persons in a vulnerable position, rather than further burdening those who have become the victims of this process, we could make use of the potentials that the ICT society offers, in ways from which the whole society would stand to gain. In an article, A Revolutionised Working Life, Fahlbeck has formulated some fundamental questions that are central for the agenda pursued here. He presents thoughts about the design of working life, "if we were faced with the option of "starting from zero"" (2000: 327) Fahlbeck's aim is to discuss the organisation of working life free from links to the present system. His attempt is to present a perspective that is as unbiased as possible (2000: 327). Fahlbeck takes his departure in persons as 'buyers of labour' and 'sellers of labour'.

He notes about this departure that it makes the article "completely value neutral and the terms are used in a strictly technical way, with no hidden meaning" (2000: 328). The merit of Fahlbeck's approach is that he frees himself from the standard departure in an employer - employee relationship. He notes that this dichotomy is not suitable for the simple reason that his scrutiny is not confined to employment relationships, but encompasses categories such as independent contractors, contract work, subcontracting or hiring out of manpower. Fahlbeck notes that 'value provider - value receiver' would be more appropriate terms. Those who work provide / create / give / sell new and additional values, whereas their opposite party receives /buys / takes these newly created values (2000: 328). Fahlbeck's approach illustrates what is required to allow for reflexivity in labour legislation; that account is taken of people's factual conditions. For this, the oversimplified categories of entrepreneurship, an employment relationship and atypical work, as a deviation from the latter do not suffice.

An independent status needs to be devised for what we today call atypical work. In devising an alternative status, the guiding principle should be that an optimal degree of autonomy be granted persons working in what today is called atypical work on a par with what is labelled the 'standard'. Whatever the constellation, a decisive criterion should be that a person is duly compensated in instances where 'atypical' work formats are resorted to in order to give the employer more flexibility and less responsibility. Another central aspect is to give recognition and appropriate guarantees for the great variety of activities that follow another logic than a breadwinning employment or business activity. Where such 'instant compensation' is not possible, and a person has to rely on social security, the same principle should apply so that the economic support should enhance a person's free choices and complement a small income on line with the Dutch scheme for artists, the Wik system.

CHAPTER 5

ART THE KEY TO A TRANSITION FROM HUMAN RESOURCES TO HUMAN BEINGS

2004 - A Journey of Exploration: Composing Europe [41]

One person, who in an admirable way has captured our time is Manuell Castells. He points to one interesting aspect of ICT society; that through new technology, it is the first time in human history that oral, written, and audio-visual expressions blend in human communication. This, he notes, is as revolutionary as when the Greeks devised the alphabet. This combination of different means of expression implies a new kind of interaction between the two brain halves, the rational and the creative and emotional one. Castells emphasises that this is something that hardly can be overestimated (1999: 334). A challenging task, therefore, is to reflect on what all this implies. Also our cultures are in a process of change. Castells points out that the strong influence of the new communications systems will lead to a new culture that will be intermitted by social interests, governmental policies and business strategies (1999: 335).

We thus live in the midst of a decisive social change that should force upon us a reconsideration of a number of issues, from the theoretical tools through which we investigate reality to institutional structures, practices and attitudes. In this context artists hold a central position. One expres-

[41] Report from the European Cultural Caravan, 4 -11.4. 2004. This paper is based on my lectio for my doctoral dissertation *To each one's due at the borderline of work - toward a theoretical framework for economic, social and cultural rights*, 2002, published in Tidskrift utgiven av Juridiska Föreningen i Finland, JFT, 6/2003: 689-692.

sion of the changed conditions of our time is the dramatic increase in artistic and culture activities. By way of illustration the number of artists in Finland has increased by 127 per cent during the period 1970–1995. Within this number the category 'other art and entertainment occupations' has increased by 349 per cent. This is one indication, among many others, of the diversification of working life that has occurred during the past decades.

Artistic work assists in displaying the changing makeup of the information society. We need to be aware that within a span of a few decades, people have been expected to transmute from passive men and women by the assembly line, subdued to cost-effectiveness in time and movement, to a person who is expected to be one's own architect of fortune, a policy aspiration now often articulated. The aspirations that people be active players reflect a decisive change of emphasis in social and political organisation, that has not yet been properly reflected in legislation and legal practices. This is as such not surprising because legal personhood is a much-neglected field in legal theory and research.[42]

This shortcoming in recognising legal personhood has gained increased topicality with the transformations in the economy and working life. But as Castells emphasises identity has, notwithstanding, become a primary organising principle. This being the case, we need to be aware of what challenges it poses. First, it is in place to give some considerations to identity. Identity is for Castells the process through which a social player primarily perceives oneself and how meaning is formed out of given cultural attributes (1999: 35). Our challenge today, as Calderon and Lasegna have formulated it, is how we, in a world simultaneously characterised by globalisation and fragmentation, are to combine new technology and collective memory, universal knowledge and a culture of community, passion

[42] See Harvard Law Review, volume 114, April 2001, number 6, Notes What we talk about when we talk about persons: The language of a legal fiction, pp. 1745-1768.

and reason (Castells 1999: 36). These are central ingredients in our responses to structural change, in our ways of seeking new venues for our lives that differ from a context dominated by large-scale industrial production. This change requires recognition of the human as a spiritual person as well as material aspects of people's lives. And who are better suited to assist us in making this change of perception than artists. As Hans-Georg Gadamer has put it: ""Art" begins precisely there, were we are able to do otherwise." (The Relevance of the Beautiful, 1995: 125) And we need to do otherwise today.

We need another renaissance. The previous renaissance was triggered by a failure of the Roman Catholic Church and the Holy Roman Empire to cater for people's spiritual and material life. We are there again, this time because of the way the bold project of modernity has been undermined in different ways. Among others, this is the case with the subsequent development in thought, such as the narrow world view and view of the human that has resulted from positivist and utilitarian orientations in thinking. Humanism was a central concern for renaissance thinkers. Humanism is what we need today too, to counterbalance the materialistic world-view that to a great extent has reduced the view of a human to a *homo economicus* or a man and woman at the assembly line. That a *homo economicus* is not a true description of human nature and human aspirations is clearly demonstrated in the great increase in artistic and cultural activities. In addition to manifesting human inclinations and people's aspirations, the great increase in artistic activities equally reflects the social change that western societies have gone through during the past decades.

Another expression of this change is that art and entertainment are among the fastest growing sectors of the economy today, as a general trend in the western hemisphere. We are thus faced with a number of challenges, for which artists can assist us in different ways. Artists are professionals for whom there are no proper categories in labour and social security legislation. So in addition to the contribution that artists can make to assist us to form identity out of the new attributes we are surrounded by, their status also offers a fruitful object of scrutiny, as artistic work requires a changed perception of work, to include also other values than purely economic ones. Also, human and social aspirations need to be considered, as they are articulated in cultural policies.

We therefore need to update of our mental software to allow us not only to see but also to realise the significance of the changes that have occurred. With a changed perception we are better suited to confront challenges and counteract their detrimental effects. And what is of equal importance, to allow us to seize the opportunities that today's reality offers. Because, as Castells notes, the development we witness today with increasing social marginalisation is in no way inherent in the informational paradigm. On the contrary, Castells emphasises that information technology holds the potential of increased productivity, a higher standard of living and increased employment, if only certain technical choices were made. The informational paradigm is socially open; it is a politically administered paradigm, the most important common elements of which are technical. The present development is thus the result of economic and political choices, through which business and governments have opted for an easy way out in the transformation toward the new informational economy. This stands in sharp contrast to the potentials inherent in the informational paradigm, Castells insists (1999: 280, 238, 247).

To give the informational paradigm contours and substance is thus a great theoretical challenge today. As one step in that direction, I propose that we make the human a starting point, instead of laws and institutions that constitute the starting point in a legal positivist paradigm. This approach will reveal how law in different disciplines signals different social values and aspirations, communicating thereby who counts for legal purposes and in what way. If we focus on personhood it will be easier to perceive the justice quality of legal regulation. It will be possible to differentiate situations and constellations in terms of fairness, as an alternative to the positivist focus on law through the legal - illegal dichotomy. It will be possible to bring to the fore what Francis Bacon has termed three fountains of injustice: mere force, a malicious ensnarement under the colour of law and harshness of the law itself. All of them are part of today's scenery.

The context one of released energies

The industrialised world, if not the whole globe, has experienced a creative chaos during the past decades. We therefore need to stand back and see what patterns emerge from individual activities and new ways of doing things. We need to pay attention to and assess how sensitive different institutional structures are to these factual changes. An enormous amount of human energies, earlier tied to assembly lines, to put it metaphorically, have now been released for people to pursue deeper human aspirations - a plan of life - rather than merely a project of gaining one's material subsistence. What we term 'unemployment', holds the potential of personal fulfilment, if we are ready to see things as they are, and are ready to remove institutional obstacles that might prevent a person from pursuing an artistic plan of life, or any other deliberately chosen direction in life. An interesting illustration of the changes societies have gone through, is how artistic activity has moved into old factories, where the Kaapelitehdas, Nokia's old factory, may stand as a symbolic illustration. There is a fairly clear link between the introduction of new technology, which has reduced the need for human labour, and the growing volume of artistic and cultural work and their enjoyment through festivals, concerts, theatre and other happenings.

Victims of our thought structures

During the past decades, much theoretical effort has been put into offering alternative views of the human being to the instrumental and atomistic ones that resulted from positivist and utilitarian thinking. This involves the whole spectrum, from reassessing political institutions and democracy to theories of social justice and ethics. All these orientations contribute by adding elements that allow us to make a perceptional transition from an atomist view of an individual to a view that takes on board humans as moral agents, or that allows us, as Miha Pogacnik has put it, to make a transition from HR to HB - from human resources to human beings.

Anna Christensen has pointed to how wage labour has conditioned social organisation more than democracy, the market economy or the family (*Wage Labour as Social Order and Ideology* 1984: 7–8). And what is worse, it has conditioned our perception in a way that has made it difficult to perceive and give value to much work that is done outside the wage labour structure. The work of artists is a striking example of this, in addition to other 'invisible' work done both in households and in civil society. Gadamer has depicted the rationale of the industrialised wage labour society, as something that separates and divides us. He points to how we are still divided as individuals in our day-to-day endeavours, notwithstanding all the cooperation necessitated by joint enterprise and the division of labour in our productive activity (1995: 40). Gadamer makes this observation in a context where he elaborates on festivals as a form of art. He points to the contrast between productive activity and festive celebrations. In festive celebrations we are not primarily separated but rather gathered together. It is true, he notes, that we now find it hard to realise this unique dimension of festive celebration. But, it is an art, and it is one in which earlier and more primitive cultures were far more superior to us.[43] We have difficulties in perceiving festivities and cultic ceremony as a kind of creation. One explanation for this is the stronghold theories and methods borrowed from the natural sciences have had on our perception. So yet again, a great part of human experience is left outside our field of theoretical perception. We therefore need to direct attention to the spiritual dimension in people's lives.

Gadamer notes that there is a widespread tendency among the general public to look at the essence of cultic ceremonies as magical practices. This, he maintains, is fundamentally mistaken. The problem lies in our modern civilisation, in the deliberate and calculating pursuit of power and material advances, the tendency toward acquiring and manipulating things to which we owe the principal achievements of our modern civilisation. "It is our account that fails to perceive that the original and still vital essence of festive celebration is creation and elevation into a transformed state of being" (1995: 59).

Now we are partakers in a process in which a new culture is being formed. This offers a historical chance to make up for much of the human and cultural aspects that have been lost in mainstream research, with repercussions for the way humans and social arrangements have been perceived. The way we perceive the legal system is central, reflected in the drafting of laws and their administration. Our challenge, therefore, is to seize the opportunity of trying to make sense of the new societal reality by which we are surrounded, and make use of the potentials it offers. At a practical level this means adapting societal structures so that they become more receptive to the factual space there is for people to pursue their plan of life. In this context the human need for artistic creation and the need for sharing such activities are central.

---

[43] Gadamer advances these thoughts in the essay The relevance of the beautiful. Art as play, symbol, and festival, [1986] 1995: 40.

Artistic work - work of a different kind

When we are concerned with artists, we are concerned with persons for whom self-realisation is a primordial aim. Artistic work is often an inner necessity, and artistic work is therefore not tradable in the sense a bread-winning job is. For this reason we cannot apply the same criteria to artistic work as to traditional economic activity, such as entrepreneurship or employment. What distinguishes artistic work from most other kinds of work is the need for personal integrity, and a respect for an artist's need to pursue this work. Charles Taylor points to this when deliberating on what he calls 'Good things', to which he accords a strong value. Our emotions enable us to have a sentiment of what the good life is. This, in turn, implies that we are able to make a qualitative difference between our desires and goals in such a way that we give some desires and some goals a higher priority than others. Some are truly important, others more trivial.[44]

Strong values involve subject-related meanings, implying that we make distinctions between purposes that are more elevated or inferior, between motives that to their nature are either good or bad. One can say, Taylor notes, that these sentiments are reflexive of the nature of the subject (1995: 125). This means that we relate distinct purposes to each person when we draw up our moral map. By drawing a moral map we can try to give shape to our life experience (Taylor 1995: 125). Strong values refer to our lives as a subject. If such a status is not allowed, if some people are denied the respect and possibility to choose, this implies a lack of respect for these persons (Taylor 1995: 145).

The scenario that is unveiled, when we look at the conditions under which artists carry out their plan of life, testifies of the inability of legal

[44] Identitet, frihet och gemenskap 1995: 123–124

systems - labour and social law in particular - to comprehend other features than those pertaining to the ideal types underpinning labour law, the business man and the male factory worker. This implies, speaking in Taylor's terms, that economic activity has been accorded a strong value, full stop. Our legal traditions and the theoretical schemes associated with them have difficulties in recognising activities that by their nature cannot be measured in economic terms, in case this activity is not 'sanctioned' by an institution. Here an 'on-off' mechanism is at play for the same activity depending on whether this activity results in a sold product or not, if it is supported by a grant or otherwise recognised or carried out within some institution. The effects of this, for persons pursuing artistic activity, can bluntly be summed up as follows: In order to be able to pursue artistic activity, one needs to be wealthy in order to afford it. Or, one needs enough physical strength to do artistic work in addition to a bread-winning job, provided jobs are available. If neither of these preconditions apply, and an artist has to rely on social security, this person will by the employment authorities first be considered unemployed, before some form of subsistence allowance will be granted, if it is. To be labelled unemployed is a blatant disregard and negation of the work an artist is doing. In addition, we here have an illustration of how a rule of a technical nature in the unemployment benefit system overrules human rights standards, such as economic, social and cultural rights.

Yet, artists are precursors for the new approaches we need. As matters now stand, there is no proper link between the role accorded art and culture through different cultural policies and cultural institutions, and the conditions of many artists. There are different support structures, yes, but they are in many respects problematic, seen from an artist's perspective. The availability of such structures does not remove the fundamental problem of a lack of recognition of artistic work in its own right. Is it a legitimate demand, then, that artists should have a right to pursue their artistic activity, considering that such a venue is not catered for in our legal or theoretical schemes?[45]

What would we base our views on, if we consider that artists should have a right to pursue the work for which they have received a professional training or for which they have an inclination or aspiration? John Stuart Mill has, in my view, captured the 'space of tolerance' we need when we approach the question of artistic work as a plan of life: "If a person possesses any tolerable amount of common sense and experience, his own mode of laying out his existence is the best, not because it is the best in itself, but because it is his own mode" (*On Liberty* 1974: 163). Mill's statement was directed against laws, institutions and practices that impeded trade. One could say that we today have moved full circle since then. A major challenge today, is to find means of correcting the imbalance caused by the preponderance of economic concerns and the effects of a global economy and a profoundly altered working life. Likewise, the economy generated around art and entertainment needs to be considered.

Furthermore, we need to take account of the propelling force that art and culture exercise in our lives. Here some random observations. In medicine, the therapeutic role of art is well recognised. Why should we not use the power of art to improve the quality of life in society at large? This was Josef Beuys' aspiration, a tradition that many artists continue to pursue today. We all experience the power of art when we participate in artistic or cultural activities. We therefore need to be aware of the significance of art for a wider public, for all of us as 'consumers' of art. Yet another expression of the significance of art; what would our knowledge of past times be if we did not have pieces of art that convey a picture of human life throughout the ages? Why then, do we have such difficulties in giving

---

45 From a 'rights perspective', artistic activity can be considered as a freedom of expression. Freedom does, however, not qualify as an answer from the social justice perspective chosen here.

recognition to artistic activity in its own right? In my view, the problem boils down to perception.

A broadened perspective

It is only by broadening our perspective on societal arrangements and by incorporating a human perspective that we can make headway. We need to take a look at the human, her plan of life, as an issue in its own right, in addition to the prevailing view of people as mere factors in or outside economic production and working life. Only by recognising the human condition, will we be able to make sense of, and seize the opportunities today's world offers. The human being is not merely the omnipotent man that walked into the theoretical landscape through Francis Bacon's pages. We are not a social atom, a person who goes about one's plans of life, controlling it and making the most profit out of it, as the utilitarian worldview has it. It should be obvious that this is not a true description of the human condition, for which artists offer a fairly obvious contrast. Gadamer also points out how extremely one-sided modern man's concept of action is (1995: 77). He proposes that Greek epic and drama remain real for us because we too live with great uncertainty. We can be alarmed by sudden transformations. At a stroke, everything can have changed. "We are too familiar with darkness, perplexity, madness, catastrophe, sickness and death, love and hate, jubilation, arrogance and ambition, the whole vast range of human sufferings and passion that the Greeks experienced as the real presence of their gods. Greek myth speaks about this fundamental experience which we all have of the way in which such things befall us". That is why it always speaks to us (1995: 77).

As a contrast to a material viewpoint, art represents the spiritual dimension in people's lives. If we turn attention toward arts, we are thus offered an alternative and more truthful picture of the human and her condition, than the one permeating much of our thought structures. Gadamer again: "We know and yet do not know ourselves in the struggle between nature and spirit, animality and divinity, a discussion that is yet inseparably united in human life. In a mysterious way, this struggle pervades all our most particular personal, psychological, and spiritual activities and combines the unconscious life of natural being with our conscious and freely chosen existence to produce a unit that is consonant and dissonant at one and the same time" (1995: 76).

Art - a key to a changed perception

In contrast to industrially produced objects, the work of art provides a perfect example of the universal characteristic of human existence - the never-ending process of building a world. In the midst of a world in which everything familiar is dissolving, the work of art stands as a pledge of order. Gadamer notes that "[p]erhaps our capacity to preserve and maintain, the capacity that supports human culture, rests in turn upon the fact that we must always order anew what threatens to dissolve before us. This is what the productive activity of the artist and our own experience of art reveals in an exemplary fashion" (1995: 103–104). This is line with the way in which Fredrik Lång pictures the transition from scholasticism to the renaissance (Lång 1999: 132–133). Perhaps are we now at a threshold similar to that of Petrarch, that Lång portrays when comparing Petrarch's and St. Augustine's view of the world. In the 14th century, Petrarch took a decisive step in the transformation from scholasticism to the renaissance. By reviving the tradition of antiquity, he sought a union of elegance and power with virtue. "One who studied language and rhetoric in the tradition of the great orators of antiquity did so for a moral purpose to persuade men and women to the good life". Petrarch says in a dictum that could stand as the slogan of renaissance humanism, "it is better to will the good than to know the truth".[46]

Tension between wealth generated by employment and art

In view of what has preceded, we have reason also within the legal traditions to critically assess the premises on which legal structures are based. We need to expand the perspective from industrial artefacts as the major feature around which society revolves. It is a challenging task, because we need different kinds of measurement than a price given an artefact, the production of which can be measured in time, costs and profit. Art does create wealth, spiritual as well as pecuniary, only it does not do so on a straight axis, like an industrial product. This is a conviction that Josef Beuys strongly advocated, as do those who follow in his tradition. In an Adam Smith lecture (1995), Richard Demarco talked on Beuy's theme 'Kunst = Kapital', Art = Wealth. Demarco refers to the way Beuys perceived of money. Beuys emphasised the circularity of money, which he compared to the circulation of blood in the human blood stream. Demarco also refers to the painter Robert McDowell, who turned into a banker. In a Keynesian tradition McDowell points to our need to take a three-dimensional view of money flows. In doing so we can see how very real and productive financial resources can be created through investments in areas such as arts or health (Demarco 1995: 19). Until the 1980s, governments had a more three- dimensional view of money. What goes around, comes around, which means that the tax income generated by public expenditure is also taken into account. After the 1980s this view has changed, making all public spending appear as a cost to the taxpayers (Demarco 1995: 22).

Through the Demarco European Art Foundation, Demarco is an active agent in the Fringe Festival accompanying the Edinburgh International

---

[46] Encyclopaedia Britannica 1997.

Festival. Based on extensive experience of these activities he offers the following insight: "The impression I have gained, however, from artists dealing with the subject of money is that they, and no doubt economists as well, really want to be valued not only for having new and insightful means of engaging us about life's fundamentals, they also want to be recognised as making a real economic contribution" (1995: 19). And they do. Demarco presents the following estimate of temporary jobs generated by the Edinburgh festival. There are some 12 000 jobs generated in relation to the festival, whereas another 10 000 temporary jobs are created in shops, restaurants, hotels etcetera. The festival attracts at least 70 million pounds in additional spending in Edinburgh (1995: 24). Why should artists not stand to gain from it as well? Demarco notes about artists, actors and also art impresarios that somehow they find ways to survive against the odds. "Artists may have a reputation for stargazing, but believe me most time is spent searching for solutions to short term financial problems, which I venture are, in the arts, more unremittingly elusive than in other fields of human endeavours". And Demarco concludes: "Economists and politicians talk about unemployment and job insecurity! They should talk to artists. In this field they are the experts." (1995: 20)

Where to direct attention

The right of artists to pursue artistic work is perhaps the most extreme conceptual contrast to the wage labour society, a logic according to which present societal structures are largely designed. Artists thus assist in opening new perspectives on existing structures, and in addition to this, they also assist in indicating the potentials of our time. We are here concerned with two poles, one from which present structures take their departure, that were created to meet the needs of industrialisation, and the factual changes surrounding us, that are the product of a high-tech society. Castells noted that it is the first time in human history that the human being is using all her senses in productive work, on a fairly large scale at least. If we want to make use of the potentials offered today, both artistic work and people's plans of life more generally, should be taken seriously. This would require that rules and practices that directly hamper artistic activity should be removed. The same goes for perception, such as is the case when an artist is labelled as unemployed, when not engaged in salaried employment. To remove obstacles is one reforming phase. Another is to create structures that facilitate artistic work. This will require an altogether new administrative culture and a new mind-set. Only through interdisciplinary approaches will we be able to embrace the new conditions in a constructive way.

CHAPTER 6

TIME TO GIVE ARTISTS THEIR DUE – A MATTER OF PERCEPTION

2004 - Mediterranean Seascapes Conference, Valletta, Malta[47]

My theme is somewhat odd in this conference concerned with Mediterranean maritime heritage. We do, however, have a few meeting points, such as the question of what our recollection of history would be without the work of artists. I hardly need to convince anybody in this audience that artistic work is work, and that it has a value, independently of whether it generates money or not. Imagine how much poorer our recollection of history would be, if we did not have the work of artists – taken in the widest sense – to convey to us past times and cultures. There is one further point that unites any research, perception, and that is what I want to talk about. In this gathering of historians, I will be concerned with a very contemporary matter: how we perceive our own time, and particularly how we perceive artistic work. Throughout time, most artists have had to struggle for their material survival while doing what they had to do – create. My concern is that there has not been much improvement in this regard, notwithstanding the human rights standards introduced during the past century, particularly economic, social and cultural rights (see Storlund 2002). A more recent phenomenon that should induce us to consider

[47] La Navigation du Savoir, Network of Historical Arsenals in the Mediterranean, 14-15 October 2004

the conditions under which artists work, are governmental policies concerning art and culture. The cultural policies of Malta, the Netherlands and Finland will here serve as illustrations of the points I will reflect on.

Perception - the starting point

The problem I want to bring to the fore is that artistic work is not recognised in its own right in labour law and social security schemes associated with working life. To give artists a status in labour law that would reflect the value accorded art and culture in cultural policy programs requires a change of perception so that artistic work is recognised as work in its own right. Whatever discipline or research questions we are concerned with, perceptions and thereby the prevailing theoretical paradigm influences how we see different phenomena, what is brought to the fore and how we deal with it. The paradigm equally acts as a censor for what questions can be put, delimiting thereby the scope of the possible. An effect of this is that law and perception largely determine what is the truth of the day. As historians you should have a good perspective on this phenomenon. David E. Cooper has caught the implications of different paradigms in a nutshell in a comparison between the approach to arts in Antiquity and during the Enlightenment. He observes that "1,500 years divide Plotinus' chapter on beauty from Hume's essay on taste (1757), but it might as well be 15,000, so different are the contexts assumed and the problems addressed)."[48]

I would argue that the (post) enlightenment theoretical legacy largely explains our difficulties in dealing with the value of art today, particularly so in a labour law context. Today we lack proper theoretical tools for perceiving other values in working life than economic ones. This delimits considerations about art and culture and the ways in which they contribute to human life. To put it bluntly, art and culture are mostly measured

---

[48] Cooper, David, ed, *Aesthetics, The Classic Readings*, 1997: 76.

in economic terms, as commercial products, or they can be seen as a means through which to improve performance in working life. We lack proper criteria for according art and culture a value of their own. One major reason why we have difficulties in talking about human values in a legal context is that western legal traditions are based on an economic rationale and thereby economic values. This is a product of the industrial revolution and of the need for a legal regulation of the new conditions in the transition from a predominantly agrarian economy to an industrial one. In this process, work became equalled with industrial work, making a blue-collar worker the ideal type for the regulation of working life. With the present transition from a predominantly industrial society to one dominated by information and communication technology (ICT) and globalisation, we are again faced with the challenge of adapting both perception and legislation to these new conditions. This is our chance to correct the deficiencies in the perception of work on which present legislation is based, and to also include other values on a par with economic ones. And here governmental cultural policies should guide us.

Identity and creativity - requisites of our time

It is high time to focus on the conditions under which artists work, because I would argue that artists have a very special mission today. Our challenge today, is to combine new technology and collective memory, universal knowledge and a culture of community, passion and reason (Castells 1999: 35). Art and culture must be a part of that answer, something that is also confirmed in national cultural policy documents. Cultural policy programs are in unison in emphasising the positive values of art and culture for individual persons as well as society at large. A big challenge lies in translating the values that art and culture represent into legislative terms in a labour market context. But not only that. In order to make a reality of governmental cultural policies, the cultural administration must reach out to other sectors of society. To achieve this, again, we need something that Malta aspires to through its cultural policy, which is to "replace the Maltese mindset of standardisation with critical values and active questioning." (National Cultural Policy in Malta 2002: 17) It requires both a change of perception and a new administrative culture. A pertinent point made in the Finnish cultural policy document, Art is possibilities, is to consider art on a par with research (Finnish cultural policy document 2002: 90).

In the following I will also make some parallels with research in this inventory of points on why we need a change of perception. How shall we go about this task of looking at things in new ways? In the Foreword to the second collection of *Malta Tales and Narratives*, Edward de Bono makes a pertinent observation. "If history provides the bones of a nation, the stories provide the flesh on the bones. Stories and anecdotes reflect the everyday life of ordinary people living in their day." De Bono says that although stories concentrate on unusual events, the background of these events illustrates the usual. He further notes that four things work together: human nature, human emotions, human values and human thinking. Thinking he divides into two parts, one being the thinking involved in human perception: how we see a situation, and what we are dealing with.[49]

If we want to be able to embrace all the aspects of human nature that de Bono mentioned, we need to recapture perceptional clusters that were lost after the Enlightenment, as illustrated by Cooper above.[50] I wish to illustrate de Bono's point with a story about how rabbit became the Maltese

---

[49] Edward De Bono, Foreword in Attard, Robert, *Malta A Second Collection of Tales and Narratives* 2001: ix.

[50] Cooper (1997: 76). I have traced the narrowing of the theoretical paradigm in Storlund, 2002, Chapter V recaptures lost clusters.

national dish. This is a story that not only gives flesh on the bones of Maltese history, but muscles, too. It is a story about how the Maltese rose up against their rulers, the Knights of the Order of St. John, when they had banned rabbit hunting. See video at the end of the chapter. This is a bottom-up perspective, that brings to the fore the conditions of ordinary men and women, in contrast to the perspective of rulers that influences the perceptional truth of the day.

It is noted in the Maltese cultural policy document that one of the most fundamental values transmitted by culture is identity. Thus, after Malta's independence from Britain in 1964, to democratise culture was considered important. And here, cultural heritage is central. In the 1990s, it became the declared policy to review culture "not as the privilege of an elite few, but as the dynamic heritage of the whole people".[51] The place where this conference is held, St James Cavalier Centre for Creativity, is an embodiment of these aspirations. There is a further important symbolic value associated with this place. It is a bastion built for defence and exclusion that now welcomes everybody, enriching our lives with art and culture. Likewise, in the newly formed Finnish state of the early 20th century, political leaders wanted to promote Finnish cultural identity through policies aimed at promoting the arts and artists.[52] Identity is clearly not something settled once and for all. In the Netherlands, the German occupation during world war II was an incentive for extra financial support to artists as a gesture to mend the disrupted relationship between the artist and society for a limited period of time.[53] The Dutch cultural policy program *More than the Sum*, states that "knowledge of our heritage contributes to

---

[51] Cultural policy finally gained its own profile when a Minister for Education, Culture and Tourism was appointed after the first elections in 1966. Malta, country profile, chapter 1, Historical perspective. http://www.creativeurope.info.

[52] Finland, country profile, chapter 1, Historical perspective. http://www.creativeurope.info.

[53] Netherlands, country profile, chapter 1, Historical perspective. http://www.creativeurope.info.

a cultural self-awareness that is essential in a multicultural society. That added value for society is the basis for a justification of support for art and culture".[54] The quest for cultural identity is just as strong today, this time kindled by the changed conditions brought about by new technology and globalisation. Manuel Castells points to how information technology has led to an increasing emphasis on identity in social and political organisation (1999: 35).

Creativity is another strongly favoured attribute. In the Finnish policy program for art and artists, creativity is seen as central among the multiple ways in which art enriches both people and communities. For the human, art offers a platform for creative self-expression and for the development of one's emotional life and self-understanding, enhancing thereby the ability to build one's identity and structure reality. For the community, art represents creative, social, cultural and economic capital. Likewise, the role of art is emphasised in the global and increasingly differentiated, pluralistic and technologically dominated information society. The innovation policy of the state should therefore be extended so that art is also seen as a strategic source for development, it is noted in the Finnish program (2002: 90). We need creativity to rid ourselves of standardised ways of thinking. And creativity is precisely what artists can contribute. On this score, the Dutch Minister of Culture Medy C. van der Laan advocates a reverse reasoning, whereby focus is placed on an increasing cultural awareness in society rather than social awareness in culture. "The focus is not on the social or political "control" of cultural life, as if the sector needs such due to an inherent weakness, but on intensifying the cultural factor in the various sectors of social life." Among others, the Minister calls for a

[54] '*More than the sum*', Cultural Policy Letter 2004-2007 presented by the Dutch State Secretary of Education, Culture and Science, Medy C. van der Laan, 2003: 2.

questioning of things we think give us security, and calls for a need to constantly calibrate different values.[55]

How do we go about it? I think that the required change of perception has to start with simple observations. The organiser of this conference, Simon Mercieca,[56] offered me one such insight, when he pointed to how a phenomenon that today is the most obvious of things was something revolutionary in its time, i.e. the Middle Ages: the identification of artists by name. Some Austrian researchers have offered similar assistance, by formulating an alternative way of capturing the artistic scene and thereby nuancing perceptions of traditional professional categories in the artistic and cultural field.[57] They opted for the following distinctions:

- High culture, artistic culture: traditional, representative art having symbolic profitability.
- Social culture: the so-called third sector in culture, which consists of process- and communication-oriented initiatives having social profitability.
- Mass culture: culture and leisure industries having economic profitability.[58]

What these researchers have done is to substitute formal professional categories with categories that take into account the context and the factual conditions in which artistic and cultural work is performed. This reveals that one and the same kind of activity assumes different values depending on the context. These are important distinctions that need to be considered in any efforts to tailor a status for artists in a labour law context. But they can equally serve to differentiate the simplistic perception

---

[55] She exemplifies with the need to pay attention to culture in education, the quality of public space, the urban investment climate and the amount of free time. *More than the sum* 2003: 2.

[56] Director of the Mediterranean Institute, University of Malta.

[57] *Pyramid or Pillars* 2002: 43, www.ericarts.org.

[58] Harauer, Robert, Mayerhofer, Elisabeth, Mokre, Monika, *Thanks for Playing Anyway*, in Pyramid or Pillars, 2002: 43.

of work that has its origin in a blue-collar worker as the ideal-type in labour law. This ideal-type can be seen as an adequate representation of traditional industrial work along assembly line principles. In contrast to this, for any work involving people, such as care functions and education or work involving ideas such as research, art and culture, the blue-collar worker as ideal-type is clearly inappropriate. The only thing that unites these different kinds of work in labour law is the formal criterion of an employment relationship. But as soon as different considerations and calculations become involved, such as quality versus profitability or efficiency, the blue-collar worker as an ideal-type reveals its inadequacy. In addition to this, work that is done outside an employment relationship, such as artistic and cultural work, is situated in a legal grey area because of inadequate legal regulation of such work. We thus need to substitute formal distinctions by substantive ones. By doing so we are able to see the work that is factually done, what values it represents, and whether it is symbolic, social or economic. Another distinction that requires careful scrutiny is the distinction between public and private that in an equally undifferentiated way lumps a variety of different functions and activities (Storlund 1992: Conclusions).[59]

As things now stand, there is a growing legal grey area in the intersection between the public and private sectors. This is an area that has been long inhabited by artists. The experience of artists can therefore help us to see factual conditions and equally help to devise new structures and practices that are better suited to today's conditions than those of the past. If we look at substantive aspects, we see that the public sector is an agglomeration of competing functions and interests. Here we have the whole range of activities: from defence, law and order, where we hear the echoes of Thomas Hobbes, and further to John Locke and other thinkers

[59] For a further inventory of this topic, see Storlund, Vivan, *Public power versus industrial democracy - the case of public employees*, IV. Conclusions 1992.

legitimating a minimalist night-watch state. Then we have education, research, art and culture that represent an opposite pole to that of law and order. In between we have a whole array of activities from care functions to road maintenance and many more.

The point I want to make is that they all represent different categories of activities, requiring different conditions for the work to be effective. Because of the varied nature of activities in the public sector, the administrative culture also requires careful scrutiny. As a legacy from past times there is a paternalistic control mentality that is at odds with many activities carried out in the public sector, and increasingly so with the changed conditions of the information and communication society. Here I see that researchers and artists are allies in the sense that their work stands for values that cannot be measured in economic terms; neither is the control mentality that permeates much public activities appropriate for the creative and innovative processes involved in art and research. The work of both researchers and artists requires a sphere of autonomy, and should consequently not be judged according to traditional administrative standards. This is a point that the Dutch Minister of Culture also referred to when questioning the need for 'control' of cultural life, as if the sector needs such control due to an inherent weakness.

Behind the notion of public power and authority, we have sediments from past times, during which different power centres have promoted their position and interest, from absolute monarchy to the role of the state as the night-watch state, safeguarding economic interests. Despite the introduction of democracy and human rights provisions, no fundamental revisions have been made to older theoretical schemes to accommodate them with perceptions relating to democracy and human rights. To this must be added today's neoliberal orientation that attempts to see almost any activity in economic terms, independently of whether activities can be measured in such terms or not. This induces conflict and misunderstanding between those who do the actual work and those who control it.

Here researchers have an important role to play to correct these anomalies, because how we go about things is conditioned by perception. Thereby it is the task of the academic community to bring theoretical reflection in line with human rights standards and cultural policies, for which there is no proper place in current practices and paradigms.

The Dutch Minister of Culture translated her plea for a strong cultural self-awareness into three priorities: less bureaucracy and more individual responsibility, more connection and interaction in cultural life, and a reinforcement of the presence of 'Culture' in society (2003: 3). It is a question of giving recognition to features that are there, although not always recognised. Because, as Philiph D. Dracodaidis has pointed out, "culture is no longer a closed world governed by inspiration and avant-garde but it is part of everyday life, whether we accept it or not.... Today, Culture is not a self-supplied world where individual principles prevail; it is an extrovert world where individual principles contribute salt and pepper, lifestyles and common understanding." (*Building Cultural Strategies for the Enlargement Countries - Myth or Reality* (2003: 28) Perhaps it has always been so, after all – for are not all the artefacts that make up the Mediterranean maritime heritage a significant instance of the embodiment of art and culture?

Videos:

Stories behind the Monuments – How Rabbit became the Maltese National Dish[60]

Peter Serracino Inglott: Discussions on art in the third millennium[61]

---

[60] https://www.youtube.com/watch?v=DDoRSWop6fY&t=13s

[61] https://www.youtube.com/watch?v=1Ckc4zlbkhk

CHAPTER 7

RECOGNISING ARTISTS' RIGHTS - A NEW CHALLENGE TO THE HUMAN RIGHTS PARADIGM

2006 - Mediterranean Journal of Human Rights[62]

Artistic work is a strange bird in our legal culture, particularly so in labour law that is permeated by the logic of industrial production. To recognise artistic and cultural work and to introduce appropriate provisions for such work is a compelling need in order to catch up with societal change. This requires a new conceptual framework that is considered in this article. Departure is taken in economic, social and cultural rights that are primarily approached through concepts devised by theories of social justice.

A person in one's own right

Artist and prostitutes are the most ancient professions of humankind, it is said. This sounds plausible. But notwithstanding a long history, and notwithstanding the human rights standards introduced during the past century, many artists and prostitutes may ponder where their rights are. Surely, they are as worthy of human rights as any other person. How come then so many artists and prostitutes live a life in hardship at the borderline of work? I will argue that we need a change of perception in order to properly address the problems facing artists and prostitutes - as well as many others. We equally need to device new structures or revise old ones, in order to accord people the legal protection that economic, social and

[62] Volume 10, Number 1, 2006

cultural rights are aimed at securing. I will here be concerned with the rights of artists - or rather shortcomings in this regard - but I will start by juxtaposing artists and prostitutes in order to illustrate the implications of two notions on which I will base these considerations; the notions 'to each one's due' and 'personal autonomy'. This will primarily be done relying on concepts provided by theories of social justice.

The reason why I wish to juxtapose artists and prostitutes is that, speaking in general terms, their situation may be characterised by needs of some kind that helps to differentiate the notion of need. For a prostitute it is fairly safe to say that prostitution has been a last resort for many a person in a vulnerable position - a means of material survival. For a person with a strong urge for artistic creation again the need is of a different kind, it is a question of an inner necessity that often goes along with a struggle for material survival. For prostitutes the gist of the problem is that society does not provide the kind of protection for persons in a vulnerable position that would give them a free choice as to how to gain their living. Here it is a question of inadequate economic and social rights that raises the issue of a fair distribution of benefits and burdens in society. In regard to artists, again, the question of cultural rights is brought to the fore, involving primarily the question that the value of artistic work should be recognised and that appropriate structures should be devised that would allow artists to carry out their work under decent conditions.

The human in a theoretical context

I will start by relying on David Miller's considerations of needs, as elaborated in his book Social Justice. Miller notes that the satisfaction of needs can be regarded either as a matter of justice or as a matter of humanity. There is no strict inconsistency between them, but they depart from different premises. If we approach the question of needs as one of humanity, the underlying premise is that human suffering should be avoided. But if the satisfaction of needs is seen as a matter of justice, a different underlying premise is required. Miller considers the premise difficult to state with any clarity, but he suggests that it may be expressed by saying that every person is as worthy of respect as every other. Although men differ in moral virtue, in merit, in personal success, in usefulness to society, there is an underlying equality, which consists in the fact that each man is a unique individual with his own aims, ideals and outlook on the world and that consequently he must be treated as such. Further, this premise is required to show why each man has an equal claim to carry out his plan of life, and hence to have satisfied the needs which are related to that plan of life. Unless the premise is granted, we cannot show why it is unjust (and not merely inhumane) to satisfy one man's needs and not the needs of another, Miller notes (1979: 146–147).

Alasdair MacIntyre can assist by throwing some light on the difficulties in finding a proper premise that would have justice as a starting point. In his book *After Virtue*, he points out how the paradigmatic shift that occurred with enlightenment thinkers, has had the effect that 'man' ceases to be a 'functional concept' (except within theology). This is because the Aristotelian understanding of nature and action were repudiated in the 17th and 18th centuries and substituted by theoretical efforts to lay bare the physiological and physical mechanisms underlying human action (1981: 54–55). A unifying notion of a person was thereby lost. Hence, we are no longer simultaneously concerned both with questions of how human action is to be explained and understood, as well as with questions of what kind of actions are to be performed, as this is expressed in Aristotle's Ethics and Politics (MacIntyre 1981: 78–79).

In law this problem is reflected in the ambiguities surrounding legal personhood, to which attention has been drawn in Notes in the Harvard Law Review (HLR). Legal personhood is there pictured as a 'grossly undertheorized field' under the title *What we talk about when we talk about persons: The language of a legal fiction* (2001: 1745–1768). The metaphor of a legal person reflects and communicates who 'counts' as a legal person for the purpose of law. Even without explicit reference to a person, laws signal this by including or excluding certain categories of individuals, either explicitly or through judicial interpretation (HLR 2001: 1746–1747). What is at stake is the social meaning of law; revealing that law does more than regulate behaviour, it also signals social values and aspirations (HLR 2001: 1760). "Courts' treatment of legal personhood communicates anxiety not only about divisive social issues, but also about the operation of law itself.... The law of the person, and especially courts' ambivalence about it, exposes the uncomfortable but inescapable place of status distinctions in even the most progressive legal systems." (HLR 2001:1766)

In seeking an understanding of the problems we face when dealing with economic, social and cultural rights, it is instructive to be aware of the role and significance of the legal metaphors we use. "Hence, the very project of the law, which depends on metaphors to make sense of its rules and to justify its use of force, is as unstable as it has ever been." This lack of a universal notion of a person is fraught with troubling normative implications (HLR 2001: 1767). Because of the implications of how legal personhood is granted, attention to this question would also make law more apt to contribute more fully to social dialogue about what it means to be human, it is noted in the HLR Notes (2001: 1768).

To be a moral agent

To remedy the uncertainty concerning the premise that Miller refers to and the ambiguities concerning legal personhood, I propose that we need to restore an Aristotelian paradigm, whereby a view of a person as a moral agent is revealed. This implies taking humans as a point of departure. In order to capture Miller's point that every man is as worthy of respect as every other, I propose the notion 'personal autonomy' as a means of assessing what is required in a particular situation to allow a person to act according to his own aims, ideals and outlook on the world. I would reduce this to a person's possibility to act as a morally responsible person. Such an assessment I consider to be prior to, and to assist in differentiating situations in a human rights perspective. By addressing the notion of personal autonomy, we are able to catch sight of persons in their life context, such as a person having to resort to prostitution when no other means appear to be available, or an artist who often has to forsake material well-being because of a compelling need to create.

If our aim is social justice, policies and actions may not further burden persons who are marginalised or stand the risk of being so, but should on the contrary correct such injustices. It is in order to capture this that I propose 'personal autonomy' as a conceptual tool, as it will be easier to reveal unjust situations and see what is required of institutional arrangements to remedy such injustices. It also helps to bring out problems associated with the way economic, social and cultural rights are legally formulated and administered. The way many social security schemes associated with working life are designed, they have not granted autonomy for persons 'dependent' on these rights. Although economic and social rights are largely correctives to classical rights and liberties, they have often been constructed in such a way that they become appendices to classical rights and liberties, rather than providing benefits over which a person would have control. This leaves persons relying on provisions aimed at securing economic and social rights, such as social security, in a dependent position. In such a position it may be extremely difficult to defend one's rights.

We can see that autonomy is no self-evident matter for, say, those who have been made redundant or hired as so called atypical workers because of employers' aspirations to improve their profit, when they rationalise their activities to this end. The autonomy in this case is the autonomy of the employer to go about his business of making and improving his profit, at the cost of the autonomy a person has enjoyed through full-time salaried employment. Autonomy here is autonomy for one at the cost of others. If focus is placed on the degree of autonomy a person enjoys at each instance, where it is infringed upon, a different logic ensues.

Wojciech Sadurski points out that if there is full respect for each person's sphere of autonomy, then everybody will share the same benefits of autonomy and the same burden of self-restraint. This again, requires a set of general rules by which it will be possible to determine if an act undertaken by somebody will result in harm to somebody else. Through such general rules, it will be possible to guarantee autonomy to everyone, in their sphere of action, which is non-harmful to others. This autonomy is not absolute, but is determined by changing social and cultural values, Sadurski notes (*Giving Desert Its Due*, 1985: 104–105). I propose that if we focus on how a person's autonomy is negatively affected by different states of affairs, and what this person would be due in order to have her or his autonomy restored, this would to a large extent meet the requirement of the general set of rules that Sadurski is in search of.

Criteria of social justice

Miller proposes 'to each his due' as the most valuable general definition of justice (1979: 20). The notion to each one's due has the advantage that it is non-substantive in character. Thereby it is easier to perceive the specific setting and conditions of any particular case. By investigating what it is that infringes on or undermines a person's autonomy, one can also see at what level remedies need to be introduced and in what form. Furthermore, the individualistic ring that is associated with the notion of autonomy is totally transformed when qualified as requiring a personal sphere of autonomy. This implies that both substantive and relational aspects are considered, in addition to bringing forth a particular institutional setting. The relational aspect also brings action into consideration, allowing us to assess human behaviour, bridging thereby the gap between the static picture of law, as revealed in a legal positivist paradigm, and the dynamic field of ethics. This focus allows us to consider the nature of the actions of different parties involved, bringing forth how different parties are affected, as was illustrated in the case of employers rationalising their activities in order to improve their profit.[63] The 'autonomy test', as I call it, is purely instrumental and can, depending on the context, be translated into different notions according to that particular context. It may place the considerations in the field of rights by assessing whether a piece of legislation, by securing the rights it does, guarantees control to a person in a vulnerable position. This raises the question whether deficiencies should be remedied through legal reform and / or changed practices in legal administration. The autonomy test may also be translated into an assessment whether there is respect for a person's plan of life, or whether a person enjoys such integrity that it allows this person to act as a morally responsible agent, placing considerations in the field of ethics. Or we might focus on inter-dependencies that may place considerations into the field of political philosophy or sociology.[64] This differentiation of diverse situations and constellations is an important first step when addressing the

---

[63] These considerations are based on Storlund 2002. The notion personal autonomy I derive from Carl Wellman's analysis of rights, see further (2002: 160-16)1. Wellman draws attention to how a right is associated with freedom and control. One cannot be really free if one is under the control of others, and one is fully free only if one has control over those who would interfere with one's action. "Perhaps the best word to capture this two-sided freedom-control is "autonomy", in the sense of self-government, for whether the possessor of a right exercises or enjoys his right is governed primarily by his own will rather than that of any alien will." By this notion of autonomy Wellman considers that a functional unity is achieved between the different elements that make up a legal right. Wellman, Carl, *Legal Rights* 1978: 219.

[64] For the notions 'ethical integrity' and 'inter-dependency' see Mason, Mark, *Ethics and Values in an Open Society: Fostering a Culture of Peace* 2003: 43-44 and Agyman, Kwasi, *The Causal and Purposeful Angles of Peace* 2003: 6. Abstracts of presentations at Joint UNESCO seminar 'Ways of Promoting a Culture of Peace', co-organised by Johanna Lasonen, UNESCO

substantive question, what someone is due. In theories of social justice different and conflicting means are available to answer the question what somebody is due, that Miller summarises in the three principles: to each according to his rights; to each according to his deserts; to each according to his needs.[65]

I will continue to focus on needs. Miller observes that the 'needs' conception of justice and the principle of equality stand in a peculiarly intimate relationship to one another but still less than an identity. The intimacy consists, first, in the fact that the equal satisfaction of needs is the most important element in bringing about equality, and second, in the fact that the premise underlying distribution according to needs, also underlies equality in the broader sense. Miller suggests that the principle of need represents the most urgent part of the principle of equality. This urgency, he notes, can be seen in our undoubted willingness to regard the satisfaction of needs as a matter of justice, compared with our uncertainty about the satisfaction of other wants. It is certainly true, Miller holds, that to satisfy everyone's needs it is necessary to mete out different physical resources to different people, because people have varied needs and wants, as the case of artists and prostitutes is intended to illuminate (1979: 149).

A real life context

The way many artists have to struggle for their material survival displays a flagrant paradox. Culture is valued in society, and it is something that no

---

chair at the University of Jyväskylä and ambassador Anja-Riitta Ketokoski-Rexed, Finland 13-14 June 2003 in Espoo.

[65] Miller observes that the conflict between these principles is not symmetrical. 'Rights' and 'deserts', and 'rights' and 'needs' are contingently in conflict, since we may strive for a social order in which each man has a right to that (and only that) which he deserves, or to that (and only that) what he needs. See Miller 1979: 27-28, Storlund 2002: 140-141.

society could either be or do without. Why then are the producers of art and culture not recognised as professional categories with a status that would reflect the particular characteristics of artistic and cultural work? Anna Christensen can throw light on this. She observes that wage labour has conditioned social organisation more than democracy, the market economy or the family (1984: 7- 8).[66] And what is worse, it has conditioned our thought structures in a way that has made it hard to perceive and give recognition for much work that is done outside the wage labour structure. The work of artists is a striking example of this. This is a problem we have faced throughout the industrial era, the effects of which have been felt in many sectors of working life, such as public services, education, research and other activities, where it is difficult to measure the relation between economic input and outcome. These misleading premises have, however, gained increasing topicality with the changes societies have undergone during the past decades transforming many societies from industrial ones to information and communication societies, with far-reaching effects on working life. There is, therefore, an urgent need to reconsider the notion of work to see also other values than the economic values associated with industrial production and business. Likewise, it must be recognised that economic gains are not merely accrued on a straight axis, as is the case in industrial production and business activity, but that there is circularity that becomes visible if we approach this issue in a Keynesian tradition. The artist Josef Beuys has drawn attention to this, a topic that has been followed up by art promoters such as Richard Demarco and Robert McDowell.[67] Over the past 20 years or so, there has been an exceptional growth in the cultural labour market, for which the following figures speak their clear language. During the period 1981–

66 Christensen, Anna, Wage Labour as Social Order and Ideology 1984: 7- 8.

67 See Storlund 2002: 159-160, Demarco, Richard, *Kunst = Kapital, Art = Wealth*, 1995: 19.

1997 the number of cultural workers in Spain increased by 3.2 million persons. In Sweden there was an increase of 60 per cent in the number of cultural workers in the period 1970–1990. In Finland, again, there has during the past 25 years been an increase of 127 per cent in the number of cultural workers, which should be contrasted to a decrease by 9 per cent of the total labour force (Karhunen 2002). This is something that Manuel Castells also has drawn attention to at a general level of the economy and the labour market, in his analysis of the changes that information technology has brought about.[68]

The human as an organising factor

The growth in the cultural sector, and the changed work formats that information and communication technology has brought about, have in a decisive way changed the nature of work in an individualising direction. To recognise artistic and cultural work and to introduce appropriate provisions for such work is a compelling need in order to catch up with social change. This is all the more pressing because of the expansion of the art, culture and media sectors. As a general trend the cultural labour market has in recent years (before the financial crisis of 2008) been expanding at a rate near to or beyond the overall growth of some national or regional economies, extending also beyond national economies to global markets. This sector, ranging in such diverse fields as the visual or performing arts, broadcasting or multimedia production "has been heralded as one which can secure sustainable employment, reinforce endogenous regional potentials and shape the future through high levels of creativity and innova-

[68] See Aoyama, Yuko and Castells, Manuel, An empirical assessment of the informational society: Employment and occupational structures of G-7 countries, 1920-2000, in International Labour review 2002.

tion in a market in which the majority of goods and services are non-sustainable". So it is noted in a project report Pyramid or Pillars - Unveiling the Status of Women in Arts and Media Professions in Europe.[69]

Considering the narrow theoretical perspective on the human and society that ensued from the paradigmatic shift introduced by enlightenment thinkers, we are greatly served by art and culture, because through them, it is possible to attain dimensions that are hidden from view in our theoretical schemes. Or, as Ferench Molnár has formulated it in an article about the arts and the state: "After all, the social function of art, in the strict sense of the term, perhaps oversimplifying the issue, is no more than the description of those processes which cannot be covered by other, objective means of social research (statistics, sociology, history, etc.). In other words, it is the development of the human soul, the slow transformation of consciousness which art - beyond and besides what is specifically aesthetic - can offer to society or to the leadership of the state." (1995: 19)[70]

But also in the aesthetic field, we face problems that might not be without consequence for how we perceive things and consequently go about them. Commenting on classical texts on aesthetics, David Cooper remarks that the paradigmatic change since the enlightenment that was influenced by Galileo and Descartes has had the effect that moral and aesthetic aspects were banished from the objective reality (2000: 76). The theoretical tradition and a wage labour rationale combine to create obstacles for perceiving the human values inherent in art and culture that would allow us to give artists a status accordingly. Hans-Georg Gadamer has lucidly de-

---

[69] *Pyramid or Pillars*, 2000:10. The authors refer on this point to the declaration of the Conference *Cultural Industries in Europe*, held under the German Presidency of the EU in Essen, May 1999 (www.ericarts.org)

[70] Molnár, Ferenc, *The Arts and the State*, in The New Hungarian Quarterly, 1979: 55.

picted the rationale of the industrialised wage labour society, as something that separates and divides us.[71] This is because of our deliberate and calculating pursuit of power and material advances, the tendency toward acquiring and manipulating things to which we owe the principal achievements of our modern civilization (Gadamer 1995: 59). Miha Pogacnik also draws attention to the processes involved in artistic creation, which he does through music. He points out how in the musical process, consciousness is lifted, moving us beyond a dialectical discourse of right or wrong, black or white and so on.[72] We are separated both by the social structures and by our thought structures. Another legacy originating in the enlightenment is the view of humans as profit making social atoms. Yes, we also act as a *homo economicus*, but neither always nor entirely. It should be obvious that this is not a comprehensive description of human nature, for which artists offer a fairly obvious illustration.

Implications of a human rights culture

By restoring an Aristotelian paradigm, we are better suited to differentiate the varied constellations pictured above. One thinker of modernity can serve us in this exercise, John Stuart Mill. He says: "If a person possesses any tolerable amount of common sense and experience, his own mode of laying out his existence is the best, not because it is the best in itself, but because it is his own mode"[73] Mill's statement indicates what is involved when we talk about autonomous persons. This should be a point of depar-

[71] Gadamer, Hans-Georg, The Relevance of the Beautiful and other essays 1995: 40.

[72] Interview with Miha Pogacnik in Storlund, Vivan, *Konsten har mycket att ge näringslivet* 2000: 19.

[73] Mill, John Stuart, Utilitarianism, On Liberty and Considerations of Representative Government 1974: 163.

ture when we consider whether economic, social and cultural rights materialise or not. This so called second generation of human rights cannot be handled in the same way as classical rights and liberties, that is, approached from an abstract and general level. On the contrary, it is precisely because of the abstract and general approach to rights' questions that problems arise, for which we continuously seek remedies in different categories of human rights.

The new human rights culture has far-reaching implications that Salvo Andò has analysed in an illuminating and comprehensive way in an article *The welfare state as a legal obligation* (1999). He notes that the state must first of all "satisfy the needs of a pluralistic society; one which is founded on an organised system of autonomous social groups" (1999: 85). Andò illustrate this, among others, with the Italian constitution that establishes a duty for the Republic to promote the right conditions so that freedom and equality of the individual and of the groups in which one's personality finds fulfilment, become real and effective.[74]

How are we to make this relevant for artists? Three different stages need to be considered. A first decisive step is to recognise the worth of every person. Second, we need to go beyond the wage labour rationale and give credit to people's efforts to enhance both their own life situation and that of others, be it through artistic work or through a variety of activities in the third sector. It is my impression that many social security schemes provide rescue for a person's material subsistence when no other means are available, but that they fail to support different efforts, such as artistic work, when this does not fit the wage labour structure.[75] The perception of work needs therefore, as a third step, to be differentiated, accompanied with different kinds of supportive measures also for

[74] Andò, 1999: 88, where he refers to articles 2 and 3 in the Italian constitution.

[75] I have dealt extensively on this issue in Storlund 2002, chapters V and VI with practical illustrations from Finland.

those who do not have full-time employment. It must be recognised that the collective level of industrial relations, at which labour standards mostly are determined, does not properly cover the great variety of work patterns today, such as artistic work, project work and work in the social economy. This being the case, the state has, in line with what Andò noted above, an obligation to remedy the injustices that follow from inefficient protection in labour and social security legislation.

Lucy A. Williams also draws attention to the need to establish a closer juncture between work and social welfare law. She points to how the perspective of welfare law remains limited to wage labour, privileging thereby collective bargaining, as the primary site of progressive initiatives for economic and social redistributions (2002:93).[76] This illustrates the problems associated with personhood referred to above; that laws signal social values by including or excluding certain categories of persons (HLR, 2001: 1746–1747). The gist of this problem is that as long as cultural workers are treated according to the same rules as persons holding an employment, this will ordinarily lead to exclusion from the benefits and safeguards embodied in collective agreements as well as labour and social security legislation.

We are advised by Aristotle on this score. He observes that justice is equality when we deal with people who are equal. "We make bad mistakes if we neglect this 'for whom' when we are deciding what is just". (1987: 195) Attention therefore needs to be directed to the forms artistic and cultural work takes. What today is called atypical work can be seen as a typical format for work in the cultural sector. The work is highly mobile and flexible, often of a trans-national nature. Actors, for example, may

---

[76] Williams, Lucy A., Beyond Labour Law's Parochialism: A Re-envisioning of the Discourse of Redistribution, in Labour Law in an Era of Globalisation (eds.) Conaghan, Joanne, Fischl, Richard Michael, Klare, Karl 2002: 93.

work for a theatre, television, performing alone, or play a role in a multimedia installation. A composer may be engaged to create a film soundtrack and, if lucky, the next day have a contract to compose for a publicly funded symphony orchestra, in addition to making own compositions, as well as performing herself. This varied picture of cultural work and the high degree of mobility between different kinds of activities both within and often also outside the cultural sector has implications in many respects. Also because of downsizing of public cultural institutions, there has been an increasing proportion of small business, of outsourcing, of self-employment, short-term contracts, freelance or part-time work (see *Pyramid or Pillars* 2002: 10).

In this setting there is not much left of labour law's premises; a clearly defined employer - employee constellation, full-time employment as well as defined working hours and working conditions. Equally, the cultural labour market cannot be considered as a homogeneous one in other respects than that it presents a rationale that differs from the wage labour rationale, and must be treated accordingly. In the project *Pyramids or Pillars*, Austrian contributors have made a differentiation of artistic work that helps to grasp the cultural sector. In reporting on artistic work the authors were, not surprisingly, faced with "[m]ethodological difficulties inherent when defining artistic and media professions according to "traditional" boundaries between the individual professions" (*Pyramid or Pillars* 2002: 43). Faced with this dilemma the authors opted for the following already above cited distinctions: high culture, "artistic culture": traditional, representative art with symbolic profitability; social culture: the so-called third sector in culture, which consists of process and communication oriented initiatives with social profitability; as well as mass culture: culture and leisure industries with economic profitability.[77] This distinction among three different kinds of artistic work can be generalised to

[77] Harauer et al. *Thanks for Playing Anyway*, in Pyramid or Pillars 2002: 43.

work at large as it differentiates the varied nature of work in a way that is as valid for the old 'industrial era', as it is for today's context, only the proportions differ. A new phenomenon today is that the share of industrial work as the sector generating economic growth has diminished, whereas art and culture are among the fastest growing sectors of the economy.

A just treatment of artists

Because focus has almost exclusively been placed on wage labour, and because the role of government in social welfare has been seen as one concerned with transfers and redistribution, attention has not been directed to the state's role in constructing labour markets, Williams remarks (2002: 93). She points out that established definitions "reinforce the socially constructed identities upon which mainstream discourse and political rhetoric are founded. By pursuing a traditional social welfare agenda primarily connected to an anachronistic image of the waged worker, and by distancing other members of society as 'non-productive', labour contributes to the stigmatisation of millions of low-waged and non-waged workers, including welfare recipients and immigrants." (2002: 94–95) A basic question for legislative policy is therefore "what legal instruments and institutions should determine who receives the protection of labour law - how courts and other arbitral forums interpret legal definitions of who should be covered by labour law".[78] Should not everybody? If we aim at justice the answer must be that everybody should enjoy the protection of law on equal terms. This requires new approaches and structures. One illustration of such a new approach is a scheme for artists introduced in

[78] Benjamin, Who Needs Labour Law? Defining the Scope of Labour Protection, in Labour Law in an Era of Globalisation, (eds.) Conaghan, Joanne, Fischl, Richard Michael, Klare, Karl 2002: 76.

the Netherlands in 1999. The Dutch scheme for artists, De Wet inkomensvoorziening Kunstenaars, WIK, departs from the recognition that artistic work does not fit the standard picture of work and that many artists are therefore unable to gain a living from their own artistic work. Thus a basic support system is provided.[79] This system has many merits and could act as a model for a variety of activities outside the wage labour structure. A major merit of the WIK system is that it is flexible. The testing of thresholds is avoided, that in existing social welfare schemes often exclude those who are in the greatest need for economic support.

Economic, symbolic and social values

To differentiate activities according to the values they represent in social cooperation, is one way of considering to each according to one's right, to each according to one's deserts and to each according to one's needs. If we look at what a person is due in the artistic field, the activities representing a symbolic value appears to be most clear-cut as they represent activities that by the polity has been designated a societal function and worth. These are institutions such as museums, theatre, opera that can be placed on a par with education and research. These activities are the least problematic. Because of their institutional standing, their activities are regulated by laws and collective agreements. This does not mean that they would be unproblematic, but to their legal and institutional structures, they accord to the legal regulation of working life.

In the entertainment and cultural industry the setting is more obscure because of the variety of ways in which economic profit is accrued, triggering questions such as who stands to gain from such products. Instead of an employer and employee-constellation we are here concerned with

[79] See Wik informatie, Kunstenaarswijzer nr 29, herfst 2000:18.

commissioners, producers and the doers. How is economic gain distributed among the different players involved? This is a highly versatile area of growing economic significance that would require another point of legal departure than the one represented by existing labour law. The same goes for activities generating social value. This sector is even more challenging than the one represented by the entertainment and cultural industries. This is because the value of such work cannot be measured in conventional economic terms, at least not in a neoliberal sense. With a Keynesian approach to economics, it is easier to make sense of the value created in activities generating social value.

If we address these questions through the notions of rights, deserts and needs, a tentative picture emerges on the following lines: Where the nature of work conforms to conventional labour standards, such as is the case for those who perform artistic or cultural work within an employment relationship, they can assert their rights in regard to their employer, a municipal orchestra, theatre, museum, etc. Here the whole array of labour standards are available, such as compensation according to established standards (collective agreements), social security provisions and different entitlements such as in-service training and so on. When artists are hired as so-called atypical workers, such as fixed-term contracts or on a freelance basis, the testing of thresholds starts. There may still be some protection to be gained from labour legislation, when an employment relationship can be identified, but here uncertainty sets in. In much entertainment as well as artistic and cultural activities, work is done on a freelance basis. Here social security associated with employment is out of reach. The same goes for artistic and cultural work that is not primarily aimed at economic profit but done for artistic or communitarian purposes. These activities cannot be approached from the same perspective as work done in an employment relationship.

A new re-distributive agenda

A new re-distributive agenda is required that takes account of the variety of values created at the borderline of work. Symbolic, social and economic values are complementary and they are all an inherent, even a necessary part of any social setting. These different values also represent different modes of operation that has not been sufficiently brought to the fore. To look at the nature of 'profitability' as symbolic, social or economic also allows a fresh perspective on the distinction between public and private. The public - private distinction easily evades from view the varied nature of activities carried out in the respective sectors, involving economic as well as social and symbolic values. This needs to be recognised and here we can be assisted by artists.

CHAPTER 8

ARTISTIC WORK - A PRECURSOR FOR WORK IN ICT SOCIETY

2005 - in Liber Amicorum Reinhold Fahlbeck

The status of artists and cultural workers is an under-research field in labour law, as is also the growing sector of cultural industries. Conceptual tools are here devised to facilitate an analysis of artistic and cultural work, with the goal of bringing this work within the ambit of labour law, in accordance with the UNESCO Recommendation concerning the Status of the Artist and international labour standards (1980).

An extended agenda for labour law

How should labour law be adjusted to reflect changes in working life manifested in the great increase in so called atypical work? Before the oil crisis of the 1970s atypical work averaged a few per cent in OECD countries. Today we talk about plus – minus 25 per cent in the western hemisphere.[80]

How should labour and social security legislation be redesigned to accord legal protection to persons working in so called atypical workformats on a par with the legal protection accorded those we term typical, that is, persons holding full-time employment of indefinite duration. This question extends beyond national labour and social security legislation. It involves international labour standards and human rights. Equally, it

[80] Aoyama, Yuko and Castells, Manuel give a survey of changes in working life in an article *An empirical assessment of the informational society: Employment and occupational structures of G-7 countries*, 1920-2000, International Labour Review, Vol. 141, No. 1-2, 2002: 123.

raises questions of fundamental prerequisites of a legal order, such as predictability, legal certainty, equality before the law, etcetera. Artistic work is a case in point. It is conceptual confusion to talk about atypical work when roughly one quarter of the working population perform work so termed, and its decrease is not in sight.

What is meant when we talk about atypical work is that the formal prerequisites of such work differ from the premise on which labour law is based, thus, full-time, long-term employment. It is evidently not a sustainable solution to continue calling work that deviates from these premises atypical. On the contrary, the conclusion that must be drawn is that labour law has not been adapted to factual conditions. An effect of this is that a growing number of persons are deprived of the protection labour law is intended to offer the working population. Thereby so-called atypical workers are to varying degrees deprived of the legal protection that a legal order is intended to secure. A fundamental problem as labour legislation now stands, is the sharp distinctions between paid and unpaid work, between 'employed' and 'self-employed' workers, between employment and unemployment, and between 'work' and other life-activities", as pointed out in a comprehensive assessment of labour law in an era of globalisation, by Joanne Conaghan et al (2002: xxvi).

Consequently, the way in which a legal system poses and answers questions concerning work generally determines who does and who does not receive the protection of labour law (Benjamin, *Who Needs Labour Law?* 2002:75). These questions involve basic legislative policy issues as to "what legal instruments and institutions should determine who receives the protection of labour law and - how courts and other arbitral forums interpret legal definitions of who should be covered by labour law", Paul Benjamin notes, scrutinising the scope of labour protection (Benjamin 2002:76).

These are big and complex issues and therefore, problems concerning atypical work cannot be addressed from the prevailing premises of labour law. To remedy the status of atypical workers in a piecemeal fashion, as has been the case up till now, is like "plugging only some of the holes in a sinking boat", as Mark Jeffrey has put it (*Part-Time Work, Atypical Work and attempts to Regulate it* 1998: 172). What is required is a comprehensive reconsideration of that part of working life that is not properly covered by existing labour legislation, collective agreements and social security schemes associated with them.

You, Reinhold, have done an admirable work in raising the question of freedom of religion in working life, pointing to how today's increasingly multicultural societies require us to look at things differently. I can think of no better forum than this book to honour you, for venturing a similar agenda for artistic and cultural work, as we over the years have been comparing notes on our efforts to obtain a better understanding of the phenomena facing us in working life. For this my sincerest thanks.[81]

New approaches required

Art and entertainment are fast growing sectors of the economy today, paralleled by a great increase in the number of persons engaged in such work. To indicate structural models and provisions in labour- and social security legislation that would cater for a legal standing for artists[82] is fraught with difficulties because we do not have appropriate conceptual tools to make artistic work relevant in a labour law context. Questions have to be put differently when art and culture is involved than when the primary function of a job is to secure one's material subsistence. For artists and cultural workers, the fundamental questions boil down to being able to do

[81] My thanks equally go to Otto A. Malms Donationsfond for the grant that allowed me to write this article and to the University of Malta, where this article was mainly written.

[82] as sought by the UNESCO Recommendation concerning the Status of the Artist 1980 and international labour standards.

one's work and to be able to accrue an income from it. To consider the work of artists and cultural workers in a labour law context requires looking at work from a perspective that is perhaps as far removed as can be from the ideal-type underpinning labour law - a male blue-collar worker.

The guiding principles for considerations about artists are to be found in the UNESCO Recommendation concerning the Status of the Artist. The recommendation departs from the recognition that artists work under specific socio-economic conditions that differ from the overall labour market. The recommendation calls for the right of artists to proper remuneration for their professional activities - free from discrimination in areas such as taxation, social security or freedom of association. Regrettably, there has not been much progress on this front since 1980, when the recommendation was adopted.[83] Much work has, however, since then been undertaken by the cultural administration in different countries, and national cultural policy documents have been adopted, that need to be made relevant in a labour law context.

An EU Commission Staff Paper Culture, the *Cultural Industries and Employment* has caught the nature of artistic work in a nutshell when noting: "Creation is the work of gifted individuals." How this gift is used, that is, the possibilities there are for artists to make a living from their work depend essentially on the value that society attaches to artistic work. Contrary to a statement made by a representative of the EU Commission, cited below (Economic profitability), who only sees art and culture in market terms, the staff paper is perceptive of the volatile field of artistic creation. "In some cases this begins with non-market activities such as public-sec-

---

[83] See Pyramid or Pillars, Unveiling the Status of Women in Arts and Media Professions in Europe, Eds, Cliché, Danielle, Mitchell Ritva, and Wiesand, Andreas Joh., 2000: 15-16.

tor cultural policies, patronage or the assistance of cultural promotion associations but creative work can also fit into traditional economic circuits, and in this case the creative artist can live off the earnings generated."[84]

Entering an under-researched area

Artistic and cultural work is an under-researched area, starting with a lack of reliable statistical information. Nevertheless, according to some studies the number of jobs in the cultural sector in the 15 EU member countries amounted to some 2.5 million in 1995. If arts and crafts are included we talk about 3 million jobs in the cultural and craft sectors, equalling somewhat more than 2 per cent of the jobs in the Union.[85]

Here some illustrations where reliable figures are available: In Spain employment in the cultural sector grew with 24 per cent between 1987 and 1994. In France the increase was 36.9 per cent between 1982 and 1990, or ten times the increase in the total working population over the same period. In the United Kingdom the growth was 34 per cent between 1981 and 1991 for all persons with a cultural job, whereas the increase in the total working population was negligible. For Germany the increase in employment of producers and artists grew by 23 per cent between 1980 and 1994. In North Rhine-Westphalia, an area with a declining heavy industry, there was an increase as high as 161 per cent in the number of cultural businesses and jobs between 1980 and 1992 thanks to special investments to this end. (EU Staff Working Paper 1998: 2-3) As noted earlier, the increase in the number of artists in Finland amounted to 127 per

---

[84] *Culture, the Cultural Industries and Employment*, European Commission, Staff Working Paper, Brussels 14 May 1998, SEC (98) 837, p. 3.

[85] EU Staff Working Paper 1998: 2. See also Rensujeff, Kaija's study concerning income and grants for artists in different professions based on a questionnaire addressed to members of art organisations and artists having received grants in 2000. p. 14. Helsinki 2003.

cent during a 25-year period, 1970–1995. Within this number, the category 'other art and entertainment occupations' increased by 349 per cent, 89 which indicates that statistical measurement has not kept pace with these new conditions. Parallel with this there has, however, as a general trend been a decrease in some cultural sectors due to cuts in public funding since the early 1990s (EU Staff Working Paper 1998: 3).

These figures should suffice to indicate that artistic work needs to be taken seriously in a labour law context. Yet, there are other factors than mere statistical numbers to argue the case of art and culture; the values that artistic and cultural work represent, as articulated in national cultural policy programs. Furthermore, the EU staff paper *Culture, the Cultural Industries and Employment* also points out that "the trends observed and the analyses carried out confirm the hypothesis that culture and the activities which surround it - directly or indirectly - are a resource for the future and an important asset for the development of employment in Europe." (1998: 27) It is noted that public or private expenditure in the field of culture should not be considered a cost purely and simply but a viable financial investment with medium and long-term prospects. Here we see that the economic value of cultural activities cannot be measured in the same way as in industrial production. It is rather in tax yield for the public purse that we see the economic value of cultural activities (EU Staff Working Paper 1998: 27).

And we have the multiplier effect. The total multiplier effect is generally estimated to be a minimum of 1 (i.e. one direct cultural job leads to the creation of one or more indirect or generated jobs). For example, culture-related employment currently accounts for an estimated 6–8 per cent of jobs of the active population of greater Barcelona, representing some 8 500 firms producing more than 6 per cent of the area's total output (1998: 26). In one way or the other, art and culture have meeting points with other activities. Tourism is one such sector. Tourism is now the world's leading industry. Employment in the tourist sector represents some 6 per cent of total employment and an estimated 2 million new jobs were expected to be created by the end of the decade, according to the EU staff paper of 1998. And here the cultural heritage plays a central part. An estimated 30 per cent of total tourist consumption depends on the existence of the cultural heritage (EU Staff Working Paper 1998: 26).

Threading a fine line

There are sensitive issues involved when dealing with art and culture in an economic context. It has to do with the integrity of the artist and the artistic process and cultural production for all the good reasons stated above. Not surprisingly concern is therefore voiced in artistic and cultural quarters; "governments must participate in conceiving an internationally co-ordinated policy against the complete liberalisation of the diffusion of cultural goods. These goods are not merchandise, as many try to argue at the negotiations in the World Trade Organisation (WTO)", Razvan Theodorescu notes.[86] The pressure for mainstreaming is very strong, which is the very antidote of artistic expression. "Culture works against homogenisation. The cultural homogenisation, so close to consumerism is to be looked after in order not to fall into the trap of homogenisation. This means that Culture has to defend itself against existing risks", says Philip D Dracodaidis. [91] Also in the EU staff paper a warning is voiced that although the cultural sector holds great potentials, there is the danger confronting the different cultural segments today, notably the globalisation of the economy and pressures leading to uniformity of cultural services (EU Staff Working Paper 1998: 15).[92]

Dracodaidis, who is a cultural management consultant, considers that a cultural policy should be accompanied by a strategy for those who carry

[86] Theodorescu, Razvan, *European Identity, Regional /National Identities and the Arts*, p. 46, in ECA, Artists sharing without Frontiers, 2003.

out the work. In order to be viable, this must start from the artists and cultural workers, a 'bottom-up' approach, in other words. As Dracodaidis puts it, "in Culture we start from the artists, from those that work for Culture, we ask them questions, we find solutions together with them, we make proposals to the national decision centres together with them. If these steps are followed, it is time for what we call the "top-down approach", meaning that the decision centres, the decision makers, the authorities must play a constructive role, which is to decide, to discuss their decisions with all the parties involved and finalise a concrete action plan duly financed. This double-key approach works perfectly well when a strategy is available." (2003:30) And here also labour law enters the picture.

Reassessing the worker as ideal-type

When venturing a theoretical and statutory framework for the labour market that takes account of present day circumstances, it is instructive to start with the ideal-type underpinning labour law. The ideal-type on which labour legislation is based is a male blue-collar worker. This ideal-type has never offered a fair representation of the varied nature of work, and decreasingly so with the current diversification of working life. Franz Neumann discusses ideal-types, basing himself on Max Weber, who pictures the ideal- type as a mental design "which is not itself a reality, but with which reality is measured and with which it is compared".[87]

Neumann puts some questions, which will assist in pinpointing problems relating to the theoretical foundation of labour law. He notes that the ideal-type is attained by eliminating certain individual features while emphasizing others that appear essential for constructing the ideal-type. And

[87] Neumann, Franz, The Rule of Law, Political Theory and the Legal System in Modern Society 1986: 87.

he asks: Why may we neglect certain historical phenomena, and consider others as essential? Does this not make the very notion of the ideal-type a purely arbitrary one? Are there any standards of measurement indicating which individual historical features are necessary for the construction of the ideal-type, and which are only incidental (Neumann 1986: 187–188).

When looking at labour law in operation in the early third millennium, we need to keep in mind those features, which in the 19th century were seen as central for the ideal-type. It was the economy and trade that had to be freed from different kinds of restraints. The focus on economic processes made contract a central legal notion in the restructuring of law, which took place through law reform in the 19th century. This was taken on board in the ascending labour law through the employment contract.[88]

And here Neumann's questions are pertinent. What kind of problems can be traced back to aspects, which were omitted from the ideal-type, and what kind of legal problems result from the way the ideal-type influenced legal regulation in different fields? The mere fact that we allow ourselves to talk about work as being atypical when it accounts for plus, minus 25 per cent, can well be seen as an indication of how an ideal-type can steer our perception and equally what consequences this may have. Gunnar Eriksson offers a way out of the impasse into which an ideal-type can lead us, by suggesting that we operate with two opposite poles.[89] On this score I will complement the ideal-type of a male blue-collar worker with

---

[88] The employment contract became a theoretical hybrid that leaves logic wanting, when combining freedom of contract with a subordination of the worker to the employer. For a discussion on this topic, see Veneziani, Bruno, *The Evolution of the Employment Contract*, p 60, in Hepple, Bob, ed. The Making of Labour Law in Europe, A Comparative Study of Nine Countries up to 1945, 1986 and Storlund 2002, Chapter IV, 4.1. 5, also at http://ethesis.helsinki.fi

[89] Gunnar Eriksson uses Max Weber's ideal-type in an attempt at obtaining a fuller picture of the history of ideas. *Platon & smitaren, Vägar till idéhistorien*, Atlantis, Malmö, Om idealtypsbegreppet i idéhistorien 1989: 184-185.

that of an artist. In this way it is possible to overcome the problem Neumann pointed to; the arbitrary way in which certain phenomena are relied on whilst others are ignored. Eriksson notes that by operating with two polar ideal-types it is often easier to depict reality. He illustrates this through the polar relationships that Ferdinand Tönnies has brought to the fore through the notions *Gemeinschaft* and *Gesellschaft* (see Eriksson, G 1989: 189).

Industrial work and artistic work - two poles

The merit of working with two poles is that any phenomenon can be placed somewhere between the two poles. In regard to Gesellschaft and Gemeinschaft, Eriksson points out that all social groups can be said to be placed somewhere between these poles, drawing their main characteristics from one of them but with varying degrees of ingredients from the other. An ideal-type is thus a caricatured picture to which similar phenomena conform to varying degree.[90] In line with this, the blue-collar worker is still valid as an ideal-type for part of the labour market, representing one pole, but it needs to be complemented by an ideal-type that captures the other pole, one that is well represented by artists.

The notions of *Gesellschaft* and *Gemeinschaft* suits well the present effort to differentiate the notion of work by juxtaposing industrial work and artistic and cultural work. As Tönnies depicts *Gesellschaft* is characterised by mechanical calculations. The corporation is a case in point that is held together by calculations based on reason and planned profit. In contrast to this, *Gemeinschaft* is organic in nature and evolves in a spontaneous

---

90 Eriksson makes an important distinction between a concept seen as a logical class concept and an ideal-type. A logical class concept implies that all its members conform to the criteria given by the definition, whereby a phenomenon either conforms to the class or is excluded. Eriksson, G, 1989: 185-186.

way, such as the family, the original village and friends. Here sentiments and tradition play a primordial role. And here art and culture find their place. The difference between the two spheres is fundamental and makes almost everything look different in these two spheres of life. So much so that there can be features in *Gesellschaft* that do not exist or are not comprehended in *Gemeinschaft*. To be a human being or to act in a specific way is one thing in *Gemeinschaft* and quite another one in *Gesellschaft*.[91]

The blue-collar worker as ideal-type can be seen as an adequate representation of traditional industrial work along assembly line principles. In contrast to this, for any work involving people, such as care functions and education or work involving ideas such as research, art and culture, the blue-collar worker as ideal-type is clearly inappropriate. The only thing that has united these different kinds of work is the formal criteria of an employment contract. But as soon as different considerations and calculations become involved, such as quality versus profitability or efficiency the blue-collar worker as an ideal-type reveals its inadequacy. We here face a phenomenon that Elizabeth Wolgast has pointed to in a critical assessment of the rights tradition. She observes how the notion of rights, where inappropriately applied, drive us to caricature the matter at hand, and forces our considerations into a grid that has room only for individuals who are autonomous, have property, make contracts, and are void of basic human sentiments.[92]

The same is true for the selective picture of work that ensues from a sole focus on an employment contract. This has practical implications for the way those, whose work does not conform to the ideal-type, are perceived and treated. Wolgast notes that our habit of emphasising individual rights obscures the focus of moral objection, rather than giving the ob-

---

[91] Asplund, Johan, *Essä om Gemeinschaft och Gesellschaft* 1991: 67.

[92] See Wolgast, Elizabeth, The Grammar of Justice, Chapter 2, Wrong Rights 1987: 28-49

jection a firm foundation (Wolgast 1987: 47). Such is the case with atypical workers, too. On the side of the industrial pole, employers mostly resort to atypical work as a means of reducing costs. This places a double burden on atypical workers as such work often results in lower income and may, in addition, lead to exclusion from different work-related entitlements and social security schemes associated with work. As long as there are no complementary structures to remedy this injustice, there is no right, neither is there a firm foundation from which to react. This constellation also applies to artistic work, with the risk that only those who have a secured economic position as an artist, or those employed by a cultural institution are visible for labour law purposes.

There is likewise the risk that all activities are viewed purely from an economic profitability perspective, undermining thereby the goals of cultural programs. In the following, I will rely on the two poles of a blue-collar worker and an artist as a means of differentiating the notion of work. I will, however, shift focus from the traditional departure in an employment contract to a consideration of the work that is factually done and the attributes associated with it. In this way the impasse caused by the prevailing premises is avoided, whereby everything that does not conform to an employment contract of unlimited duration is labelled atypical – end of story. This is where my story begins.

If we introduce an ideal-type for work - rather than the worker - and complement our considerations of work as industrial production with artistic work, we will be able to place any kind of work between the two poles. We then move between the poles of working in order to gain one's material subsistence to one of realising a personal plan of life, artistic creation. Thereby we allow space for a variety of forms of work, including the different values it generates encompassing economic as well as symbolic and social profitability. In this way we avoid the trap of forging reality by pressing it into simplistic templates, as pointed out by Wolgast above.[93] To bluntly capture the present scene, the protection of labour and social security legislation is available when one happens to have a full-time employment of unlimited duration. With the great increase in fixed-term or part-time employment and all other variations of atypical work in industrial production, we see that already at the industrial pole, the ideal-type falls short of providing proper legal protection for a growing number of persons. Here we talk about big numbers, whose problems have received due attention in labour law and industrial relations research. This, however, is not the case with the status of artists and cultural workers.

Cultural industries signposts for the new economy

The artistic pole is not peopled by the same numbers as the industrial one, yet we are talking about an increasing number of people, as indicated above. What does this sector look like? One research project that gives a picture of the new cultural economy is a Dutch study of creative industries in the region of Eindhoven, Het creatief DNA van de region Eindhoven. The creative industries are in the project defined as "those activities which have their origin in individual creativity, skill and talent and which have a potential for wealth and job creation through the generation and exploitation of intellectual property."[94] One characteristic of the professions involved is that they have a high level of education (Eindhoven study 2003: 25). It is a heterogeneous and under-researched sector that is mapped out through a survey and in-depth interviews. The findings show that in the region of Eindhoven there are some 8 500 enterprises employing about 30 000 persons in the creative industries. This amounts to some

---

[93] For more of this, see Storlund 2002, Chapter IV.

[94] *Het creatief DNA van de regio Eindhoven, Feiten, cijfers en conclusies*, Etin adviseurs, Tilburg, juni 2003: 7. In the following referred to as the Eindhoven study.

8 per cent of employment opportunities, which exceeds employment in sectors such as construction (7 per cent), education and information technology (both 5.5 per cent). The estimated turnover is 1.2 billion euro, totalling 3 per cent of the turnover in the region.[95]

The authors of the study remark that there is a growing awareness that culture and economy combine in the creative industries and that this is of great importance both for the economy and for culture. It is seen as one of the most promising sectors with a strong ability to generate added value and employment. With the presence of a strong creative industry the region is better geared for its future development. This is, on the one hand, because of the way in which the creative sector may contribute to other sectors and, on the other, due to the significance the cultural sector has both for people's lives and the working climate in the area (Eindhoven study 2003: Foreword). This illustrates the point that art and culture should not merely be measured in economic terms. Yet the economic element is clearly there.

At a macro level the creative industries generate both an economic turnover and work for artists. This work has many positive connotations. It is capital extensive, knowledge intensive, labour intensive and tears less on the environment than many other activities. There are numerous examples of investments made in areas with a declining heavy industry that has transformed them into new ICT clusters, such as Barcelona, North Rhine-Westphalia and Glasgow, Rotterdam and the city on the Maas. With reference to this development the Dutch Minister of Education, Culture and Science, Mendy C. van der Laan emphasises, in her policy letter for the years 2004–2007, that creativity is a crucial production factor in the

[95] Eindhoven study. The sectors involved were artisanship, architecture, visual arts and antiques, literature and printing, film, video and photography, leisure software, music, television and radio, performing arts, advertisement and design. 2003:1, 7.

knowledge economy that is vitally important for the development "from a generic technology policy to an active innovation policy".[96]

It is not merely a question of technology, but increasingly a question of smart combinations of technology and factors such as artistry in design and creativity in the structuring of information. "Cultural innovation is often the secret behind the commercial success of numerous products and services", the Minister notes.[97]The Maltese cultural policy document also recognises the evolving notion of 'cultural worker' and 'cultural industry' and the need to introduce cultural and artistic management on a professional basis.[98] One institution created to this end is the Centre for Creativity, St. James Cavalier. Its role is to contribute to the country's economic and social development and prosperity by promoting artistic creativity as an alternative means of entertainment, self-actualisation and empowerment.[99]

Characteristics of the cultural industries

One outstanding characteristic of the creative industries is small size, the Eindhoven study shows. About half of the enterprises in the Eindhoven region are one-person enterprises. All in all 87 per cent have a personnel of less than 10 persons. Also, the turnover is low. This is partly due to the

---

[96] See Cultural Policy Letter 2004-2007. In Rotterdam, the local Development Corporation is pursuing a two-track policy. Favourable accommodation conditions have been created for audio-visual companies, and the city is also encouraging investments in film and television production via a fund with an obligation to spend locally. An independent film commissioner is responsible for bringing international productions to the city on the Maas to reinforce the regional economy and the city's dynamic image 2003:14.

[97] Cultural Policy Letter 2004-2007, p. 14.

[98] *National Cultural Policy in Malta*, 2002, Council of Europe, Steering Committee for Culture, pp. 2, 1

[99] National Cultural Policy in Malta, 2002, p. 4.

share of visual artists, representing many individual artists that have a fairly low turnover (2003:2). Another category that keeps the level of turnover down is foundations, among which most are small and have a low turnover. The involvement of foundations also brings along voluntary work that plays an important role in the activities of foundations. In this way unpaid work has a clear economic input (2003: 12–13). The enterprises in the Eindhoven region are young. Almost 37 per cent of them have existed for five years or less. Enterprises that have existed for more than 20 years count for 17 per cent of the creative industries (2003:2). Specific to this sector is also that many work at home, close to 40 per cent of them do so. This is partly explained by the difficulty to find business localities that they can afford (2003: 2, 27). Not surprisingly, the findings of the Eindhoven study also show that public structures are not yet geared toward these small-scale activities, but rather tailored for business life in its conventional form. By way of illustration, contacts with the Chamber of Commerce are scarce. Only 2 per cent had had frequent contacts with the Chamber, whereas 41 per cent had had occasional contacts (Eindhoven study 2003: 32). This is one practical example of the need for different administrative sectors to adapt to these new conditions, as this is a new sector of the economy.

For self-employed it is through cooperation with others that they manage the commercial side of their business (2003: 22). The creative industries also represent a new business culture. Few entrepreneurs in the creative industries aim at profit maximation. Aspects such as taking a pleasure in one's work, artistic freedom and the possibility to develop one's creativity are valued higher than pecuniary aspects. As is the case with many artists, some of the entrepreneurs have a commercial activity for the sake of an income that allows them to do artistic work (Eindhoven study 2003: 23). To take a pleasure in one's work rather than focussing on profit maximation does evidently not mean not working hard. On the contrary, the survey shows that people in the creative industries work long hours. About half of them work more than 40 hours a week, 25 per cent more than 50 hours a week (Eindhoven study 2003: 25). The deep interviews revealed devotion for working on a product. Focus thus lies on creativity and professionalism (2003: 22). It is a personal matter whether an entrepreneur in the creative industries sees him/herself primarily as an artist or an entrepreneur. Many of them are more concerned with the creative process than the market aspects of it. For them contacts with other people in the creative field is central (Eindhoven study 2003: 22). Two major orientations can thereby be seen in the creative industries, a market oriented one and one focussing on self-development (Eindhoven study 2003: 20).

Thus, there is in the creative industries a combination of mainly economic and social profitability. It is important to make this distinction to avoid that the creative industries are lumped as one streamlined profit-generating entity, of which more below. It is also important to differentiate the picture so that different categories and settings are given due consideration in terms of both legal prerequisites and practical arrangements. In addition to the combination of economic and social profitability in the new creative industries, also symbolic profitability plays a part, if we use this term to represent public or private funding, which I choose to do here. Thereby both the combination of different kinds of activity and their ability to generate an income is brought to the fore.

A need for supportive structures

The Eindhoven study reveals that the creative industries have received little attention in the regional economy. Other sectors can count on more attention and financial support, such as the high-tech sector. Yet, the creative industries are an economic factor to count with. And here we have an interesting illustration of 'how art works'. The authors of the study note that it is above all by way of strengthening other sectors and smoothening regional economic fluctuations that the creative industry contributes to the region. "It is time for a widening of the horizon", they note (Eindhoven study 2003: 38). The Eindhoven study also reveals a structural inequality that runs throughout the whole artistic and cultural sector, that requires attention and new approaches. Artists and small entrepreneurs have difficulties in obtaining funding for their activities. A great majority of the creative industries do not receive any subsidies (80 per cent). This does however not exclude that there might be possibilities for obtaining funding. Some 20 per cent obtain subsidies or funding for their activities and this is mainly the case in the cultural sector of the creative industries.

Here the structural inequality can be seen in that it is the bigger enterprises that obtain funding. Some 42 per cent of enterprises with 10 employees or more had received funding, whereas this was the case for merely 15 per cent of enterprises with 2 - 9 employees and 13 per cent among self-employed. The conclusions drawn in the report is that either big enterprises have easier access to subsidies, or else the rules are more suited for them. It is the big companies that determine the structures (Eindhoven study 2003: 38). Because of the small scale of the activities in the creative industry, there is a need for support structures of different kinds, to promote contacts with other businesses, to create networks, to find new openings for the products and services and to find the right subcontractors. In fact the foundation that carried out the Endhoven survey, the Stichting ALICE, was established in 2001 to support the creative sector (Eindhoven study 2003: 2).

Another Dutch example, to which the EU staff paper on the cultural industries and employment refers, is a bureau for artists and technicians in the performing arts and audiovisual media (Landelijk Bureau Kunsten & Media). In addition to job offers, the bureau provides services and training courses to help artists become self-employed; programmes for the acquisition of professional skills; and a database providing information and listing opportunities on the market for products and services (1998: 18). The EU staff paper points to the need for investment in training for cultural workers to sustain the development of the sector. As many jobs in this area are insecure and are strongly dependent on special skills in new technologies, it is essential to maintaining employability (1998: 18). In addition to the artistic and technological aspects, the EU paper also points to the need for training for new tasks such as administration and management in the broadest sense.

When setting up a business it is also important to have information on the legal, employment and economic aspects, including how to obtain funding. To share experiences of good practices is important as they then can be compared and transferred. This is the idea behind the measures the Commission has been developing for some years, to enable cultural operators to compare notes with a view to promoting the creation of new jobs, according to the EU staff working paper on cultural industries (1998: 19).

Economic profitability

The Eindhoven study shows that there is economic profitability in the creative industries. But again, it is not a question of clear-cut categories; we rather move on a gliding scale between the different categories of profitability. An artist moves into the sphere of economic profitability when a product sells. However, economic profitability is often generated around the work of artists rather than in a way from which they could directly profit. Authors and the publishing industry is a good illustration of this, particularly in a small country. Vivi-Ann Sjögren, an author belonging to the Swedish-speaking minority in Finland has pertinently pointed out how authors' manuscripts keep the publishing business running. Yet authors get the smallest economic share of it.[100] This is particularly the case when we talk about small markets. Another factor that affects an economic return is simply chance. This is something the Czech author Arnos Lustig has pointed out. He considers that all his books are equally good, yet one of them sold in big numbers.

These are examples of the kind of phenomena at work in the cultural field, of which we need to be aware to avoid the ensuing kind of generalisation. At a hearing on the cultural industries held by the European Parliament, Mr Reinhard Büscher, a representative of the European Commission, stated as the position of the Committee on art and culture, that cultural industries are a sector of the economy just like the other ones, big business with 100 billion euro turnover per year. He regretted that there were deficiencies in productivity obstructing even more success in the field of cultural industries. Büscher mentioned the Scandinavian book market as one example, where the productivity is very low. This results from too many books for too small markets. Competitiveness is the key to economic success and it need not contradict cultural development "because the taste of the majority of the general public is the main criterium for the free market", Büsher is reported saying.[101]

Büscher's statement triggers the question what cultural diversity there would be if countries with a small population like Iceland, Greenland or Malta would have as a primary criteria that the book market be profitable business. It is imperative that any form of cultural expression be assessed on its own merits in its proper context. In a position paper that the European Council of Artists, ECA, had made for this same parliamentary hearing, it is pointed out that the development of the cultural industries over

---

[100] Sjögren, Vivi-Ann, *Befängda frågor*, p. 25, Hufvudstadsbladet 22.4.2004.

[101] Cited by Laher, Ludwig, in Appendage Europe, National Artists' Umbrellas between Networking and Not Working, p. 57, in ECA, Artists sharing without Frontiers 2003.

the past decades had unproportionally favoured big cultural events. The ECA further states in its position paper that "cultural industries and private sponsorship cannot fully replace the obligations of the public and the state to encourage a flourishing cultural climate. Both public and state involvement are under all circumstances essential. Any discussion concerning cultural industries in Europe ought to reflect on the manifold interdependencies between political institutions, cultural industries and the artists." (Laher 2003: 58)

Social profitability

The most challenging task in a labour law perspective is to make sense of the social profitability of artistic and cultural work, as well as other work carried out outside the public or economic arenas. This is a legal grey area that is rapidly growing due to the great increase in artistic and cultural work, but also due to the downsizing of activities in the cultural sector representing symbolic profitability. This is the borderline of work because labour legislation does not recognise activities carried out in the intersection between employment, entrepreneurship and unemployment. A functional definition of this group could be artists and cultural workers who are not able to, or have difficulties in accruing a living wage from their work. Yet they contribute to the value generated by art and culture, as this is officially recognised in cultural programs and brought forth in studies referred to here.

Socio-economic conditions of artists and cultural workers

There is an urgent need to scrutinise labour and social security legislation and the effect existing rules have on the conditions of artists. In her cultural policy document, More than the Sum, the Dutch Minister of Education, Culture and Science also raises the question of bureaucracy; the need to reduce bureaucracy and to create more space for art and culture. She proposes that an assessment be made of existing regulations with the questions: "Which rules affect Education, Culture and Science institutions? How high are the resulting costs? Which rules result in the greatest amount of irritation and the most work?" (Cultural Policy Letter 2003: 5) Such an assessment should also be made at the level of individual artists. A consequence of not recognising artistic and cultural work means that the social profitability of their work is ignored. We here have the paradox that whilst the cultural industries are generating increasing return, most artists are working under deteriorating conditions, which makes it difficult for them to concentrate on the quality of their work (see Laher 2003: 58).

I cannot but draw a parallel here between a destitute workforce at the early stages of the industrial revolution and the position of a growing number of atypical workers today. Nonetheless, the observation that artists have difficulties in concentrating on the quality of their work highlights the decisive change in the nature of work in today's context. Because artistic work does not guarantee an income, many artists also work in other professions, ranging from art-related work to a bread-winning job without a connection to an artist's real profession (multiple job-holding) (see Rensujeff 2003: 38). According to a study on the income-formation of Finnish artists in the year 2000, 37 per cent were able to do their artistic work, either through an income derived from it or through grants. 52 per cent performed other work related to their artistic field, whereas 21 per cent obtained an income from other work (Rensujeff 2003: 41). A musician noted as one reason for doing other work, that this allows him to plan the economic side of his life in quite another way than being a freelancer (see Rensujeff 2003: 43). Predictability is a scarce asset in the artistic world. Another aspect of working as an artist is the solitary nature of the work. Thus, one reason given by a visual artist for having an employment in addition to her artistic work is this social aspect; her need to feel that she is part of a social context (Rensujeff 2003: 42).

But there is also a high level of unemployment among artists. A pertinent question that Swedish actors put is why they should be paid unemployment compensation when they could do their work with that same money. Questions of this kind need to be formulated to expose inappropriate structures. An urgent matter to attend to is to see how artistic work could be facilitated because unemployment rates are high whilst at the same time the cultural industries is a growing economic sector. In the arts, unemployment rates are higher than the national average, especially in the case of performers. In the United Kingdom unemployment in the cultural sector increased from 8 per cent in 1991 to 11 per cent in 1994 compared with 9.5 per cent over the same period for the rest of the economy. In reality, unemployment might be higher, around 16 per cent. In Sweden unemployment increased from 6.1 per cent in 1981 to 12.6 per cent in 1987.[102]

Of the 250 000 composers in the European Union, only 10 per cent have an income amounting to a minimum living wage that allows them to work as full-time composers (EU Staff Working Paper 1998: 21). Another factor that aggravates the situation for artists is the inadequacy of the criteria authorities operate with in establishing unemployment for free artists that neither have an employment nor commissions. Free artists are often considered as self-employed with the consequence that they do not have access to unemployment compensation. In her study of the income formation of Finnish artists Kaija Rensujeff points out that for an artist to obtain unemployment compensation, she or he may often have to show that the artistic work has ceased. A further problem is that those artists

[102] EU Staff Working Paper on Culture, the Cultural Industries and Employment 1998: 20, citing Cultural trends 1995; Cultural policy in Sweden, Council of Europe, 1992.

who have a bread-winning job alongside their artistic work may not show up in statistics. Furthermore, many artists do not register as unemployed as they have no chance of obtaining unemployment compensation. This caters for hidden unemployment that is seen as a great problem (2003: 34).

During 2000, 20 per cent of Finnish artists were registered as unemployed jobseekers for different periods of time, compared to the general level of unemployment of 10 - 13 per cent. Visual artists scored highest with an unemployment rate of 38 per cent, followed by dancers 34 per cent, artists in the film sector 28 per cent and multiple sectors and actors both 23 per cent (2003: 35). Among artists that had registered as unemployed jobseekers, 13 per cent were denied unemployment compensation (2003: 38). Although artists in general have a high level of education this does not, in contrast to other professions, have a positive effect on their employability (2003: 36).

Cultural work should also be considered in national employment plans in accordance with the Employment Title of the Amsterdam Treaty (Article 127). Through a multidimensional approach to culture and employment that recognises the different values involved, also social cohesion may be considered, whereby the activities of the Community Structural Funds enters the picture. In the EU staff paper on cultural industries it is pointed out that this could offer new opportunities for development that would enable the Union's citizens to fully express their cultural identity (EU Staff Working Paper 1998: 28).

Comprehensive structures required

Measures need to be taken at many levels to facilitate cultural and artistic work. To avoid that these only become peace-meal measures, comprehensive schemes are required to cater for the requirement of the UNESCO Recommendation concerning the Status of the Artist, that artists should enjoy the protection of labour law and social security. The only comprehensive scheme I am aware of that recognises this is the Dutch scheme introduced through The Income Provisions for the Artists Act (Wet op de Inkomensvoorziening voor Kunstenaars), the so called WIK scheme. This scheme provides artists with a basic income (70 per cent of welfare payments) while they at the same time can work and sell their products.[103]

In my reading of the WIK scheme, it has a number of merits and it could offer a model also for other vulnerable groups in the labour market. The scheme departs from the understanding that artistic work does not fit the standard picture of work. Thereby it differs from many other social security schemes where there is no recognition of the specific nature of artistic work.[104] After certain formal criteria are fulfilled, and an artist receives the WIK support, the system operates in a way that appears to avoid testing thresholds. This testing of thresholds to determine whether a person is entitled to a certain work-related entitlement is a by-product of so called atypical work. This generates a high degree of bureaucracy with no certainty that an atypical worker will be successful in obtain the entitlement in question. This is particularly so because employers resort to atypical work in order to reduce their costs and this may also have spill over effects for social security.

The inherent logic is such that however much the qualifying thresholds are lowered, if systems are not all inclusive, those who are most vulnerable will be excluded. In addition to the complicated bureaucratic processes this generates, there are also misunderstandings between public officials and artists, as the Finnish study on the income-formation of artists reveal. Artists feel that they are not taken seriously as professionals

[103] Netherlands cultural profile, 8.1.1 Special artists support schemes, Wik informatie, Kunstenaarswijzer nr 29, herfst 2000:18.

[104] For a tentative problem inventory for Finland, see Storlund 2002: 207-214, Chapter VI, Social security - support or guillotine.

and that they are forced into legal categories where they consider they do not belong (Rensujeff 2003: 32). The WIK scheme appears to avoid that trap (see Wik informatie 2000:18). The WIK system was introduced in 1999 as a four-year scheme that could be used during a 10-year period. With this support an artist could have an income from her/his work amounting to 125 per cent of the subsidy, whilst still retaining it. If an income exceeded that amount the artists could exit the system, for example when receiving a commission, a grant or any other more substantive income, and return when the extra funding ceased (WIK 2002: 18). This scheme is continued in a slightly adapted form through a new act.

At a level of principle, I do, however, have reservations about the WIK scheme. This is because it is designed as a social security scheme. Here again we are faced with a conceptual mismatch, as the purpose of the scheme is to allow artists to do their work and to assist them to establish an enterprise. The proper nature and place of such a scheme should be in line with the economic support given to high-tech enterprises, shipping, agriculture and any other sector that a government chooses to support. The Eindhoven study also shows that some artists involved in the creative industries relied on the WIK scheme (Eindhoven study 2003: 38).

We here move along the borderline between social and symbolic profitability, and it can be in place to draw a parallel to research at this juncture, as research is not something from which one would expect immediate economic return. On the contrary, research is seen as having a value in itself, and professors would hardly like to conceive of their income as social security. As both research and artistic and cultural work is assigned a societal value, it is a waist of societal resources that either of them be unemployed. Again, we are faced with a conceptual mismatch because by definition artists make art and researchers do research. These are activities where the logic of industrial production does not apply. Instead it is, as Dracodaidis has put it, a direct and sustained personal investment that is the basis of any cultural work.

Also, in the process there is a meeting point: "Culture has uncontrolled maturation periods that will (or will not) lead to the final result, say a work of art. This means that the direct and sustained personal investment is the basis of any cultural aspect." (Dracodaidis 2003: 28) The labour market is traditionally viewed as the meeting point of supply and demand for employment but in the cultural sector setting up a business is often the surest way of obtaining a job, as it is the artist's investment in his or her project that becomes the best guarantee of employment. This is equally true both for individual artists and for collective cultural projects where everyone plays an important role in the running of the project and in the creation of jobs. The cultural labour market is primarily a market for the creation of new activities, goods or services (EU Staff Working Paper 1998: 17).

Funding - cost effectiveness and predictability

Where artistic and cultural work does not generate an income, this work is dependent on funding in one form or the other. The activities representing symbolic profitability are in this respect most clear-cut as they are financed through public budgets. Also from a labour law perspective, this sector is most clear-cut as much work, such as in a symphony orchestra, a theatre, a museum etcetera mostly is performed in an employment relationship. When artistic work is performed without an employment contract, we enter the legal grey areas revealed above. Funding in the form of grants is there for the purpose of allowing artistic work to be done. It is, however, important to be aware that this is not an option but a chance. In other words, it is not something an artist can count on, only hope for. Based on observations made I would venture a rough estimate that some 25 - 30 per cent of those who apply for funding receive a grant. For them all is well for as long as the funding lasts. The time and effort put into applying for the grant paid off. Now their work is visible. It is an on-off situation.

The problematic side of applying for funding is the time and effort that is put into this for the 70 - 75 per cent whose applications are turned down. For those who do not have a monthly salary running, the time spent on preparing an application, is extremely expensive time, as it is off the time doing the artistic work an artist should do in the first place, or off the spare time dedicated to artistic work for artists who have a bread-winning job. The study on the income-formation for Finnish artists in 2000 reveals that a total of 27 per cent of the applicants had received grants during that year. There is a great variation among different artistic categories that also reflects their ability to accrue an income from their work. The work of authors and visual artists are most distanced from a standard model of work and this is also reflected in the allocation of funding. Among authors applying for funding, 79 per cent received an average amount of 6 432 euro, scoring highest, followed by visual artists with 44 per cent, receiving an average of 6 702 euro (Rensujeff: 2003: 56).

The business of applying for funding also raises questions of efficiency and cost-effectiveness in a person's professional endeavours. In addition, it raises a number of intricate philosophical questions concerning the autonomy of the creative process, what criteria to apply, etcetera that goes beyond the scope of this paper. Focus will here be placed on how efficient and realistic present practices are. The EU program Culture 2000 may here exemplify a couple of points; on the one hand that support structures are tailored for big players and on the other, how unrealistic expectations thereby are placed on singular artists in search of funding for their activities.

The purpose of Culture 2000 is to promote trans-national co-operation in Europe. This requires a collaborative partnership among cultural organisations in participating European countries. All participants are expected to contribute in terms of ideas, expertise, contacts, time, personnel, resources and finances. Each co-organiser must bring a minimum of 5 per cent of the overall project costs to the central kitty.[105] Where does that leave individual artists? As the Eindhoven study revealed, in the creative industries artists have a low turnover, which means that they have to put long hours into their work in order to make ends meet. So how realistic is it that individual artists would stand a chance to contribute to a common cultural space in Europe?

Catherine Boothman who presented the Culture 2000 programme at a meeting of the European Council of Artists gave advice on how to go about it: As only organisations can apply for funding from the programme, artists that have worked together can register as a company or enter a contractual relationship with a production company. (For an artist working on a freelance basis, setting up a company may have negative economic implications). I will cite Boothman's advice for preparing a proposal in order to highlight the time and effort that goes into applying for funding, and the costs in terms of time and money this implies for those whose applications are turned down. (There is evidently a value in the contacts that are established and maintained during the preparation of the application, but this is uncompensated input.)

Here Boothman's advice:

" -Make sure you have strong, discursive relationships with your prospective co-organisers so that everyone is involved equally in planning the project and aware of their responsibilities.

- Make sure all Co-organisers are aware that they each have to come up with 5% of the overall costs of the project.

---

[105] Boothman, Catherine, The Experiences of the Culture 2000 Programme as a tool for Unifying Europe - Expectations for the Future, in ECA, Artists sharing without Frontiers 2003: 36.

- Draft detailed descriptions and operational plans for the project so that all your Co-organisers can work on the preparations.
- Circulate up to date drafts of your estimated costs and estimated income regularly between the Co-organisers so that people can work on a small strand of the budget or keep an eye on the bigger picture.
- Meet your Co-organisers face-to-face, and work on the final project proposal together.
- Build conditional arrangements with other people or organisations who will be necessary to your project but who do not have the same involvement as Co-organisers in designing the overall project (e.g. possible subcontractors, such as a web design company, or a partner like a local authority that may be providing space or some other resource for part of the project).
- Identify your target general participants (e.g. mid career visual artist; young people with disabilities).
- Identify your public audiences. - Build agreements with other Co-financers (e.g. commercial sponsors; regional and national public agencies).
- Identify expected revenues the project will create (e.g. ticket sales; workshop registration fees) " (Boothman 2003: 37)

In addition to all the work that has gone into these preparations, there is the further hazard whether additional funding will be obtained or not. I feel that even researchers would sigh faced with these requirements. Yet, in the academic world there are longstanding contacts and cooperation among universities. This is not necessarily the case in the new cultural fields. As the Eindhoven study shows the enterprises are young and already at a local and national level they lack proper networks. Therefore, there simply must be more rational ways of promoting the common cultural space in Europe than in the way presented here. It is to be hoped that better ways are found as EU has on its agenda to develop new methods for support (see Boothman 2003: 38).

Sponsorship is yet another element, where new forms of cooperation need to crystallise. In the Netherlands a code for sponsors of cultural events has been drawn up, entitled culture sponsoring. The most important aspect of this code is that in principle the sponsor is not allowed to influence the actual content of the activity organised by its cultural partner.[106]

A balance sheet

It is a fairly bewildered picture that emerges out of this new territory in working life. With the increasing use of projects as a work format, an increasing number of people throughout working life are faced with the host of problems raised here; inadequate legal protection and a lacking ability to go about one's work in an autonomous and rational manner. "The institutions which finance contemporary art have a very important role to play in preserving the freedom of the artist. Their commissions or grants must help the artist to create, free from market conditions."[107] With these words Dan Dediu voices the concern of artists. A cultural producer, again, has pointed out that applying for funding may extend over several years, and when funding is finally obtained, the persons originally involved may have moved on to other tasks.

Much work needs to be done at a conceptual as well as legislative and administrative level to facilitate artistic and cultural work. For this we need a new legislative and administrative culture that includes rather than excludes. We need guidance from artists for a new mindset that will allow us to seize opportunities in the new environment we live in today - as opposed to the environment and measures that were seen as necessary

---

[106] Netherlands, Cultural profiles, 7.3. http://www.creativeurope.info

[107] Dediu,Dan, *The Influence of Financing Strategies on Contemporary Arts*, in ECA, Artists sharing without Frontiers 2003: 44.

one century ago. Yet again, as Hans-Georg Gadamer has put it ""Art" begins precisely there, where we are able to do otherwise" (Gadamer 1986: 125).

CHAPTER 9

CONDITIONS FOR AN ACTIVE CITIZENSHIP - A PROBLEM INVENTORY

2006 Conceptual study for a project on civil participation[108]

The power that stems from civil action lies in people's aspirations and needs to act for themselves and their kinships to secure and improve their quality of life. Civil activities cannot be questioned without questioning the right of everybody to strive for the good life for themselves as well as for their kinships and the society in which they live. This observation Aaro Harju makes in his book about civil society as a joint venture, as well as its challenges.[109] He has in this quote pinned down a state of affairs that at a common sense level is self-evident, and yet it is an extremely complex question. The challenge is to identify what it is that impedes such aspirations.

There is today a widespread concern about decreasing civil involvement in society. Sociologists have been in the forefront in voicing this concern, with Robert D. Putman as a leading authority. In his book *Bowling alone* he paints a sombre picture of civil involvement in the early 21st century. Similar concerns have motivated the Finnish government to launch a program for civil participation. The objective of the program was to improve electoral participation and provide opportunities for active civil participation between elections. The program also placed emphasis on

---

[108] Experiences of civil activities at Pappilantie, Espoo. A project carried out within the framework of the Finnish Governmental Civil Participation Policy Programme, financed by the Ministry of Education, 2006.

[109] Yhteisellä asialla 2003.

those groups whose participation and influence had remained low in the past.

Parallel with these concerns, however, we have persons in the so-called third sector who struggle to be able to do their work. And there are many of them. Finland is considered a promised land for civil activities. Consequently, there appears to be a discrepancy between the concerns for lacking civil involvement in Finnish society and factual conditions. This discrepancy reveals a paradox that needs to be scrutinized. To put if metaphorically, there appears to be some obstacles between 'supply and demand' that need to be cleared. I will henceforth use the notion 'supply and demand' for short, to pinpoint discrepancies between the quest for civil engagement and the obstacles facing those who are engaged in such activities.

Form versus substance

There is a risk that by focussing on form rather than substance, we might not see factual activities that are there, if we lack formal criteria to capture them. Lack of proper criteria may also have legal repercussions, revealing legal grey areas. Activities in civil society is a case in point. When we talk about civil participation, we are concerned with what Harju described above, that is, people's aspirations and needs to act for themselves and their kinships to secure and improve their quality of life. At a formal level, this is done through elections, but at a level of substance such aspirations are transformed into activities in civil society, and here a not negligible body of activities go on. It is not only a question of bowling clubs, but also a considerable amount of services that are provided by third sector organisations, involving employed personnel, volunteers and different groups of people for whom the work is done. According to research made by the international Johns Hopkins university, some 82 000 persons were employed in the third sector in Finland in 1997, out of whom 25 000 worked part-time. Compared to overall employment in the whole service sector, this amounts to some 10 per cent. When compared to employment in the public sector, employment in the third sector amounts to 13.5 per cent. If voluntary work is also considered, the shares are approximately doubled (see Harju 2003:33)

Here we encounter the problem of legal categories, which is one central factor that needs to be considered when scrutinizing the obstacles between 'supply and demand'. In this case it is because labour law is not attuned to the great variety of work that is factually done, and increasingly so because of changing societal conditions. As unemployment is a great political concern, a first thing to do in order to improve the situation should be to recognize the work that is factually done, and facilitate such work both through legal and other means. In his book *The Rise of the Creative Class*, Richard Florida has attributed decreasing civic involvement to the new societal conditions in which we live, where information and communication technology, ICT, has overtaken industrial production as the dominant feature of our time, and thereby the culture that goes along with it. His analysis is pertinent and needs to be taken seriously. Yet, he gives only one part of the picture of changing economic and social conditions, although a very important one. Further parallel venues therefore need to be explored. It can be helpful to start at a philosophical level to see what guidance can be obtained to the riddle of the discrepancy between 'supply and demand' in civil involvement.

Conditions for an active citizenship - perception the first step

One fundamental question to be put is: what are the conditions that will allow persons to act as active citizens? This is something that changes over time, where different kinds of structural and legal as well as cultural restraints condition people's abilities to take an active part in civil life. To get a perspective on the challenges facing us today, it is instructive to see how philosophers and other thinkers have addressed these questions during previous époques. Civil society was a central theme among enlightenment thinkers and beyond. How philosophers and sociologists approached civil society captures in an interesting way different historical contexts, and thereby different phases of development. The constraints enlightenment thinkers were faced with involved an accumulation of old power structures from church and aristocracy to royal power and mercantilism. The rule of law, free markets, democracy and freedom of association where seen as means to overcome obstacles deriving from these old power centres. All these issues that we today take for granted, involved in their time great controversy, particularly so freedom of association.[110]

It was then, up till the 19th century, a question of adapting structures and attitudes to the realities of commerce and industry. Now, the conditions have again changed in so fundamental ways that we need to reassess the conditions for an active citizenship. Evidently, it is the conditions of a society dominated by information and communication technology, ICT, as well as globalisation that now provide a changed societal context. Florida has in a perceptive way captured the new rationale that the ICT society represents, by looking at how new technology is transforming work, l, community and everyday life. It should be stressed here that his field of research is regional economic development, and that he thereby looks at social change from an economic perspective. He insists, however, that it is not technology as such that is the driving economic force, but creativity. This constitutes a decisive shift from a focus on physical assets of previous époques, to human assets today that needs to be reflected at a perceptional level.

[110] On the controversy of freedom of association, see Storlund 2002: IV.6. *The combination of labourers.*

According to Florida's classification, more than 30 per cent of the American working population work in occupations that involve creativity, and he notes that this group, "the Creative Class has shaped and will continue to shape deep and profound shifts in the ways we work, in our values and desires, and in the very fabric of our everyday lives." (Florida 2002: ix) Florida observes: "A new social class, in short, has risen to a position of dominance in the last two decades, and this shift has fundamentally transformed our economy and society - and continues to do so." (Florida 2002:82) Describing his research process, Florida gives an illustration of the kind of change of perception that is required to grasp the new reality in which we live. "As I delved more deeply into the research, I came to realise that something bigger was going on. Though most experts continued to point to technology as the driving force of broad social change, I became convinced that the truly fundamental changes of our time had to do with subtler alterations in the way we live and work - gradually accumulating shifts in our workplaces, leisure activities, communities and everyday lives. ... it became increasingly evident to me that the emerging Creative Economy was a dynamic and turbulent system - exciting and liberating in some ways, divisive and stressful in others." (Florida 2002: x- xi)

Florida says that unless we design new forms of civic involvement appropriate to our times, we will be left with a substantial void in our society and politics that will ultimately limit our ability to achieve the economic growth and rising living standards we desire (Florida 2002: 316). In view of Florida's observations, our challenge today is to enhance the liberating potentials of information and communication technology, and, what is equally important, to see what obstacles there are to this, as well as to devise structures and practices that will facilitate creative activities throughout society. These challenges are illustrated through a project that metaphorically could be pictured as 'Pappilantie in the shadow of Nokia'. The project departs from the position of people who have been the victims of economic and social change, or of persons that do creative work at the borderline, as opposed to the success stories that constitute the driving economic force that Florida pictures.

Florida is well aware of the detrimental effects this development has had on a large part of the population and he warns for the social divide, of which more later. First, however, the new dominant class needs to be considered. Florida observes: "it struck me that the members of the Creative Class do not see themselves as a class - a coherent group of people with common traits and concerns. Emerging classes in previous times of great transition had pulled together to forge new social mechanisms and steer their societies. But not this group. We thus find ourselves in the puzzling situation of having the dominant class in America - whose members occupy the power centres of industry, media and government, as well as the arts and popular culture - virtually unaware of its own existence and thus unable to consciously influence the course of the society it largely leads." (Florida, 2002: xi) It is time for the Creative class to grow up and take responsibility. But first we must understand who we are, says Florida (2002: xii).

The book itself is primarily a description of this new creative class, with only occasional reference to those who have paid for this development. It is that latter aspect that I primarily draw on here. To shed some light on the challenges facing us today it can be of interest to contrast them to John Stuart Mill's views of the challenges of his time, the 19th century. J. S. Mill attempted a synthesis of central philosophical orientations in his time and offers thereby a subtle analysis of that previous period of profound change, which brought along the rule of law, freedom of trade, democracy and freedom of association. This is how J. S. Mill's biographer, Nicholas Capaldi, summarises Mill's views. "Mill came to believe that genuine social reform originated in self-reformed actors, individuals whose self-consciousness became the prototype for society as a whole. ... All lasting political reform is not accomplished directly, through partisan activity, but indirectly, through the reform of the culture." It is a matter of the moral transformation of individuals who reconstruct the arguments on all sides of the controversy (Capaldi 2004: xii).

Florida observes that today's creative class has the power, talent and numbers to play a big role in reshaping our world. "Its members - in fact all of society - now have the opportunity to turn their introspection and soul-searching into real energy for broader renewal and transformation. ... [T]he task before us is to build new forms of social cohesion appropriate to the new Creative Age - and from there, to pursue a collective vision of a better and more prosperous future for all (Florida 2002: xi, xii). Florida recognizes that the task of building social cohesion in this new context is not an easy one. "To build true social cohesion, the members of the Creative Class will need to offer those in other classes a tangible vision of ways to improve their own lives, either by becoming part of the Creative Economy or, at the very least by reaping some of its rewards. If the Creative Class does not commit itself to this effort, the growing social and economic divides in our society will only worsen, and I fear that we will find ourselves living perpetually uneasy lives at the top of an unhappy heap." (Florida 2002: xii)

In the same vein, J. S. Mill saw that a market economy is not just about making money. He considered that unless as many individuals as possible are part of it, liberal culture will breed its own self-destructive Frankenstein. Mill accepted the idea that his time was dominated by the technological project, and that a free market was the most efficient means for achieving the productive benefits of it. He equally considered that a free market economy and private property could be maintained only if there were limited government, individual rights, the rule of law, and toleration. "The extrinsic value of the technological project is the production of the material conditions that make possible the institutionalisation of individual autonomy, and individual autonomy is the intrinsic goal of that project, the moral quest of modernity. ... Unless autonomy is recognized as the intrinsic goal, a free market economy will undermine the very moral foundations that it requires for its own functioning." (Capaldi 2004: 198) The concept of "autonomy" is the key to understanding Mill, notes his biographer Capaldi.

When autonomy is the ultimate goal and when wealth is seen as a means to autonomy, then the pursuit of wealth properly understood is not an inevitable source of conflict. In order for one autonomous person to preserve his or her autonomy, it is necessary for him or her to interact with other autonomous persons. "What this means is that the pursuit and preservation of autonomy obligates us to promote autonomy in others.... It is the recognition that our ultimate objective must be the pursuit of universal autonomy. This is why Mill became a critic of the psychological and ethical egoism that is inherent in Jeremy Bentham's utilitarian thinking." Mill was of the view that social sciences must be related to more fundamental truths about human beings and, interestingly enough, he notes that it is ultimately the artists who explicate the norms (Capaldi 2004: 199). This is in line with Hans-Georg Gadamer's by me often cited observation: "Art begins precisely there, where we are able to do otherwise." (Gadamer [1986] 1995: 125)

In Mill's time merchants and industrialists felt their autonomy restricted by the old power structures. In this regard, the changes that Florida brings to the fore are different, in the sense that the new creative class occupies positions of power throughout society, in industry, media and government, as well as the arts and popular culture. Florida observes that class is today considered a dirty word, but he insists that creative workers already constitute a de facto class by virtue of their dominant economic role and function. But, he notes, any concept of personal identity requires a well-defined notion of how one relates to others: what one's obligations are to other people, and what one expects of them (2002: 315, 316).

On Florida's point about personal identity and a well-defined notion of how people relate to each other, Mill has this to say about his own time and the effects of utilitarianism captured in Bentham's seductive formula 'the greatest happiness of the greatest number'. Mill considered that by itself, the resolution of the issue of happiness, only solves the problem of how and why individuals come to pursue some ideal. What needs still to be resolved is the problem of how the pursuit of one's individual ideal can be made compatible with the common good or the pursuit of someone else's ideal. The problem of the individual good and the common good can be resolved only if my ultimate ideal is compatible with everyone else's ultimate ideal. This requires both a common set of conditions and the transcending of any kind of paternalism. One individual's autonomy is not only compatible with, but also permits and ultimately requires, everyone else's autonomy. "It is this conception of autonomy ("freedom"), that explains Mill's peculiar conception of and passion for equality, his abhorrence of philanthropy, his defence of liberty, and his sense of public responsibility, both local and international", his biographer notes (Capaldi 2004: 61- 62).

Today's new creative class does not face the formal constraints upward mobile people did in Mill's time. The formal requisites are more or less in place, the rule of law, free markets, democracy etcetera. But here we encounter a cultural obstacle, the mentality of 'the organizational man'. Florida has pertinently pointed out how the rationale of the 'organizational man' today impedes creative efforts. The 'organizational man' has its origin in giant "fordist" organisations - big, vertically integrated command-and-control bureaucracies. Florida points to how this organisational model came to be introduced also in places other than factories and that its spread had powerful social effects, through its finely honed division of tasks, of hierarchy and bureaucracy. "Whether people made things or pushed paper, they filled prescribed slots: "Work, don't think". Even if you had a high-order thinking job, you were paid to think only about certain things in certain ways. The giant office towers with massive administrative, managerial, executive and clerical staffs were the vertical equivalent of the factory." This constituted a change in everyday life that William H. Whyte has captured in his book *The Organization Man*. How the industrial logic has permeated the whole of society is something that John Kenneth Galbraith has shown in his book *The New Industrial State* (Florida 2002: 64).

Also the public sector became permeated by this philosophy. Florida makes a very pertinent point when noting that initially this system contributed to more efficient ways of operation. But there comes a point, when a system reaches its zenith, where after the system becomes counterproductive. This could today be said about the project economy, where the 'organisational man' is one of many problems. This will be considered later. First, let us see how Florida pictures the working of the 'organisational-man' culture. "Despite the initial creative efficiencies of this new system, the eventual creative limits were obvious... Large organizations were beset by the conflict between creativity and control. The bureaucratic values of the period often function to snuff our creativity on the factory floor, smother or ignore it in the R&D (research and development) lab and discourage entrepreneurship by wiping out small competitors and raising high entry barriers. As hosts of occupations were "deskilled", layers of command and control were imposed to keep workers in line and ensure efficiency. ... Scientists and engineers in corporate R&D labs saw their innovations scoffed at by corporate managers. ... The organizational system, as a means of harnessing human creativity, had proven to be inexorably self-limiting. The dominant form of organization was now the integrated, hierarchical, command-and-control behemoth - not a good form for eliciting creativity from the vast ranks of pigeonholed employees." (Florida 2002: 65)

The project economy - trust versus control

One central phenomenon of our day that invokes the control mentality of the organisational man is the whole business of project funding. To work in projects was initially a way of releasing creative energies that otherwise would be trapped in the command and control mentality. However, as an increasing amount of work today is performed in the form of projects, all over the societal spectrum from research, artistic and cultural work to social activities, the control mentality has emerged in new forms. Basing herself on research done by the organisation psychologist Hanna-kaisa Länsisalmi, Anna-Liina Kauhanen asks: Where did the creative class disappear? And her answer is: To the project hell of white-collar slaves. She points to the detrimental effects that the project economy can have on creativity.[111] The project economy involves a number of intricate issues that would require careful study. One such aspect is efficiency. The question of being able to effectively do what one is supposed to do. This is particularly relevant for artists and activities in civil society. There is a risk that the liberty initially involved in project work is frustrated because of the conditions under which funding has to be obtained.

Börje Mattsson, who for more than a decade has been working with projects aimed at activating unemployed persons and immigrants, mostly refugees, points to how projects reveal the amount of ideas that people have, and are eager to act upon. Also, the great number of projects there are, reveal all the ideas and energies that have been hidden under the surface, because there has not been any structures to channel them. Projects offer a very good alternative to public structures. The problem is their limited duration. There is the risk that the day a project ends, the participants will again walk around with empty hands. Mattsson insists that the

---

[111] Helsingin Sanomat, Talous 4.9.2005.

substance matter of a project needs to be a process that does not come to an end, and that we need new structures to cater for that.[112]

Here we could have something to learn from one of the pioneers of today's technological project, John Seely Brown, former director of Xerox PARC. He has pictured the creative economy as "the ability to leverage the community mind" by providing the physical and social context required for creativity (Florida 2002: 138). Control hardly contributes to this. Instead we should take advice from J. S. Mill on how to enhance a creative culture. Mills ideal of a good society is, as noted earlier, based on personal autonomy. This presupposes that people are as free and independent and self-sufficient as possible. It is only when they cannot help themselves that government intervention is needed and justified. Capaldi aptly notes that what Mill contributed through this notion, was a framework for asking the relevant public policy questions (Capaldi 2004: 148). A central policy issue in today's context is to unravel the obstacles between 'supply and demand'; a general concern for lacking civil involvement in society versus people's struggle in civil society, to be able to do the work that they have a zeal for doing. To pin these issues down, the concerns voiced in the Finnish governmental program on civil participation will be contrasted to opinions voiced by third sector organisations in a survey of the third sector in some EU member states.[113]

Citizen Participation Policy Programme

Citizen Participation Policy Programme is one of four policy programmes adopted by Prime Minister Matti Vanhanen's government in 2003. Its purpose is to strengthen Finnish democracy from its basis through the cooperation of several Ministries. The programme aims to reinforce the

---

[112] See Storlund 2002, VI.13.1.3 *Projects an opportunity and a curse.*

[113] Matti Kari ja Jari Markwort, Kolmas sektori EU:ssa ja eräissä euroopan maissa 2004.

functioning of representative democracy and encourage civil participation. The objective is to improve electoral participation and provide opportunities for active civil participation between elections. The programme placed particular emphasis on those groups whose participation and influence have remained low in the past. So how should the objectives of the policy program be translated into concrete practice? A study made by Matti Kari and Jari Markwort of third sector organisations in the EU and some European countries, offers a frame for the question.

The study reveals that third sector organizations at a general level face a common set of problems. To obtain funding for their activities is a major problem. Donations have decreased and when public funding is obtained the autonomy and freedom of action can be jeopardized. When organizations resort to business activities as a means of funding their primary activities, their status as a third sector organisation may be at risk because the delimitation of business activities is fluid (Kari & Markwort 2004: 12–13).

Here third sector organisations find themselves in a legal grey area in several respects. Part of it has to do with the recent trend of third sector organisations' involvement as service providers in the social and health sectors, as public authorities have difficulties in producing the necessary services. In this situation, organisations face an increasing number of players who produce these same services on a commercial basis. The tax relief that third sector organisation enjoy, is considered to give them an advantage that distorts competition. However, if third sector organisations are forced into free competition, they loose their character as third sector organisations (Kari & Markwort 2004: 12–13).

This is one example of a general need to make a distinction between different kinds of activities in society, to identify what values they represent, as well as to accord structures and means that are appropriate for them. Social and cultural values need to be able to compete on equal terms with economic values. To achieve this requires the change of culture that both J.S. Mill and Richard Florida point to above. There is a constant process of change going on, of which we need to be aware. Kari's and Markwort's study offers an interesting account of the attitudes toward the activities of third sector organisations since the 1970s. And here it is of interest to recall Aaro Harju's observation in the opening paragraph of this problem inventory of factors that impede an active citizenship; that civil activities cannot be questioned without questioning the right of everybody to strive for the good life for themselves as well as for their kinships and the society in which they live (Harju 2003: 41).

With this in mind, let us look at attitudes toward third sector organisations during the period 1970–2005. In the period 1970–1985 there was a proliferation of organisations and their activities. This was a period characterised by conflict. Formerly, voluntary organisations had been praised for their sacrificing work, but now the new organisations were seen as a threat as well as disturbance to democratic institutions. Public authorities opposed them (Kari & Markwort 2004: 12–13).

The following period the authors distinguish is 1980–1995, a period characterised by negotiation. By the early 1980s there had been such an expansion among third sector organisations that governments could no longer ignore them. This initiated a period of negotiation, during with different advisory and joint bodies were established for the purpose of establishing formal links between third sector organisations and the public sector. These mechanisms for negotiation still persist and they are an important means in practical cooperation. Some third sector organisations do, however, criticise these bodies, saying that they are not true channels for exercising influence, but rather means through which public authorities feed ready-made policy guidelines (Kari & Markwort 2004: 12–13).

The last period, 1990–2005, represents new public management, whereby third sector organisations are made cooperating partners as service providers through joint ventures, compacts and service agreements.

The issue here is governance, where public power steers. This has generally been seen as a neoliberal practice or one of economic rationalism, but the authors observe that this form has emerged due to pressures from several directions. Whereas conservatives promote privatisation, more progressive quarters favour better conditions for organisations to provide services, so that the services would be more responsive to people's needs (Kari & Markwort 2004: 12–13).

This new form of cooperation between third sector organisations and public authorities has generated two kinds of interpretation. On the one hand, it is seen that the third sector now also has more political power, as the production of services is no longer the privilege of the public sector. Also third sector organisations are now able to participate in developing public policy. On the other hand, it is argued that third sector organisations are simply made to implement decisions taken by the public. Through contracts, third sector organisations have come too close to public power and can thereby not bite the hand that is feeding them. There is also talk about actors in the third sector suffering from 'participatory fatigue'. After all contractual obligations have been fulfilled, there is not much energy left for their proper non- profit activities. Kari & Markwort observe that during these different periods, traits of the previous ones are still present (Kari & Markwort 2004: 12–13).

The above account offers a good illustration of the notion of autonomy, where we recall that Mill insisted that personal autonomy requires both a common set of conditions and the transcending of any kind of paternalism; that one individual's autonomy is not only compatible with, but also both permits and ultimately requires, everyone else's autonomy (Capaldi 2004: 61–62). It is in the social sector that autonomy is mostly lacking.[114] This is a field where a rethinking is badly needed along the lines Florida indicates. And here Mill's observations about the French revolution of

---

[114] See Storlund, 2002, chapter VI, Social security - support or guillotine.

1848 may serve as guidance for the mindset required in contemplating approaches to the third sector that would be more in tune with the aspirations of the Finnish governmental program on citizen's participation. Although critical to socialism, Mill considered that its advocates should get a fair hearing. He observed that they had "generally very wild and silly notions and little one can sympathize with except the spirit and feelings which actuate them." However, Mill's point was that if they were not able to express their views the underlying economic issues would not be addressed or resolved, and the end result would be universal disaster (Capaldi 2004: 221).

We equally need to give different quarters a fair hearing as we are faced with a changed economic and social context of the same magnitude as the one John Stuart Mill addressed. Increasing involvement in the third sector since the 1970s reveals what the Finnish governmental program advocates, active citizens who strive to improve societal conditions. Should we not call this a sign of maturing democracy? But here, at first, the activists were faced by an administrative culture that was not ready for its active citizens. This illustrates J. S. Mill's point that all lasting political reform is not accomplished directly, through partisan activity, but indirectly, through a reform of the culture. It is a matter of a moral transformation of individuals who reconstruct the arguments on all sides of the controversy (Capaldi 2004: xii).

The two ensuing periods of negotiation and cooperation can be seen as a process whereby a new culture is emerging, but still with many open questions. One pivotal issue is the concern expressed about too close a relationship between public authorities and third sector organisations, so that organisations thereby cannot bite the hand that is feeding them. Equally important is the observation that they risk losing their identity as non-profit organisations and will thereby be unable to pursue their original tasks. Both issues raise the question of restrictions on their autonomy.

How should this be remedied? Here the question of trust enters the picture. Trust is a central notion in considerations about civil society and social capital. The issue at stake here is whether authorities have trust in actors in civil society, and their ability to pursue their tasks in a responsible manner. If trust is lacking, and third sector people are not able to react, to bite, in other words, this implies a restriction on their autonomy. This restriction can in part be due to a control mentality that is not in tune with aspirations for an active citizenship. In part it can also be due to legislative and administrative constraints.

The new tasks assumed by third sector organizations, coupled by privatisation and out-sourcing, has resulted in new constellations that, yet again, brings us into legal grey areas. Esko Romppainen has addressed the changing role of organisations from a legal perspective, asking whether they are able to work for the public good, or whether they have become accountable servants of the state and municipalities. Addressing a conference organised within the frame of the Finnish governmental program on civil participation, he points to a need to identify the tensions that have occurred due to their new roles, and means of solving them (2005). To preserve the autonomy of organisations, allowing them to retain their original function in the new division of work that has occurred during the past decades, new distinctions need to be made that reflect the substantive context, rather than formal legislative rules. What is needed today is to focus on the substantive aspects that are required for an active citizenship, in other words, the degree of autonomy persons have in third sector activities. One could say that the danger facing activities in civil society is on the one hand a control mentality that is often seen in public administration, but also among funding agencies. On the other hand, organisations' need to become economic players, have put them in a weird position that is often not in line with the philosophy of their activities, and as noted in the account of changes in the third sector, consumes the energy that they should use for their original purpose. Here distinctions need to be made that recognize the social nature of third sector activities.

How to go about it?

Florida considers that the creative class has three fundamental issues to address. They are: Investing in creativity to ensure long-run economic growth, overcoming the class- divide that weakens our social fabric and threatens economic well-being, as well as building new forms of social cohesion in a world defined by increasing diversity and beset by growing fragmentation. We can meet them only by ensuring that the creativity of the many is tapped and that the benefits of the creative age are extended to everyone, says Florida (2002: 318).

Florida further makes a disturbing observation about this sea change that has occurred in our societies. He notes that people have come to accept that they are on their own, that the traditional sources of security and entitlement no longer exist, or does not even matter (2002:115). What can be an exciting challenge for a young and upward mobile highly educated person, takes on altogether different connotations for somebody who has been laid off from industrial work, or an over-indebted person who became a victim of the 'casino economy', who now simply struggles to survive from day to day. It is people in life-situations like this that many third sector organisations cater for. Hyvä Arki is one of them (The good daily life). Or take artists who are not part of the success stories that Florida describes. They are many, and we also find them in the association of visual artists, Suna. Hyvä Arki and Suna are two small associations that, metaphorically speaking, exist in the shadow of Nokia, this high-tech hub populated by the creative class located in the same city, Espoo. The organisations partake in the Pappilantie Project, a project that in an interesting way illustrates the issues Florida raises.

The association Hyvä Arki, caters for people who find themselves in a difficult stance in life, more often than not because of long-term unemployment. This is a consequence of the structural changes in the economy from one dominated by industrial production to a society dominated by information and communication technologies, that they feel they are not part of. In the artists' association Suna members struggle, as artists mostly do, to be able to do their artistic work. What unites the people involved in these associations is that their autonomy is limited, although in different ways. One aim of the project is to differentiate the notion of personal autonomy and point to means of enhancing the conditions of these different groups to allow them to participate more fully in social life. The degree of autonomy, or control of one's life that a person enjoys is conditioned by a variety of factors, ranging from legal provisions to people's conduct and attitudes.

Putman, who has made extensive investigations into the riddle of decreasing civic engagement, also points to the effects of economic insecurity in his book *Bowling alone* (2000: 192–193)."It is also true that financial worries and economic troubles have a profoundly depressing effect on social involvement, both formal and informal ... The Great Depression triggered the only significant interruption in the rising tide of civic participation and social connectedness during the first two-thirds of the 20th century. Contrary to expectation that unemployment would radicalise its victims, social psychologists found that the jobless became passive and withdrawn, socially as well as politically. As my economic situation becomes more dire, my focus narrows to personal and family survival. People with lower incomes and those who feel financially strapped are much less engaged in all forms of social and community life than those who are better off." (Putman 2000: 192–193)

It is organisations like Hyvä Arki that are able to give distressed people some form of social context, although it does not always take the form of voluntary action but offers also a social context for them as visitors. If tapping human creativity is the key to economic success, then having large numbers of working and service class people who don't do much creative work is tantamount to wasting a resource, says Florida. Members of the creative class thus have an economic interest as well as a moral imperative to reduce class divides, not just through charity or government transfer payments, but by tapping the creativity of the many, ensuring thereby that all are integrated into the creative economy. Florida notes that the motive of human dignity is here aligned with economic motives (2002: 321).

The present attempt to analyse what obstacles there are between a publicly recognised wish for an active citizenship and third sector agents' struggle to be able to carry out their work, can in short be pinned down to obstacles relating to culture on the one hand, and legal and institutional arrangements on the other. With the widened social responsibilities assumed by third sector organisations, coupled with the spread of the project economy, persons involved increasingly find themselves in legal grey areas, squeezed between public authorities and the pro-profit sector. It is as if agents in the third sector would not enjoy legal personhood on equal terms with people in the public and pro-profit sectors. This has to do with culture, with perception and thereby with the question of how we fabricate meaning. Zygmunt Bauman has pertinently pointed out that all societies are factories that fabricate meaning (Bauman, Det individualiserade samhället, 2002: 10). The cultural connotations associated with the notion of the good life may illustrate this.

The good life as an intellectual challenge – a cultural matter

After this tour d'horizon of conditions for an active citizenship we will return to Harju's observation that civic activities cannot be questioned without questioning the right of everybody to strive for the good life for themselves as well as for their kinships and the society in which they live (2003: 41). As noted above, this is so self-evident, and yet such a complex question, as I have attempted to indicate above. A change of culture is the starting point, as Mill pointed out. Attitudes toward the notion of the good life may here illustrate this point, as opposed to the Protestant ethics that permeates our culture in ways that makes it difficult to endorse the good life. Already Aristotle drew attention to the difference in focus between business life and people's aspirations for a good life. To Aristotle the role of the state is to secure the good life. "[T]he aim and the end is perfection; and self-sufficiency is both end and perfection." (Aristotle, 1987: 1252b27, 59)

The good life, which Aristotle has designated as the ultimate purpose of government, requires a certain minimum supply of necessities. Property is one prerequisite, which he considers necessary in order to satisfy basic needs. Property is thus a means for the end of satisfying basic needs, and thereby there is also a natural limit to the acquisition of property. By Max Weber's time this acquisition of property that Aristotle criticized had gained the status of a virtue, as he pictures as the Protestant ethics. Weber will for this reason be given the floor for the following lengthy exposé on the economic culture:

"Man is dominated by the making of money, by acquisition as the ultimate purpose of his life. Economic acquisition is no longer subordinated to man as the means for the satisfaction of his material needs. This reversal of what we should call the natural relationship, so irrational from a naïve point of view, is evidently as definitely a leading principle of capitalism as it is foreign to all peoples not under capitalistic influence. At the same time it expresses a type of feeling which is closely connected with certain religious ideas. If we thus ask *why* should 'money be made out of men', Benjamin Franklin himself, although he was a colourless deist, answers in his autobiography with a quotation from the Bible, which his strict Calvinistic father drummed into him again and again in his youth: 'Seest thou a man diligent in business? He shall stand before kings' (Proverbs 22:29). The earnings of money within the modern economic order is, so long as it is done legally, the result and the expression of virtue and proficiency in a calling; and this virtue and proficiency are, as it is now not difficult to see, the real alpha and omega of Franklin's ethic...

In truth this peculiar idea, so familiar to us today, is in reality so little a matter of course, of one's duty in a calling, is what is most characteristic of the social ethic of capitalistic culture, and is in a sense the fundamental basis of it. It is an obligation which the individual is supposed to feel and does feel towards the content of his professional activity, no matter in what it consists, in particular no matter whether it appears on the surface as a utilization of his personal powers, or only of his material possessions (as capital)." Andreski, ed. *Protestantism and the Spirit of Capitalism*, 1983: 114–115) .

An interesting testimony of this Protestant ethics, is given by James Truslow Adams in his book *Our Business Civilization*, of 1929. He closes his analysis of how American society fabricates meaning with a chapter on 'The Art of Living'. "As one moves about the world in order to test life in its great foci, in New York or Washington, London or Paris, Prague or Vienna, one cannot but be struck by the differing degrees in which various people have attained to the practice of this most difficult of all the arts ('the art of living'). In America, indeed, there seems to be hardly any appreciation at all on the part of most people that such an art exists." Adams observes that it is not without significance that Europeans talk about 'the art of life', whereas if such a discussion is pursued in America, it is usually done under the caption "the business of life" (1929: 289).

Comparing the art of living with the work of artists, Adams concludes: "everything, tangible and intangible, is a "tool" with which the artist in life may produce thought or emotion, and so modify the life itself conceived as a product of art. It is evident that whoever would practice an art of living is likely to be overwhelmed by the wealth of his material and by the unlimited choice of tools with which to mould it into specific forms." (1929: 291) Adams refers to the freeing effects of the renaissance that allowed all the arts to flower, and he notes that they, in the late 1920s, are freer from the tyranny of old ideas than at any other period in history, to order their lives according to art. If there is such an art, Adams notes, "evidently the first thing of all is to decide what we want to make, what sort of life is worth while, what sort of thoughts and emotions." (Adams 1929: 292)

We here have some illustrations of Bauman's point about society as a fabricator of meaning (Bauman 2002: 10). Bauman notes in his book *The Individualized Society*, that each societal order can be seen as a network of channels through which people search for a meaning of life and through which the formula is transmitted. It is transcendental energy that keeps this enormous activity going that we call 'the social order'; it makes it a necessity and functional at the same time (2002: 13). Bauman further notes that the core of a social order is made up of the task of redistributing the culturally created resources and the transcendental strategies. It is, furthermore, the task of a social order to regulate access to these goods, to transform these assets into the most important 'factors of stratification' and the central measure of socially determined inequalities. The social hierarchy with all its privileges and deprivations are constructed on formulas of life available to different groups of people according them different values (Bauman 2002: 13).

It is not a mere coincidence that social capital and its value have received increasing attention during the past decades. There is a clear connotation to the changes (western) societies have gone through during the past decades, with new technology and globalisation as major driving forces. This, again, is in the most tangible way seen in working life, and thereby in people's material conditions. Bauman has caught the implications of these changes in a nutshell under the heading Local Order, Global Chaos. He there considers the implications of globalisation on our abilities to go about our plans of life, in terms of the degree of predictability we have in going about our daily 'business of life'. Things are in order if one does not need to think about the order of things, or think of it as a problem, less so as a task. As soon as we start thinking of order, it is a sure sign that something, somewhere is in disorder: something is about to slip out of our hands and much effort is required to recreate order. What this boils down to is a clear and un-ambivalent degree of probability. When there is no probability that certain things will happen, when there is only a 50 per cent chance that a certain thing will happen then one can talk about chaos, says Bauman (2002: 43).

The project economy is one such factor. To be able to predict and thereby control what one does is what appeals to us most in the case of order. In opposition to this, the apparent lack of connectedness between what one does and what happens, between 'doing' and 'what happens' makes chaos repulsive and frightening (Bauman 2002: 43–44). And this is what has occurred in the transformative processes societies are in right now. The conditions under which people shape their individual existence, that determines their choices and their consequences are beyond their own control. This raises the question of the borderline between people's actions and the conditions under which they act (Bauman 2002: 15). This is highly relevant for people's abilities to act as active citizens.

Control of one's life = personal autonomy.

Bauman points to how the new world order called globalization has turned the old order on its head, entailing a downgrading of order. In this new world, order is a sign of lack of power as well as subordination. This new global power structure is driven by the opposing powers of mobility versus stability, accidental occurrence versus routine, as well as freedom from restrictions versus attachment to them (Bauman 2002: 47). We thus need to focus on society as a fabricator of meaning and revise a number of notions that are out of tune with today's reality. One characteristic of civil activities is that they often aim at remedying the deficiencies in the functioning of both the public and pro-profit sector, and increasingly so today. Civil society has thereby assumed a number of functions that both the public and private sectors have catered for before. Along with this, a host of legal ambiguities are revealed because of the legal grey areas in which actors in civil society go about their tasks. Attention should therefore be placed on how different laws and practices affect the autonomy of identifiable persons.

By taking the degree of autonomy a person enjoys as a point of departure, human beings become the organising factor on equal terms, irrespective of societal sector or legal discipline. It will then be easier to locate the different tensions and knots, cultural as well as legal and institutional, that require remedies in order to unleash human energies. Because, as Harju pertinently points out, social capital is not accrued by itself, however much attention researchers give this notion. The accumulation of social capital requires concrete action that enhances trust among people and strengthens human interaction. Large and encompassing social networks are means to this end (Harju 2003: 69).

CHAPTER 10

CONDITIONS FOR DEMOCRACY - ECONOMIC, SOCIAL AND CULTURAL RIGHTS IN FOCUS

2007[115]

Our constitution ... favours the many instead of the few; this is why it is called a democracy. Thucydides II, 37.

Democracy can only be achieved when people have confidence in each other and when they are confident that they can conclude binding agreements, like businessmen do, without one profiting from the other more than what is to their joint advantage and in their joint interest.

In these words Fredrik Lång has pinpointed central prerequisites for democracy in his book about Pythagoras, *Mitt liv som Pythagoras* (2005: 60). How well does democracy materialise today, in the sense pictured by Lång? In this paper I will scrutinise this question from a human perspective, with particular emphasis on the effects of changes that have occurred during recent decades and their reflections in working life and social security. How have these changes affected people's ability to go about their life in the way described above? I will further look at civil society from the point of view of work carried out there and suggest means through which deficiencies in people's conditions in part could be remedied through a universal basic income. A human perspective on these questions implies a bottom up approach that differs from mainstream, where laws and institutions constitute a point of departure. In a mainstream approach the

[115] Unpublished

effects of legislation are not easily perceived. In a human perspective unfair effects on people are revealed. Unfair states of affairs thereby become the point of departure. Human rights standards, particularly economic, social and cultural rights will provide a point of reference for an assessment of the material conditions for democracy that Lång refers to.

Social change and people's conditions of life

The changes societies have gone through during past decades, mainly marked by information and communications technology (ICT) as well as globalisation, have had far-reaching consequences for people's conditions of life. This is particularly visible in working life, as work constitutes the principle basis for people's material existence. These changes have thereby in decisive ways influenced people's ability to go about their life in an autonomous way. Uncertainty has become a distinct characteristic. Those who have a job often live in constant fear of losing it. Because of the ways in which unemployment compensation and other social security provisions associated with working life are designed, these support systems may generate as much uncertainty as certainty, which should be their basic function.

Furthermore, an increasing number of people are dependent on external funding for their work, lacking thereby certainty about their possibilities to do their work. It is commonplace to talk about the risk society. The changes alluded to above have generated various legal grey areas and constitutional inconsistencies, whereby risk has, one could say, become people's daily companion. But it does not need to be so. Existing structures could well, with presently available resources, be redesigned in more rational ways that would offer more security and predictability and thereby increase people's autonomy. Solutions could be found that would benefit everybody. What is basically required in order to come to grips with these problems is a change of perception, as well as political will. There are clear human rights standards to rely on for this.

Locating the problems

Art and entertainment has during past decades become one of the fastest growing sectors of the economy. In 2003 culture and the creative sector contributed 2.6 per cent to the GDP in the EU. Between 1999 and 2003 the growth of this sector was 12.3 per cent higher than the growth of the general economy.[116] This is one central illustration of the shift from an industry-dominated economy to one dominated by information and communications technology. The changes are profound, which is also illustrated by the fact that Shifting of Power Equation was chosen as the theme of the World Economic Forum at Davos in January 2007.

A task ahead is thus to update perception and institutional arrangements to this new rationale. With this development there has been a considerable reallocation of rights and obligations among different players in society, in the economy, working life, the public sector and civil society. These changes have partly come about through legislative reform, such as flexibilisation in working life, privatisation and the liberalisation of trade. The negative effects of this development can to a large extent be seen in civil society. Changes have largely been inspired by the neoliberal trend that gained ground in the 1970s. One major problem caused by this trend is that almost any social phenomenon is approached as a commodity, whereby its value is primarily measured in economic terms. This is harmful for many kinds of activities, particularly so for activities in civil society and also for art, culture and research. For all of them the motivations and

---

[116] The Economy of Culture in Europe, Study prepared for the European Commission (Directorate-General for Education and Culture), October 2006: 61.

aspirations are not economic in origin, but social, cultural or intellectual. Civil society, art and culture, along with research, represent cradles of innovation that often generate means of operation or products that are subsequently taken on board by the public sector or business life.

A crucial question is what the conditions are, under which work of a social nature, art, culture and research are pursued. With the present trend of pressing whatever activity into a product-format or measuring it in economic terms, there is a danger that creativity is suppressed in its cradle. One central problem is that the changes that have occurred have not been accompanied by any comprehensive reconsideration of the distribution of rights and obligations among the different players concerned. This being the case, there are growing legal grey areas that need to be addressed. This has to start with an updating of the conceptual tools through which we address different phenomena. At a conceptual level the nature of different activities must be a point of departure when assessing the distribution of rights and obligations. Characteristic of activities in civil society, as well as art and culture, is that they to their origin often are located in the social economy. This area, in the intersection between public and private, lack proper recognition in legal terms, and the social economy is also at a conceptual level a fairly under-researched area.

International legal standards

International legal standards that actualise in the social economy are found in human rights instruments, particularly provisions concerning economic, social and cultural rights. A deepening of the cultural aspects is to be found in the UNESCO Convention on the Protection and Promotion of the Diversity of Cultural Expressions. Furthermore, international labour standards apply. The purpose of the International Labour Organisation, ILO, and its standards is to promote social justice and secure decent conditions of work. These standards are threatened by internationally regulated economic standards, such as the standards of the World Trade Organisation, WTO and the European Union, EU, as well as policy guidelines of the Organisation for Economic Co-operation and Development, OECD. We are here faced with two different sets of activities with associated norms that represent different logics; those belonging to the sphere of economic, social and cultural rights on the one hand, and on the other classical rights and liberties, which serve as theoretical foundation for economic activities.

Legal deficiencies

New public management, NPM, is one means through which an economic rationale has come to invade spheres of life throughout society, in ways that infringe on fundamental rights. This is particularly visible in the case of economic, social and cultural rights, because this category of rights has not, at a conceptual level, been properly incorporated in theoretical schemes on equal terms with classical right and liberties (Storlund 2002). The way NPM has infringed on the values the public sector stands for has by Leena Eräsaari been analysed in the case of Finland in an article about new public management as the father of evils in the public sector.[117] Also in civil society the effects of NPM are felt, threatening the autonomy of organisations. A fundamental problem pertaining to this new context is that legal regulation has not been up-dated to reflect the differentiation of working life that has occurred during past decades. The criteria on which the administration of working life and associated social security are based can bluntly be reduced to the status of a person as employed, unemployed or suffering from working inability. From there, there is an equally blunt leap to entrepreneurship. The growing sector of what we call atypical

---

[117] Eräsaari, Leena, in Helne, Tuula &Lahti, Markku (eds) Vääryyskirja 2006)

work, much of which is situated in the intersection between an employment relationship and entrepreneurship, is largely uncovered by legal regulation, and social provisions related to that work. At a practical level, these legal deficiencies have adverse effects both for those who are unemployed and for the growing number of persons who work in the intersection between a conventional employment and entrepreneurship. These same problems are repeated in civil society, which is an important but often neglected arena of work. The issues raised in this paper are large and complex. The purpose of this paper is to link different aspects of work and social security that ordinarily as discussed in separate contexts.

Legal standards involved

Because of lacking legal adaptation to changes in working life, those who have been adversely affected may be deprived of the basic prerequisites of a legal order – predictability and legal certainty. Such effects are manifested in multiple ways but at a conceptual level they can be expressed as having disproportionately interfered with a person's autonomy.[118] An autonomy test reveals in what ways different legal provisions or institutional arrangements and practices affect a person's situation. This ranges from feelings of being denied one's human dignity, through the material conditions required for a dignified life, to the material conditions required to be able to pursue a profession of one's own choice. Here focus is placed on human rights standards and constitutional provisions, against which the deficient legislation now in place should be assessed and thereafter rectified.[119]

---

[118] The notion personal autonomy is developed as a conceptual tool for assessing economic, social and cultural rights in Storlund 2002.

[119] For an analysis and illustrations of these questions see Storlund, Vivan, *Kansalaisvaikuttaminen totta vai tarua. Ruohonjuuritason arviointi Espoon Pappilantiellä*, Appendix, 2007

The Finnish constitution may offer an illustration of the kind of requirements we are dealing with. The constitution opens with the following provision: "The constitution shall guarantee the inviolability of human dignity and the freedom and rights of the individual and promote justice in society."[120] This provision should guide any assessments of the effects of legislation as well as institutional arrangements and practices. To disentangle the legal and bureaucratic improprieties that have resulted from the simplistic premises in labour and social security legislation, I will start with social security schemes, as these are root causes for many injustices. The way social security schemes are designed and administered, they restrict recipients' possibilities to go about their lives, and are therefore perceived as both humiliating and unfair. They also have the effect of suffocating much creative energy. This is both sad and ironic, as new ideas are called for that later may lead to new work or entrepreneurship.

Social security standards

Most western social welfare schemes have been developed after world war II. A major impetus for them is to be found in the Philadelphia Declaration of 1944, which assigned the International Labour Organisation "the solemn obligation ... to further among the nations of the world programmes which will achieve ... the extension of social security measures to provide a basic income to all in need of such protection and comprehensive medical care."[121] After the Philadelphia Declaration, social secu-

[120] 11 June 1999 (731/1999), Section 1, after the statement that Finland is a sovereign republic.

[121] E/C. 12/GC/20/CRP. 1, Committee on Economic, Social and Cultural Rights, Thirty-sixth session, Geneva, 1– 19 May 2006. Item 5 of the provisional agenda General Comment No. 20 *The Right to Social Security* (article 9) Rapporteurs: Maria Virginia Bras Gomes & Eibe Riedel, p. 2.

rity was subsequently recognised as a human right in the Universal Declaration of Human Rights of 1948. Article 25(1) states that "Everyone has the ... right to security in the event of unemployment, sickness, disability, widowhood, old age or other lack of livelihood in circumstances beyond his control." These provisions were further elaborated on in the International Covenant on Economic, Social and Cultural Rights of 1966.[122]

In 2001, the International Labour Conference affirmed that social security "is a basic human right and a fundamental means for creating social cohesion, thereby helping to ensure social peace and social inclusion".[123] In a document for the 36th session of the United Nations Committee on Economic, Social and Cultural Rights in 2006, essential elements of the right to social security are spelled out. In these general comments on social security the general rapporteurs Maria Virginia Bras Gomes & Eibe Riedel note that "it should be borne in mind that social security should be treated as a social good, and not primarily a commodity or a mere instrument of economic policy" 2006: paragraph 10, 4) These are important aspects to consider when assessing the extent to which present social security schemes and practices are in conformity with the provisions of the covenant. The task of the Committee on Economic, Social and Cultural Rights is to review existing legislation, strategies and policies to ensure that they are compatible with obligations arising from the right to social security. If these standards are not met, legislation should be repealed, amended or changed if inconsistent with covenant requirements (Bras Gomes & Riedel 2006: 13).

---

[122] International Covenant on Economic, Social and Cultural Rights, adopted and opened for signature, ratification and accession by General Assembly resolution 2200A (XXI) of 16 December 1966, entry into force 3 January 1976, in accordance with article 27.

[123] Resolutions and Conclusions concerning social security, International Labour Conference, 89th Session, 2001. Maria Virginia Bras Gomes & Eibe Riedel, p. 3.

Adequacy and accessibility of social security

The adequacy of social security and accessibility to it are two aspects of social security that are central for this paper. This is how they are treated in the General Comment (No. 20), by the rapporteurs, Maria Virginia Bras Gomes and Eibe Riedel (2006:4):

Adequacy. "Benefits, whether in cash or in kind, must be adequate in amount and duration in order that everyone can realize their rights to family protection, an adequate standard of living and access to health care as contained in Articles 10, 11 and 12 of the Covenant. In addition, State Parties should be guided by the principle of human dignity, contained in the preamble, and the right to non-discrimination, which may influence the levels of benefits and the form in which they are provided. A variety of methods can be used to determine the adequacy of benefits. Considering the changes societies go through, the report aptly stresses the need to review regularly the criteria used to ensure that beneficiaries are able to afford the goods and services they require to realize their Covenant rights.

Accessibility – Coverage. "All persons should be covered by the social security system, including the most disadvantaged or marginalized sections of the population, in law and in fact, without discrimination on any of the prohibited grounds." As will be seen below, social security schemes may, because of the way they are designed, lead to a number of deadlocks and absurd situations. In practice they also lead to discrimination that may, however, be difficult to pin down because of inadequate legal regulation and the deficiencies that thereby follow in social security schemes. It is, for this reason, important that the General Comment paper emphasises aspects of adequacy and accessibility.

Another important point mentioned in the comments is that an assessment should be made both in law and in fact. In this way problems that arise because of lacking or deficient legal protection can be brought to the fore. States parties have an obligation to "take steps to remove de facto discrimination on prohibited grounds, where individuals and groups are excluded from access to adequate social security." States should ensure that legislation, policies, programmes and allocation of resources facilitate access to social security for all members of society (Bras Gomes & Riedel 2006: 5). When legislation does not properly reflect factual conditions, this has the effect that many persons do not qualify for different entitlements. On this score it is noted in the General Comment: "States Parties should give special attention to those individuals and groups who have traditionally faced difficulties in exercising this right". Among them 'marginalised workers' are singled out.[124]

Thereby what we call atypical workers is given its proper name, marginalised workers. One reason why people are marginalised is that labour and social security legislation does not properly recognise the work they are doing. Legislative shortcomings have led to a situation whereby the distribution of rights and obligations of different parties, in the sense Lång referred to in the beginning of this paper, are badly distorted. The present distribution of rights and obligations often lead to so unfair outcomes that they need to be calibrated to better fit today's conditions. For this reason, we need new approaches to work and its legal regulation that will enhance people's opportunities to work with appropriate legal protection. A first thing to do is to consider the work that is factually done. Second, we need to accord work other values than merely economic ones. In this attempt to bring forth alternative perspectives on work, I will draw on work done in civil society and discussions about a basic income. These considerations of work in civil society and a basic income are additional to and will thereby complement the traditional perception of work as one car-

[124] Bras Gomes & Riedel, 2006: 5, in particular women, the unemployed, marginalised workers, injured workers, people with disabilities, older persons, children and dependents, minority groups, refugees, asylum seekers, internally displaced persons, non-nationals, prisoners and detainees.

ried out in an employment relationship. To set the scene, I start by pointing to how the conventional view of work runs short, as well as the injustices it creates, before moving to alternative grounds.

Misconceived premises

Industrial work has originally provided the model for the legal regulation of working life. This made the male blue colour worker the ideal-type, the standard being fulltime employment, and even permanent. These premises are shaking in their foundations today. The reasons for the present changes are multiple. I will here single out three parallel phenomena that in different ways have deeply affected working life. Aspirations to increase flexibility in working life become a distinct feature in the labour market in the late 1970s and early 1980s. After that we have continued to talk about work formats that deviate from the 'standard' as 'atypical', although its share has increased from a few per cent in the 1970s to such considerable levels that 'atypical' is, since way back, an anachronism. The introduction of information and communications technology, again, has radically changed productive processes. This has made people assume altogether new and active roles in work processes that are at odds with the still prevailing organisation of work and managerial strategies. The human has largely become an organising factor, which is as well largely neglected.[125]

For its part, globalisation has mainly conditioned markets, where free competition has assumed the status of a mantra. Massive layoffs are the hallmarks of globalisation and free competition, legitimated by economic and productive reasons. In addition to the loss of jobs and the constant

[125] Florida, 2002, Castells, 1999: 35 . For an analysis of the implications for working life see Fahlbeck, Reinhold, *Towards a Revolutionised Working Life* 2000 and *Ett revolutionerat arbetsliv? Informationssamhället och arbetslivets omvandling* 1998.

insecurity that an over-emphasis on free competition has brought along, it has also intruded in spheres where it does not belong. Competition has been allowed to invade different spheres of life where human values should be a point of departure, not economic ones.

Economic activity versus working life

A continued series of extensive layoffs have led to a public debate about the social responsibilities of business life. According to views expressed by business leaders their social responsibility is to be as competitive as possible. In this way they can best serve their country, they say. For ordinary people the most tangible expression of this social responsibility in business life, appears to be a blanco license to dismiss people in their efforts to improve their competitiveness. This right has its theoretical foundation in property rights.[126] The rights dismissed persons have, as a correlation to employers' right to dismiss, is a right to unemployment compensation. This compensation will vary according to a person's employment history, either as income-related or a low flat-rate compensation. Whether a person is entitled to a higher (income-related) or a lower compensation is something that the person concerned often has not been able to influence. This will depend on what opportunity a person has had to work and thereby qualify for income-related compensation. This, again, is conditioned by employers' efforts to reduce their costs by employing persons in so-called atypical work formats.

A secure economic position for employees has thereby been lost in the process geared toward enhancing employers' competitiveness, leaving employees with no factual say. Yes, there are negotiations preceding

[126] For an analysis of this question, see Storlund, *Reflexive Potentials in Industrial Relations and the Law – Collective dismissal: An Illustration*, in Ralf Rogowski, Ton Wilthagen (eds.) Reflexive Labour Law, 1994: 287-289.

layoffs but their practical outcome is often that the employer simply "blows the horn before he runs over' his employees". In this process we have seen a growing number of marginalised workers emerge. One could say that they have become victims in a double sense. First they have been deprived the security involved in conventional employment. As proper corrective measures have not been introduced in social security, they are in addition deprived of entitlements that persons in a more secure position are entitled to. This is a problem that the rapporteurs for the Committee on Economic, Social and Cultural Rights also draw attention to: "States parties should take steps to ensure that the social security systems cover marginalised workers, including part-time workers, casual workers and the self-employed, and those working in the 'informal sector'. Where States are constrained by lack of available resources, schemes should be established to provide a minimum level of coverage for those without access to social security, although the aim must be to incorporate the excluded into formal social security systems." (Bras Gomes & Riedel (2006: 6)

Deadlocked work ethics

Whatever the form of unemployment compensation, to all of them is attached an obligation that is at odds with the freedom the employer has had to dismiss for economic and productive reasons; the requirement that anybody who receives such benefits has to be available for fulltime employment. The implications of this provision are far-reaching and they are questionable in many respects, legally and practically as well as ethically. Ironically enough, this obligation is seen as a way of enhancing people's work ethics, whereas in practice it deprives a person of the autonomy to go about one's life and try to make the best out of a difficult situation. There is thus a severe asymmetry between the rights and obligations of employers, on the one hand, and corresponding rights and obligations of the working population, on the other. The provision that people should be available for fulltime employment is cynic for several reasons, first of all because fulltime employment is hard to come by. The insistence on which this provision is adhered to, has the effect of stalling the system in ways that is detrimental to the whole of society. For people seeking new venues for their lives, it becomes an obstacle because they have no autonomy over their compensation. Instead they are submitted to a heavy bureaucratic control apparatus. It would appear that the less opportunities there are for fulltime employment, the more severe the 'working line' obligations have become.[127]

In addition to the humiliation 'unemployed jobseekers' are submitted to, the control bureaucracy is also a waste of societal resources that could be used in constructive ways. This represents a pattern that the historian Ferdnand Braudel has pointed to in his book *The Wheels of Commerce* that appears to repeat itself throughout time. Braudel observes that it would be misleading to think that confronted with the mounting strength of the economy, productive as it has been of so many revolutionary changes, other sectors, as well as society as a whole, should not continue to play their part. The social response, he notes, rarely constituted acceleration for change, but more often barriers. Forces of resistance or drags on change survive and exert their influence for centuries on end (1982: 461). This illustrates a confrontation between different social groupings and the interests they represent. This confrontation can either be solved through accommodation among the different interest groups or aspirations can be suppressed through the means of authority or plain domination through power.[128]

---

[127] See Birnbaum Universell grundinkomst och den svenska välfärdsstaten: Mot en ny generation av inkomsträttigheter? 2005: 342-345.

[128] Storlund, Vivan, *Trade union rights – what are they?* 1992. Cases studies illustrate these different approaches.

The constellation we are faced with today is one where the deregulation of capital flows and working life has increased the autonomy of players in business life. Here it is not enough that deregulation of working life has had adverse effects on the working population, infringing on people's autonomy. In addition to this, their situation is further aggravated by the way social security schemes operate. Instead of being a compensation for lost revenue and job opportunities, over which they could decide in an autonomous way, they are submitted to a control apparatus that has not caught up with human rights standards.

The logic of social security schemes

The social security schemes were designed at a time when industrial production was the driving force of the economy, and industrial work the ideal type of work. The need for social security was then primarily a temporary matter in-between jobs. Social security schemes are based on the 'working line' principle. This means that a person's right to unemployment compensation will be dependent on that person's work history. As people to decreasing degrees are able to influence their own work history, the system does not conform to the generally held view that social security is based on solidarity. As Simon Birnbaum points out in the case of Sweden, there is a clear tension between a commitment for general civil rights to an income, and an emphasis on the social rights of the working population. This tension surfaces as soon as there are citizens who do not have a steady attachment to the labour market. The normative link between the 'working line' and the duty to work has become more severe and referred to with increasing frequency during the past years (2005: 329). Birnbaum points to a need for a moral-philosophical discussion about this state of affairs, as well as a just weighing among different distributive principles (2005: 337).

Misconceived solidarity

Through her empirical research on exclusion from unemployment benefits, Anna Christensen has shown that married women with children often are victimised by the system. This is the case in instances where they decline to take up a new job, because working hours or the distance to the job makes it difficult to combine work with family responsibilities and childcare. Staffan Marklund and Stefan Swallfors have confirmed Christensen's analysis. They have pointed out how the linkage of social security to wage labour has led to a duality in the social security system.[129] The system discriminates against people who do not hold salaried employment, or who work only for short periods. They observe that "the dividing line in the dual welfare structure goes between stable labour market participants and the non-working or irregularly working reserve-army of house-wives, students, handicapped and old." (1987: 17)

Marklund's and Swallfors' study was published in 1987, before the disintegration of industrial work patterns set in in a visible way. Already then, they showed on the basis of their empirical research that the size of this marginal group varied between 10 and 40 per cent in the welfare programmes they had researched, comprising retirement pension, sickness insurance, family insurance and unemployment insurance. Thus, they confirm Christensen's analysis that wage labour is the major determining factor in the Swedish welfare system, and not political democracy or any ideology of charity or solidarity. Marklund and Svallfors thus conclude that contrary to common opinions about the Swedish system as an all-encompassing welfare state, there are in fact large parts of the population, who do not qualify for the core welfare system (1987: 39). A more recent

[129] Marklund, Staffan, Svallfors, Stefan, Dual Welfare - Segmentation and Work Enforcement in the Swedish Welfare System, 1987: 14.

testimony of the Swedish system, by Jansson et al. in 2000,[130] reveals that no appropriate updating has been made of the social security systems to take account of the diversification of working life. The social security schemes that were developed in Sweden during the 20th century presuppose that people have a steady salaried employment. A person who has had an employment during a certain period of time, and is then prevented from working because of illness, unemployment or some equivalent reason, will be entitled to a support that is dependent on how much he or she gained while working, provided he or she is again looking for a job. Those who have not yet managed to get work for a sufficiently long period of time, fall fairly short of rights. This is a big injustice that mainly young people encounter, but also, say, parents who have chosen to take care of their children, researchers who have lived on scholarships for some years, immigrants who have not yet managed to find a place in the Swedish labour market, as well as long-term unemployed who have exhausted their right to income-related unemployment benefits. The social allowance that constitutes the last safety net is means-tested and often perceived as humiliating.[131]

The less opportunities a person has had to work and thereby to earn entitlements, the more austere the systems appear to become. At the same time as social security entitlements are based on an obligation to work, to qualify for an entitlement, the logic of the system is such that it presupposes passivity. One has to show that one is ready to take on fulltime employment! Here there is thus no symmetry between the increased room of manoeuvre that employers have gained and the treatment of those who have become its victims. What is required is to release people's creative

130 Jansson K, m.fl. *Försörjningstillägg* ...En utredning om medborgarlön till Miljöpartiet de Grönas kongress 2000. Miljöpartiet de Gröna, cited in Reinikainen, J*ouni, Social rättvisa per medborgarlön? Den egalitära liberalismen I miljöpartiets distributiva ideal*, 2005: 366.

131 Jansson K, mfl. (2000), cited in Reinikainen, Jouni, 2005: 366.

energies that are now suffocating under a heavy bureaucracy, as well as to offer support for different kinds of activities, paving thereby the way for the potentials that today's technological society holds. A host of problems also originate in the grading of different support systems and the order in which they are available. This creates problems on two fronts. On the one hand, such a system generates unnecessary bureaucracy as it leads to an excursion from office to office. For a person in need of economic support the time involved in this excursion may be fatal. So it can also be because of the criteria a person has to meet in order to qualify for a social allowance as a last resort. An effect of this system may easily be that when crisis strikes, one has to 'lose it all' before the last resort, a social allowance, is available.

The effects of the ways in which social security schemes are designed, are the same in country after country. So we can switch over to Philippe Van Parijs for an analysis of the effects of these systems. He has developed a model for a basic income for all, which has been motivated by the injustices present systems lead to, as well as the "unemployment trap" it easily becomes. He points out that this problem has been stressed by social workers but generally overlooked by economists (2000: 4)[132] ; by lawyers as well, I might add. For recipients of social security the system leads to great uncertainty. Van Parijs points to the perils involved in looking for or accepting a job. What deters people from getting out to work is often the reasonable fear of uncertainty, because the regular flow of benefits is often interrupted. Administrative time lags – especially among people who may have a limited knowledge of their entitlements, and "the fear of going into debt, or for people who are likely to have no savings to fall back on – may make sticking to benefits the wisest option" (2000: 4).

[132] Van Parijs, Philippe, *A Basic Income for All. If you really care about freedom, give people an unconditional income*, net version, p. 4. Originally published in the October/ November 2000 issue of Boston Review

Another major problem associated with social security schemes is that people in practice are deprived the possibility to improve their living conditions with additional earnings. This is in violation of the Covenant on Economic, Social and Cultural Rights, Article 11, Section 1: "The States Parties to the present Covenant recognize the right of everyone to an adequate standard of living for himself and his family, including adequate food, clothing and housing, and to the continuous improvement of living conditions." The practical effects that social security systems have should also be contrasted to constitutional provisions. Here, by way of illustration, the Finnish constitution: "Section 19 - The right to social security. Those who cannot obtain the means necessary for a life of dignity have the right to receive indispensable subsistence and care." Also here, dignity is a criterion that should guide the design of social welfare schemes. Practice looks different. Because support systems have not been updated to take account of new conditions, one can say that people are held hostage of a system that is no longer representative of factual conditions in working life. And not only individual people, but also society as a whole, as present systems and practices in practice sacrifices lots of human energies and creativity.

Differentiating values – the case of civil society

One problem that has become accentuated because of the strong focus on competitiveness, is that most activities are considered from an economic point of view even though their nature do not fit such descriptions. This is the case with social and cultural activities, which are largely found in civil society. These activities should not be considered on a par with business life. As activities in civil society derive from people's own aspirations, they represent in a genuine way citizens' goals and needs. Burton A. Weisbrod, who has studied the non-profit economy, notes that these are goals that have not been 'bargained away' in a political process (1991:

5).[133] Nor have their activities been tailored to ensure profit. Thereby they are more responsive to the interests of poorly organised groups than both the private and public sectors are. Weisbrod points out that organisations serve important social aims that neither the private sector nor the government can fulfil very well (1991: 5). Yet, as indicated above, there is an intricate relationship between NGOs and the public sector, but as intricate is also the relationship to business life, where questions of competition is the crucial issue. Weisbrod has fittingly pointed to how we in the societal division of labour lack a proper perception of work in civil society: "Public policy toward nonprofits – to the extent there is one – can be described most aptly as confused. Government simultaneously encourages and discourages nonprofits – subsidizing them and restricting them, proclaiming their virtues and distrusting them. This is not surprising, since there is little consensus as to what goals society should achieve by fostering nonprofits. And without a consensus there cannot be tests of whether goals are being reached or even approached." (1991: 7) Weisbrod approaches non-profit organisations in an economic perspective, where the question of competition stands at the core.

If we approach these same questions from a bottom-up perspective, things look different. People have a reason for doing what they do. Aaro Harju has captured the essence of activities in civil society in the following observation, to which I return again: "The power that stems from civil action lies in people's aspirations and needs to act for themselves and their kinships to secure and improve their quality of life. Civil activities cannot be questioned without questioning the right of everybody to strive for the good life for themselves as well as for their kinships and the society in which they live."[134] Here we are talking about human and social concerns

---

[133] Weisbrod, Burton A., The Nonprofit Economy, 1991: 5.

[134] Harju, Aaro, *Yhteisellä asialla* - (Joint venture, civil activities and their challenges), 2003: 41.

as opposed to economic ones. That is why it is so important that NGOs are able to determine their goals and preserve their autonomy in any dealings with the public or private sectors.

The social economy

Because of the incentives for and nature of work done in civil society, it should be recognised as a social economy that exists on equal terms with the public and private sectors. A typical feature of this sector is that economic profit associated with employment (seen from an employer's point of view) and entrepreneurship are lacking – at least as a point of departure. In contrast to business life, where a profit is an aim, the social economy is driven by human aspirations and needs. We are here concerned with two different values guiding two complementary functions. We do, however, lack proper criteria to differentiate work along these parallel lines, due to the simplistic premises on which the perception of work is based. This forces different kinds of work into categories that are inappropriate for the incentives and the forms work take in civil society. To underscore the motivations and values governing activities in civil society, I therefore choose to talk about the activities going on there as the social economy. This gives the greatest leeway to capture activities of different kinds that are not properly covered by existing legislation, or when it does, does so in a way that misrepresents the nature of these activities.

Artistic and cultural work represents one kind of activity that illustrates the kinds of problems we are faced with, when legislation is not in tune with factual conditions. With the fast growing creative economy there has evidently been a corresponding increase in the number of artists who are at the origin of this boosting economic sector. We recall that in Finland the number of artists increased by 127 per cent between 1970 and 1995. Within this number, the category 'other art and occupations' increased by 349 per cent.

A reserved sphere for human and social concerns

Due to its human-centred focus, civil society is the societal sector that best has been able to respond to needs deriving from social change. The organisations at Pappilantie, the Organisation street, are good illustrations of this. They have been founded during the past 20 years and precisely in order to respond to people's needs. Harju has in a pertinent way characterised such activities: Many organisations produce activities that may be interpreted as service production, but that are done in an area where there are no markets. It is thus a question of activities that take place in-between traditional activities in civil society and professionally produced service.[135] This distinction between two activities that to their external form might look similar, but to their rationale differ, is in line with the observation made by Aristotle about two kinds of property, the one that is needed in the family for the good life, and the one that is accumulated for its own sake. This distinction sheds light on the problems of perception involved.

Aristotle's distinction can be expanded to cover civil society as well, as it operates on equal terms with the family. The point of departure is people's needs and aspirations, not economic gain. Thus defined, activities in civil society should be characterised as the social economy that operates as non-profit, parallel with public services and services produced pro profit. As the aims of activities in civil society differ from those done for profit, the criteria applied for these activities must not be the same as for activities geared toward profit. Instead criteria that reflect the nature of these activities should be applied and where lacking, such criteria should be developed. On the same score, a demarcation needs to be made to cor-

---

[135] Harju, Aaro, *Kansalalisyhteiskunta ja markkinat*, Kansalaisfoorumi, Verkkolehti, Editorial 7.11.2005.

responding activities in the public sector where the autonomy of organisations must be the guiding principle. The social economy is a growing phenomenon that needs to be mapped out and analysed. This is important for several reasons. On the one hand, demarcations need to be made to the public and private sectors respectively, as indicated above. Along with such clarifications, also new modes of operation and a new culture are required. Also legislative adaptations need to be made on many fronts.

When activities in civil society are met with demands for free competition, such demands must be balanced against the different values that civil society represents and room must be given for other than economic values in any considerations of activities in the social economy. There are of course no clear-cut boundaries between different types of activities, and emphasis may move from one category to another. The central point is that this must be made the object of a contextual assessment rather than blindly applying formal criteria, as now widely is the case. In his analysis of the non-profit economy, Weisbrod notes that "there can be no such thing as sound public policy toward nonprofits alone – policy can be wisely constructed only if it recognizes the ways that nonprofits interact with other elements of the economic system." On this score he presents recommendations for public policy aimed at stimulating a much needed policy debate on the appropriate activities, financing as well as regulation of non-profit organisations (1991: 160). What public policy requires, he says, is a procedure for continued reappraisal of the social rules that constrain and encourage the non-profit economy relative to the other components of the economic system (1991:161). Weisbrod presents two goals that guide his proposals: (1) to insulate nonprofits from pressures to deviate from the social role they can and should play in a modern, mixed economy, and (2) to help move the economy to a better balance of institutional responsibilities among private enterprises, governments, and nonprofits. "I believe nonprofits should be more restricted in some ways, more encouraged in other ways", he says.[136]

One important observation Weisbrod makes in presenting his proposals is that public subsidies should encourage the desired activities without distorting the means of carrying them out (1991: 165). This is a danger that lurks in contractual relationships between the public sector and NGOs, as dealt with above. But there is also an inherent danger in the 'project economy', of which NGOs are largely dependent for funding their activities. The project economy is in many respects a nuisance both for organisations and individuals who are dependent on external funding in order to be able to do the work they are there to do. The whole project economy would require a critical analysis that would consider, among other things, autonomy-aspects and cost-effectiveness. To secure funding in the form of projects may infringe on the autonomy of applicants. Cost effectiveness, again, should be measured by taking into account the whole administrative apparatus that is upheld to scrutinise the viability of applications, as well as the time that has gone into making the applications, by people who already are in a harsh position because they are dependent on funding for being able to do their work.

The nature of work in the social economy

In addition to the intricate relationships there exist between the public sector and NGOs as well as between them and pro-profits, activities in civil society constitutes yet another legal grey area when it comes to work. A conceptual point of departure is often that work in civil society is voluntary work. And so it also is, but this is not the whole story. Further, work in civil society is often seen as hobby activities. So it also is, yet far from all of it is. A number of clarifications are here in place. It is important to

[136] For his concrete proposals see 1991: 163-167

give proper recognition for the work done in civil society out of its own premises. Aaro Harju, who is a major player in Finnish civil society, has drawn attention to general attitudes toward work in this sector. There are many who do not see this work as professional work. Engineers are professionals and so are nurses, but those who work for the wellbeing of others, who are engaged in work that is important for a well-functioning society, they are not necessarily seen as professionals. This work is easily given the label of hobby activities, attitudes that can be seen among authorities and politicians, who take decisions that influence the preconditions for work in civil society. Many politicians and decision-makers consider that work in civil society should preferably be done without compensation, or with only minor compensation. Aaro Harju questions this view by arguing that organisational work is demanding professional work (Editorial, 31.05.2006).

Here, again, we need to be attentive to standards laid down in the Covenant on Economic, Social and Cultural Rights. Article 7 recognises the right of everyone to the enjoyment of just and favourable conditions of work. I will here single out aspects of article 7 that are at particular risk because of the conditions under which much work is done in civil society.

Among just and favourable conditions of work the article singles out: (a) Remuneration which provides all workers, as a minimum, with: (i) Fair wages and equal remuneration for work of equal value without distinction of any kind... (ii) A decent living for themselves and their families ... (b) Safe and healthy working conditions; (d) Rest, leisure and reasonable limitation of working hours and periodic holidays with pay,...(Article 7).

Yet another observation about work in civil society that Harju makes, needs to be brought to the fore that underscores the value of work in this sector. The great advantage of work in civil society, Harju notes, is the liberty it entails. It allows people to device their own activities making use of their know-how. Work can be made very challenging. This is why many innovations have their origin in civil society, which public authorities have later taken on board (Editorial 31.05.2006).

Calibrating values

It is important that work in the social economy is considered out of its own premises and the values steering these activities. It must be recognised that this work seldom brings an immediate economic return. Its indirect return, however, may be considerable. Because organisations and other actors in civil society are responsive to people's needs, they assume the function of correcting shortcomings in services offered both by the public and private sectors. In addition, public authorities increasingly rely on organisations to complement their services. Yet there is this ambivalence about non-profit organisations that Weisbrode spelled out above. Here the question of funding activities in the social economy becomes crucial. Although voluntary work is valuable, there is a risk that voluntary workers are used as cheap labour, dumping legislated or agreed labour standards. Furthermore, such activities need to be directed and administered. This presupposes employed persons who, as Harju points out, do a demanding professional work. Neither should voluntary work be deprived of the professional character, which it often has, although not necessarily.

There is thus an important element of labour standards in the work carried out in civil society that needs to be recognised and adhered to. To meet these standards, funding must be secured. Otherwise, particularly in the case of cooperation agreements, these may become so asymmetric that it places the fulfilment of agreed stipulations in jeopardy. Here it is also in place to recall the observation about the material conditions for democracy, with which this paper opened: "Democracy can only be achieved when people have confidence in each other and when they are confident that they can conclude binding agreements, like businessmen do, without one profiting from the other more than what is to their joint advantage and in their joint interest." (translated here) (Lång 2005: 60)

Enhancing people's possibilities to work – artists an illustration

I have chosen to talk about the social economy in order to also include individual work in cases where such work is not recognised in labour and social security legislation. This is largely the case with artistic and cultural work. National cultural policy programs emphasise the value of artistic work for individual persons as well as society at large. This is also confirmed in the UNESCO Recommendation on the Status of Artists (1980) and the UNESCO Convention on the Protection and Promotion of the Diversity of Cultural Expressions (2005). Furthermore, the International Labour Organisation emphasises that artist should be entitled to appropriate labour standards. Notwithstanding this, artists along with other professionals who work without an employment relationship or with activities that does not secure a status as an entrepreneur, are in practice deprived of a status and entitlements that other professionals are accorded in labour and social legislation. This is discriminatory toward them. Moreover, it is in violation of provisions of the Covenant on Economic, Social and Cultural Rights. Article 6 states that the states parties should recognise the right to work, which includes the right of everyone to the opportunity to gain his living by work which he freely chooses or accepts, and that states should take appropriate steps to safeguard this right.

The steps that need to be taken are to enlarge the present restrictive concept of work. Artistic work is in this respect a fruitful point of departure. In Finland, the value of work is spelled out in the governmental program for art and artists, *Art is possibilities*. Because of the values art generates as well as its innovative nature, the program suggests that artistic work should be considered on a par with research. Would somebody expect a researcher to secure a living on market terms? Hardly. For both professions there are different funding schemes. The problem is that they are not sufficient to sustain the activities of all artists and researchers. When funding is not available for persons pursuing these professions they are 'sucked up' in the 'wage-labour logic'. One illustration of this problem is that the Finnish cultural administration has five criteria for different forms of artists' work. The labour and social administrations have merely two, employed or unemployed. When artists and researchers have to turn to social security to secure their living, they are forced into the 'working line' obligation to be available for fulltime employment, with no regard for the work they are factually doing. This is a negation of the professional work an artist or a researcher is doing in cases where it is not done in an employment relationship, or funding is not available.

This may force a person into work that is not of one's own choice, or alternatively be deprived of social protection. It should be fairly obvious by now that existing structures and the conceptual tools that sustain them are out of tune with present day circumstances. This is something that the rapporteurs on the right to social security (Article 9) Maria Virginia Bras Gomes and Eibe Riedel are well aware of. It is noted in the document that in the implementation of their Covenant obligations, and in accordance with Article 2, Section 1, of the Covenant, States parties are required to utilize "all appropriate means, including particularly the adoption of legislative measures." The authors point out that every state party has a margin of discretion in assessing which measures are most suitable to meet its specific circumstances. The Covenant, however, clearly imposes a duty to take whatever steps are necessary to ensure that everyone enjoys the right to social security, as soon as possible. Furthermore, it is pointed out that any national measures designed to realise the right to social security should not interfere with the enjoyment of other human rights.[137] The duty

[137] General Comment (No. 20) for the meeting of the Committee on Economic, Social and Cultural Rights paragraph, p. 13

to take steps imposes on states parties an obligation to adopt a national strategy or plan of action to realise the right to social security. The strategy should: "(a) be based upon human rights law and principles; (b) cover all aspects of the right to social security and the corresponding obligations of States parties; (c) define clear objectives; (d) set targets or goals to be achieved and the time-frame for their achievement; (e) formulate adequate policies and corresponding benchmarks and indicators." Furthermore, states are expected to regularly review its social security to ensure that it is consistent with the requirements set out in the document (Bras Gomes & Riedel 2006: 13).

A universal basic income – a remedy

With the changes that have occurred during past decades, we can see three parallel economies developing. They have existed before, but their volume has grown to such extents that this phenomenon needs to be addressed and analysed to see what conclusions need to be drawn from it. In addition to the 'traditional employment relationship', we have so-called atypical workers that the social rights document aptly labels 'disadvantaged workers'. There are, furthermore, a number of employment enhancing schemes that may dump labour and social standards. In addition to this there is voluntary work. As to its substance, the same work may thus be performed in any of these categories, whereas remuneration and social security varies. This is in violation of the Covenant on Economic, Social and Cultural Rights that presupposes equal pay for work of equal value. To exit this impasse, a first thing to do is to consider what values are involved in the work done, and devise means of financing them, so that people are allowed to do the work of their own choice. Because work in the social field mostly stems from people's own needs and aspirations, their activities need to be accepted for what they are. A universal basic income could be a first step to remedy much of the problems that people outside the conventional working life encounter. It would correct some of the most blatant injustices and nuisances. In addition to this, there are also arguments about rationality and cost-effectiveness for advocating a basic income.

For those who intuitively or overtly reject the idea of a basic income, I wish to propose some points of repair to present-day states of affairs. Suppose that the social allowance that today is the 'last resort', where made the primary support scheme when people face economic problems. Suppose also that the limits to an income accrued when touching some form of social benefits, were removed. Then we would have an accommodating system, whereby people in a flexible way would be able to improve their economic position. This would make the heavy bureaucracy that today is tailored to control people obsolete, releasing thereby resources for positive ventures. With a general basic income, even more resources that now go into the bureaucracy would be released for purposeful activities. Philippe Van Parijs has developed a scheme for a universal basic income, UBI, that I will here rely on to indicate means of exiting the impasse we are in today when it comes to enhancing people's opportunity to do the work they want to do (2000).[138]

Van Parijs' considers that a basic income would serve as a powerful instrument of social justice. His argument is that a UBI would promote real freedom for all by providing the material resources that people need to pursue their aims. At the same time, it would help to solve the policy dilemmas of poverty and unemployment, as well as serve ideals associated with both the feminist and green movements (2000: 1). Social justice is the conceptual foundation of Van Parijs' scheme. Social justice, he notes, requires that our institutions be designed so that they secure real freedom to all. This presupposes that a person has the necessary resources to make use of her liberty, to have access to the means she needs in order to do

[138] For an elaboration on this question, see Van Parijs 2000: 6.

what she wants to do. Such a system should be designed so as to offer the greatest possible real opportunity to those with least opportunities, subject to everyone's formal freedom being respected (Van Parijs 2000: 5).

Through a universal basic income, Van Parijs sees that one could avoid the risk of increasing poverty that is inherent in many strategies for reducing unemployment. He points out that a basic income would not subsidise passivity. Quite the contrary: a basic income could release human activities that today are suffocating under a heavy control bureaucracy. A basic income would thus be one solution for much wanted or needed work. It could serve as an income support for persons who are doing socially or culturally important work, such as artists, researchers and persons working in civil society. It would equally constitute one step toward securing the provision in the Covenant on Economic, Social and Cultural Rights about the right to work of one's own choice. Van Parijs considers that, when fighting to reduce the impact of economic inequalities it is essential to propose, explore, and advocate ideas that are both ethically compelling and also make economic sense, even when their political feasibility remains uncertain. "Sobered, cautioned, and strengthened by Europe's debate of the last two decades" he has presented his model for a universal basic income.

To recapture the logic inherent in current social security schemes dealt with above, here is van Parijs' list of more or less stringent variants of requirements that a person must meet in order to be eligible for some form of social compensation, to which his scheme offers an alternative: "if she is able to work, she must be willing to accept a suitable job, or to undergo suitable training, if offered; she must pass a means test, in the sense that she is only entitled to the benefit if there are grounds to believe that she has no access to a sufficient income from other sources; and her household situation must meet certain criteria – it matters, for example, whether she lives on her own, with a person who has a job, with a jobless person, etc. By contrast, a UBI does not require satisfaction of any of these conditions." (Van Parijs 2000: 3) As a contrast to the prevailing social security schemes, van Parijs refers to child allowances and old age pensions that offer an alternative to existing means-tested allowances. Where such exists, they already serve as a restricted model of a universal basic income, he observes. With his model, a wide range of existing benefits can be abolished or reduced. And for most people of working age, the basic income and the increased taxes required to pay for it, will largely offset each other.[139]

Van Parijs sees that his model would be a solution to many problems associated with work in civil society. It would vitalise activities in this sector, and give actors greater leeway for their activities. Van Parijs sees also that a universal basic income could be an important step toward adherence to provisions of the Covenant on Economic, social and cultural rights.

Van Parijs also contrasts a basic income to subsidies paid to employers. With a UBI, workers will only take a job if they find it suitably attractive, whereas if a subsidy is paid to employers it would make unattractive, low-productivity jobs more economically viable. "If the motive in combating unemployment is not some sort of work fetishism – an obsession with keeping everyone busy – but rather a concern to give every person the possibility of taking up gainful employment in which she can find recognition and accomplishment, then the UBI is to be preferred" (Van Parijs 2000: 6). Van Parijs mentions a frequent objection to a UBI; that it would have perverse labour supply effects.[140] He suggests that a first response should be: ""So what?" Boosting the labour supply is no aim in itself. No one can reasonably want an overworked, hyperactive society. Give people of all classes the opportunity to reduce their working time or even take a

---

139 Most likely in the form of an abolition of exemptions and of low tax rates for the lowest income brackets Van Parijs, 2000: 8.

140 van Parijs mentions that, in fact, some American income maintenance experiments in the 1970s showed such effects.

complete break from work in order to look after their children or elderly relatives. You will not only save on prisons and hospitals. You will also improve the human capital of the next generation. A modest UBI is a simple and effective instrument in the service of keeping a socially and economically sound balance between the supply of paid labour and the rest of our lives" (Van Parijs 2000: 8).

CHAPTER 11

A GLOBAL BASIC INCOME - COMPENSATION AND INVESTMENT

2009[141]

Incentives for a basic income

A major incentive for a universal basic income is to cater for the growing sector of work that is performed in the intersection between full-time long-term employment and entrepreneurship. A basic income coupled by support-structures to facilitate work, as well as more cost- effective ways of financing projects (particularly EU-financed ones) would make all the difference. A basic income could be seen as a general compensation for any kind of work not duly recognised, and for the uncertainties people in working life are subjected to for reasons outside their own control. Furthermore, a basic income would act as a buffer for persons trying out entrepreneurship.

The case of artists

Culture and the creative sector are among the fastest growing sectors of the economy, but they have for long been fairly under-researched areas. A study entitled The Economy of Culture in Europe (2006) is one important contribution to the research that is gradually emerging in this

[141] Unpublished

field.[142] In that study the researchers collected statistical data on the quantifiable socio-economic impact of the cultural and creative sector. Here are some results of the study:
- Turnover: The cultural and creative sector turned over more than € 654 billion in 2003, compared to ICT manufactures € 541 billion in 2003 and the car manufacturing industry, € 271 billion in 2001.
- Value added to EU GDP: the cultural and creative sector contributed to 2.6 per cent of EU GDP in 2003. During that same year Chemicals, rubber and plastic products accounted for 2.3 per cent of the contribution to EU GDP, Real estate activities 2.1 per cent, Food, beverage and tobacco manufacturing 1.9 per cent, Textile industry 0.5 per cent.
- Contribution to EU growth: the overall growth of the sector's value added was 19.7 per cent in 1999–2003. The sector's growth during this period was 12.3 per cent higher than the growth of the general economy.
- Employment: In 2004, 5.8 million people worked in the cultural and creative sector, equalling 3.1 per cent of the total employed population in EU25. And also, while total employment in the EU decreased in 2002–2004, employment in this sector increased by 1.85 per cent.

Characteristics

The share of independents is more than twice that in total employment (28.8 per cent against 14.1 per cent) (this tells nothing about their income). 17 per cent temporary workers, compared to 13.3 per cent in total employment, whereas the share of part- time workers is one out of four against 17.6 per cent in total employment. These employment figures are obviously reflecting the economic growth in the sector, but when compared to what is considered 'standard' work, work in the cultural and cre-

142 http://www.cultural-economy.eu/2006

ative sector will to a large extent be so called atypical, with all the problems involved. Another distinctive feature is that people working in this sector generally have a high level of education, with 46.8 per cent possessing a university degree, whereas the percentage in total employment is 25.7 per cent. This triggers the question how human capital is treated in present day structures, considering also their economic contribution to society. (For a closer look at artists position in working life see above Chapter 8).

Purpose of a basic income

Ordinarily, considerations about a basic income are approached from a social security perspective with focus on the costs that such a scheme would involve. My point of departure is working life with focus on the profound changes that have occurred since the late 1970s. Despite reforms in labour legislation and associated social security aimed at catering for these changes, they have not accorded the whole working population the support and security that labour and social security legislation is intended to provide. Due to the restructuring of the economy and thereby also a changed working life, a growing number of people have become dependent on social security. As existing social security schemes were originally designed for the industrial society, they now harbour a host of paradoxes and nods that could be unleashed through a basic income. Therefore, human rights standards should be a point of departure. The goal of the basic income I envisage is to empower people, to give them the possibility to pursue their own plans of life. A secured and sufficiently high basic income will have a number of positive spin-off effects, individual as well as societal, such as increased wellbeing, and a spurring effect on the economy, above all at the local one.

A virtuous circle

In addition to the legal problems that a basic income could compensate for, there are also wider societal gains to be achieved. In their research on the welfare state Robert Hagfors and Jouko Kajanoja have introduced the notion of a virtuous circle that is generated by good social coverage. Their underlying hypothesis is that (1) a developed welfare state diminishes inequality, (2) diminished inequality creates generalised trust and other forms of social capital, (3) this in turn means more wellbeing among people, and (4) more wellbeing results in support for the welfare state. Hagfors and Kajanoja assume that a feeling of protection against risks among people is one of the main phenomena underlying the hypothesis of a virtuous circle. They further assume that this feeling is generated by specific social security measures of the welfare state and by the social capital strengthened by the welfare state.[143]

The notion of a virtuous circle provides a theoretical framework that allow Hagfors and Kajanoja to link together diverse strands of research on social welfare, social capital and protection against risks, and thereby also to test a number of well-known hypotheses empirically (Hagfors, Kajanoja 2007: 3). One of their objectives is to analyse statistically how the interdependencies between different forms of social capital and the levels of public social expenditure change as other features of the welfare state

---

[143] Robert Hagfors and Jouko Kajanoja *The Welfare State, Inequality and Social Capital*, Paper presented at the ESRC Social Contexts and Responses to Risk Network (SCARR) Conference on "Risk & Rationalities", 29–31 March 2007, Queens' College, Cambridge. Hagfors and Kajanoja have gathered empirical evidence (datasets comparing OECD countries) for testing their hypothesis. They present data about dimensions describing (1) the welfare state (share of social expenditure, replacement rate i.e., decommodification, extent of universal services, etc.), (2) inequality (Gini coefficient, poverty, power distance, income mobility, etc.), (3) social capital (generalised trust, trust towards institutions, participation, mutual aid in civil society, etc.) and (4) well-being (objective and subjective measures), and present an analysis of the connections between these dimensions.

are introduced into the analysis. The incentive for this approach derives from findings suggesting that trust between citizens and community-mindedness are strongest in the Nordic countries and weakest in countries where the level of social security is lowest (2007: 3). In their analysis of how social policy can be used to reduce inequality in a way that benefits society as a whole, Hagfors and Kajanoja look at equality not only in economic terms, but also as a differential ability for people to shape their life and to enjoy freedom of choice, or as differences in people's potential for social mobility and for overcoming their innate social and economic hurdles (2007:4).

Caroline West's research on happiness fits well into this picture. According to multiple research results every extra dollar that people get with an income between zero and $ 27 000 makes an enormous difference to their happiness, whereas every dollar that people earn over $ 40 000 makes very little difference. West thus considers that there is a strong argument for aggressive redistribution of income from people who earn more than US $ 40 000, to people who earn between zero and $ 27 000.[144]

Another major building block in Hagfors' and Kajanoja's virtuous circle is social capital and trust. It is primarily in civil society that these are generated. Here danger lurks in the present trend, whereby public authorities more or less hand over tasks to organisations. In this situation it is of vital importance that they are properly compensated for this work. A basic income would be a step in this direction. A basic income or civil salary has been discussed for a long time, but it has been tried out only in fragmentary ways. In view of the profound changes societies are now going through, it would be important to try out a global and unconditional basic income as one means of rectifying existing imbalances. An additional incentive for trying out a basic income is the worldwide financial crisis.

[144] Caroline West, 30 May 2009 The Happiness Machine, The Philosopher's Zone, Radio Australia. http://www.abc.net.au/rn/philosopherszone/stories/2009/2580932.htm#transcript)

While taxpayers' money is used to save financial institutions from a crisis caused by reckless behaviour, innocent people lose their jobs, homes, pensions, or in other ways the control of their lives. In this situation one would do well to also secure the economic position of citizens. It would be of utmost importance to secure the life conditions of those who are most vulnerable.

The wider context - business versus work

Business and work are two sides of the same coin. Yet we do not appear to have any conceptual schemes where the two sides would be linked. This being the case, profit and compensation for the work done stand unrelated in an assessment of different states of affairs. Yet we know there is a link. In 1897 the sociologist Vilfredo Pareto claimed that income toward the wealthier end of the social spectrum is distributed in such a way that much of a nation's wealth is held by a few individuals. Pareto expressed this imbalance in terms of the so-called 80:20 rule: 80 per cent of the wealth is possessed by 20 per cent of the people. He observed that this income distribution held true for many countries, regardless of their political system or taxation regime. The 80:20 principle has further come to be regarded as a rule of thumb for management decisions: 80 per cent of your benefit will come from 20 per cent of your outlay, 80 per cent of your results will be due to 20 per cent of your workforce, and so forth. (Ball 2005: 307–308). This triggers the question, if this is so, will it mean that when factories are closed down, laying off hundreds of workers, this is done to ensure the 80:20 ratio? The production is then transferred to low cost countries where the 80:20 ratio can be ensured. It is in this kind of wider context that a basic income should be considered.

Illustration – Namibia

In Namibia research has been carried out that places a basic income in perspective. This research is summed up in a paper Promoting employment and decent conditions of work for all – Towards a good practice model in Namibia, by Z. Kameeta, C. Haarmann, D. Haarmann and H. Jauch, presented to the United Nations Commission for Social Development, 45th session, 7–16 February 2007.

This research shows that people in disadvantaged communities carry a disproportionably high burden for caring for other people. The informal social security system effectively imposes an informal tax on the poor. There is a linear correlation of the richest households supporting other households with only about 8 per cent of their income while the poorest households spend up to 23 per cent of their meagre incomes on other poor people. In economic terms this constitutes a regressive tax on the poor that diminishes their ability to save and invest, diminishing thereby the chance to enhance their own economic opportunities.

The absence of substantial amounts of cash in the local economy prevents businesses and local projects from becoming successful and sustainable. Especially in small rural communities, the limitation on the demand side to actually pay for goods provided furthers the monopoly situation of larger businesses, exploiting the little cash there is. These monopolies are very effective in outmanoeuvring upcoming new business into bankruptcy, and then raising prices again.

The effects of foreign investment - the case of Ramatex

The Namibian government invested about N$ 120 million in public funds to set up infrastructure for the company Ramatex. The researchers' assessments of the effects are the following: "The financial support that

Ramatex received from the Namibian government is equivalent to the salaries of all workers for 40 months – more than 3 years! A huge investment by any standard which could only be justified if Ramatex' operations in Namibia would lead to long-term sustainable jobs of decent quality. Otherwise one may well argue that the huge public investments could have been spent more efficiently on other programmes aimed at job creation." (Kameeta et al. 2007: 18).

The Ramatex operations in Namibia have been characterised by many controversies. Many of the conflicts and tensions have remained unresolved and Ramatex has contributed to the emergence of a large number of "working poor" in full-time employment, unable to meet even their basic needs. This stands in sharp contradiction to the Namibian government's stated objective of promoting decent work in line with international labour standards (Kameeta et al. 2007: 18). The authors of the report conclude that the hope that the private sector would become a large-scale job-creator with substantial impact on employment has not been fulfilled. It has thus become clear that economic growth and "sound" macro-economic indicators, which Namibia has indeed achieved since Independence, did not translate into sustained benefits for the majority of the population (2007: 20). Also, experiences from South Africa show that governments' efforts to create jobs have not been effective. The cost of a South African workfare programme amounts to several times the cost of a basic income grant, yet it fails to distribute benefits to those most in need of social assistance (Kameeta et al. 2007: 21).

The authors of the Namibian report, in which they advocate a basic income, point to the generally held view in conventional economic theory that a basic income might "undermine labour force participation by reducing the opportunity costs of not working". When empirically tested against the cash transfer systems in South Africa they found that: Social grants provide potential labour market participants with the resources and economic security necessary to invest in high-risk/high- reward job search.

- Living in a household receiving grants is correlated with a higher success rate in finding employment.

- Workers in households receiving social grants are better able to improve their productivity and as a result earn higher wages (2007, p. 22).

In regard to their model for a basic income "The Basic Income Grant", BIG, the authors maintain: "it is more than an income support programme. It provides security that reinforces human dignity and empowerment. It has the capacity to be the most significant poverty-reducing programme in Namibia, while supporting household development, economic growth and job creation. The cost is ranging from 2.2 per cent to 3.8 per cent of national income." Over time, Namibia's economy will benefit from the long-term growth impact of the Basic Income Grant (2007:23). This report was presented in 2007.

Namibia basic income pilot project

In 2008 a Basic Income Grant was tried out. Otjivero, a deprived village, was chosen for the pilot project. The balance sheet after the scheme had been tried out for half a year was unambiguously positive. Here is some evidence reported by the Swedish journalist Jacob Zetterman in an article in the net journal Dagen.se 21.11.2008[145] And what was the result after half a year of payments? Did it turn out, as the critics feared, that people who get money for free become passive and shy working; that in the long run, it leads to society's collapse; that the only ones to profit from the concept are alcohol dealers and prostitutes? No, not according to the authors of the report. According to them there are now more people working at Otjivero, and there has been several start-ups since the basic income was

[145] http://www.dagen.se/dagen/Article.aspx?ID=160382

introduced. The malnutrition of children under the age of five has decreased from 42 per cent to 17 per cent. More children are attending school and the payment of school fees has doubled. The number of school dropouts has decreased from more than 30 per cent to 5 per cent.

More people can afford health care. The local health clinic has reported that its income has increased five times as much, when more people can afford health care. Thanks to an improved diet the medicines for HIV-infected persons are more effective. Further, poverty- related violence has decreased by 20 per cent, according to the first half-year report. The basic income has up till now proved to be a success, and Bishop Kameeta, who directs the project, said in a speech cited in the article that they now could look towards a promised land that is said to exist beyond the desert march of the poor Namibians. – "It was a society that stood up against poverty and assumed its dignity, this is what we saw."

The Namibian experience illustrates the virtuous circle created by social welfare, that Robert Hagfors and Jouko Kajanoja are researching. In their research they discuss how successful social policies can be used to influence public attitudes to support the allocation of resources towards social policy; i.e., how social policy can be used to reduce inequality in a way that benefits society as a whole. "We find empirical evidence supporting or – to be more cautious – not denying our hypothesis" Hagfors and Kajanoja conclude (2007:2).

The production of welfare

The Namibian basic income can thus serve as one illustration of the kind of positive effects a basic income generates that Hagfors and Kajanoja are in search of in their model for the production of welfare. Hagfors and Kajanoja further assume that just as public expenditure on health and social protection as well as on education, directly affects people's wellbeing, so does social capital, too, albeit in an indirect way. According to research

(Frizell 2006), a decrease in inequality is reflected, in terms of social expenditure, as reduced public spending on health care, as the Namibian example also reveals. On the other hand, a decrease in inequality and an increase in social capital create motivation in society to invest in human capital. More education ultimately contributes to higher productivity. Increased productivity is directly linked to gross domestic product (GDP) growth. These positive effects not only appear as better public health and higher productivity, but they are also reflected in various welfare indicators. (2007:5).

The virtuous circle is used to refer to the propensity of actions with positive effects to function in a self-reinforcing manner. In the welfare state context, this means that to the extent that a welfare effort has a positive effect on wellbeing and the reduction of inequality, the citizens are willing to maintain and even to intensify such an effort. Reference to this idea is, among others, made in the 2006 World Development Report (chapter 6:108) (Hagfors and Kajanoja 2007: 6).

A basic income could make all the difference

All in all, a basic income would serve as a buffer for work in the expanding sector between an old standard employment and entrepreneurship, from the cultural and creative sector, and people with irregular employment through to people with entrepreneurial aspirations. This is all the more important as there are lingering false expectations about people's ability to accrue an income from their work. To become an entrepreneur appears to be seen as a general solution to the decline in industry. But how realistic are such expectations? Scott A. Shane gives evidence of this in his book The Costly Myths That Entrepreneurs, Investors and Policy Makers Live By (2008: 9). Scott's message is that in order to make well founded decisions one needs to know facts and dispose of myths (2008:6). Basing himself on extensive statistical data mainly from the US but also from other parts of the world, he shows that it may take up to 6–7 years before an enterprise has established itself (2008: 73). Scott's study also shows that entrepreneurs earn much less than people in an employment relationship. The median income for people who have had an enterprise for 10 years is 35 per cent lower than for people who work for somebody else. Although the difference may diminish (25 years 25 per cent) an entrepreneur will ordinarily earn less than the beginning salary for somebody, who does the same work in an employment relationship (2008: 101). A basic income is precisely the kind of buffer that is needed to allow people to try out entrepreneurship.

A global problem requires global solutions

On a worldwide scale, the satisfaction of everybody's basic needs, and the self-sufficiency that goes along with it, could have tremendous preventive effects on measures that people may resort to in desperation. Heiner Michel sums up the scenario we are faced with in 2008: globally, 850 million people are mal-nourished - taking into account the current food crisis the number will have certainly increased; 1 billion people are living in extreme poverty below the $ 1 per day purchasing power parity–poverty line; another 1.5 billion below the $ 2 purchasing power parity-poverty line, these are together 40 per cent of the world population, forming a global under class; 10 million children die each year before reaching their fifth birthday, mainly because of poverty and easily and inexpensively curable illness; 115 million children do not receive even basic primary education.

Costing simulations made by the International Labour Office, ILO, suggest that less than 2 per cent of the global GDP would be necessary to provide a basic set of social security benefits for all the world's poor (ILO, 2008:3). If all the positive effects of a basic income would be incorporated in a calculus like that of Hagfors' and Kajanoja's virtuous circle, would not costs turn into benefits?[146]

* * *

The Basic Income Earth Network is a worldwide network of researchers advocating a basic income. It started in 1983 as the Basic Income European Network. By 2004 the scope was extended to the rest of the world as Basic Income Earth Network. The BIEN is involved in the publication Basic Income Studies (BIS).

---

[146] Keynote address by Bishop Dr Z Kameeta about the BIG trial in Otjivero http://www.facebook.com/video/video.php?v=1110435337885

CHAPTER 12

BASIC INCOME: HOW IT FITS IN THE POLICY FRAMEWORK FOR GREEN JOBS

2011 - in Green Jobs from a Small State Perspective. Case Studies from Malta[147]

"Prosperity for the few founded on ecological destruction and persistent social injustice is no foundation for a civilized society." Tim Jackson, Prosperity without growth

Abstract

The basic argument in this paper is based on the premise that when green is the qualifying criterion for work rather than profit or economic growth, the world of work and the economic scenario in which it has to operate assume a different dimension. The focus of this new dimension is here placed on work performed in the intersection between employment and entrepreneurship. This is a grassroots level hibernation sphere for innovation and thus also a fertile breeding ground for green jobs. A green job in this context is being associated with meaningful work. What makes work meaningful is its potential to enable the worker to participate meaningfully and creatively in the life of society in less materialistic ways.

Work in the intersection between employment and entrepreneurship can be characterised as 'meaningful', as there is some value attached to it that the pursuer considers worth striving for, as opposed to merely a bread-winning job. Such work represents both personal aspirations and

[147] Green European Foundation, GEF and Fondazzjoni Ceratonia, Malta.

human and social concerns. James Robertson sees this kind of individualised work, 'ownwork', as he calls it, as the future mode of employment (*Future work* 1985 / 2006).

How work in this sector should be compensated is a big challenge, to which a basic income could be a solution. In addition to securing people's subsistence, a basic income would serve multiple purposes such as providing start-up funding both for work aimed at profit and non-profit work. A basic income would furthermore serve the environment in multiple ways as it facilitates people's individual work that often is small-scale and thereby mostly local and light. In Robertson's words ownwork will enhance the informal economy, which will become one of the main areas for further economic growth and social progress (1985/2006).

A reassessment of the notion of work is generally called for. This should be linked to green economics that challenges the narrow scope of mainstream economics. Green economics look for solutions that simultaneously address poverty, climate change and biodiversity within an equitable framework. It is a question of re-orientating ourselves and our economics, "manoeuvring it back onto its rightful course to a better "life-world" result," says Miriam Kennet (2008: 19). Research in Namibia and South Africa as well as a basic income project in Namibia illustrate the potentials of a basic income as a means of facilitating new venues for subsistence and work. In affluent societies a basic income would greatly enhance the creative sector and activities in civil society. A basic income would assist in levelling the very uneven playing field we face on many fronts.

The bigger picture

There are both economic, environmental and governmental system failures that need to be assessed and the issues renegotiated. To do that we need, on the one hand, new paradigms to allow for alternative approaches to the problems we face, on the other, we need new social instruments to correct these failures, basic income schemes being one of them. Joseph Stiglitz and James Robertson who have been in the economic epicentre, as well as Tim Jackson, whose major focus is sustainable development, will here paint the bigger picture, and offer their alternatives to present day impasses. Nobel Price winner Joseph Stiglitz was economic adviser to the American President Bill Clinton 1993–1997 and senior vice president and chief economist at the World Bank 1997–2000. He gives us the promise 'Another World is Possible' (Chapter 1) in his book Making Globalization Work (2006). Furthermore, he was involved in the World Commission on the Social Dimensions of Globalization, appointed by the International Labour Organisation, ILO, and chaired by presidents Benjamin W Mkapa (Tanzania) and Tarja Halonen (Finland) (2004). Thereafter he directed the Commission set up by the French President Nicolas Sarkozy, to consider the measurement of economic performance and social progress. Main members of the commission were Amartaya Sen and Jean-Paul Fitoussi). The report was presented in September 2009.[148] Stiglitz considers that the latter commission's report (here called the Stiglitz commission) and its implementation may have a significant impact on the way in which our societies look at themselves and, therefore, on the way in which policies are designed, implemented and assessed (2009: 9).

James Robertson, again, gives us a model that combines a new economic order with a basic income. He has arrived at these models after extensive experience of how things work in practice. He started as a policy-making civil servant in Whitehall in the 1950s and 1960s, during the decolonisation process, of which he had first hand experience. "It was a very exciting time for a young man", Robertson tells.[149] Then he worked in the

---

148 www.stiglitz-sen-fitoussi.fr

149 at http://www.jamesrobertson.com/about-james-robertson.htm

Cabinet Office, participating in the central processes of government, "getting a privileged bird's-eye, worm's-eye view of how they worked." Thereafter he gained experience of mergers in the public service, which were "very educative and very frustrating." After that he turned to the private sector getting involved with management consultancy and systems analysis. He set up the Inter-Bank Research Organisation for the British banks (1968–1973). His next excursion, as he puts it, was to stand for Parliament in 1974, in support of the Campaign for Social Democracy, "Another learning experience." The lessons he learned was that, "although effective processes of conventional politics and government may still be needed to implement radical changes, different processes of 'pre-political' action are needed to get radical changes on to mainstream policy agendas." As part of this agenda he has, among others, co-founded the New Economics Foundation, nef.

Through his work Prosperity without growth? Transition to a sustainable economy (2009), Tim Jackson links together different strands. He points to how narrowly government has been associated with material aims, "hollowed out by a misguided vision of unbounded consumer freedoms". T. Jackson considers that the concept of governance itself stands in urgent need of renewal. He sees the current economic crisis as "a unique opportunity to invest in change". The short-term thinking that has plagued society for decades should be substituted with the challenging task of "delivering a lasting prosperity" (2009, Foreword).

What kind of prosperity

For T. Jackson prosperity means that human beings should flourish within the ecological limits of a finite planet. "The challenge for our society is to create the conditions under which this is possible. It is the most urgent task of our times." (2009, Foreword) Jackson considers government to be the principal agent for protecting our shared prosperity, in contrast to the narrow pursuit of growth that "represents a horrible distortion of the common good and of underlying human values." (2009: 11).

The Stiglitz commission moves along these same lines. Its report is, first of all, addressed to political leaders. "New political narratives are necessary to identify where our societies should go." (2008: 10) The Stiglitz commission advocates a shift of emphasis from a "production-oriented" measurement system to one focused on the well-being of current and future generations, i.e. toward broader measures of social progress (Stiglitz, 2008: 10). The small island-state Vanuatu captures in an excellent way the effect of looking at things differently. According to the conventional way of measuring well-being, the gross domestic product, GDP, Vanuatu has been classified as one of the least developed countries in the world. Yet the quality of life for most people according to Anita Herle is remarkably high.[150] "Nobody is hungry and there is a food security that comes from local access to fertile gardens. There's no homelessness, everyone is cared for within extended family units. There's relatively little violence, and disputes are resolved within communities by traditional leaders." (Herle 2010)

Namibia may illustrate the reverse of this picture. There it become clear that the economic growth and "sound" macro-economic indicators that Namibia had had since independence, did not translate into sustained benefits for the majority of the population (Kameta et al. 2007: 20). This can be seen in the operations of the international company Ramatex. This company has contributed to the emergence of a large number of 'working poor' in full-time employment, unable to meet even their basic needs. This stands in sharp contradiction to the Namibian government's stated objective of promoting decent work in line with ILO standards, Kameeta et al. note (2007: 18). The hope that the private sector would become a large-

---

150 Thinking about other cultures, transcript of radio program, Radio Australia, Philosopher's zone, 11.9.2010.

scale job-creator with substantial impact on employment has not been fulfilled (Kameeta et al. 2007: 20).

Well-being assessed

The Stiglitz commission recommends that when evaluating material well-being, one should look at income and consumption rather than production (Recommendation 1). Likewise, the household perspective should be emphasised. (Recommendation 2). The commission notes that without this change of focus one may get misleading indications about how well-off people are, which might result in wrong policy decisions (2008: 12–13). The effects of foreign investment may be illustrated by Namibia and the case of Ramatex as well as a South African workfare program. Governments have not fared much better in the affluent part of the world when it comes to promoting citizens' well-being. The pattern is the same. Analysing the global crisis, social protection and jobs, Joseph Stiglitz notes (2009: 3) that the level playing field has been destroyed for years to come because of the bailouts, not only of financial institutions but also the promise that this could be the case with big companies, as signalled by the US and Western European governments. "This has changed the propensity of these companies to undertake risk, because if they undertake big risks and lose, taxpayers pick the losses up. If they win, they get the profits."(2009 : 3)

What are we left with? Stiglitz observes: "The people in the global economy have the same skills as before the crisis, and the machines and real resources are the same as before the crisis. The problem is that there is an organizational failure, a coordination failure, and a macro-economic failure." (2009: 11) Robertson has developed a model for monetary reform that would correct the failures Stiglitz refers to. A basic income is part of the equation and together they would cater for financial stability - an alternative to bailing out banks. This is how Robertson sees the new economic system and a basic income interact. Writing in 2009 Robertson notes that there is growing awareness of the need for "quantitative easing", financial jargon for getting central banks to create large sums of money and pump them into the economy. The question for today's policy-makers is how and where are they to be pumped in? "If central banks themselves were accustomed to keeping the money supply at the right level, and if arrangements already existed for the regular distribution of a Citizen's Income, the answer would be easy: vary the size of the Citizen's Income as required. This would inject the money into the economy where it would circulate quickly and would directly benefit those who most need it in economic downturns." (2009: 6)

Robertson's scheme is based on taxing the value of common resources as an alternative to present taxes on incomes, profits, value added and other financial rewards for useful work and enterprise. Public spending would in his scheme be shifted to distributing a citizen's income, as a share in the value of the common resources, "away from perverse subsidies and heavy spending on big governmental and business organisations to provide dependency-reinforcing services to welfare consumers." (2009: 2) And here the perception of work is central as a diversified view of work offers an exit from the organisational failures pointed to here.

A diversified working life – a diversified view of work

The uniform view of work that was typical for the industrial society is no longer valid. Work is today increasingly performed in some form that is a deviation of the old model of 'long-duration, full-time employment'. There is therefore an urgent need to reassess the notion of work, its compensation and regulation. In addition, there are strong economic, social, cultural and environmental reasons for a new approach to work, as highlighted above. In practice one can talk about at least two parallel working lives:

- the 'traditional' work performed in an employment relationship,

- work performed outside an employment relationship such as freelance work, artistic work, research without funding, voluntary work, developing a product or trying out a business idea.

An employment relationship forms the basis for labour legislation with associated rights and obligations at work, and also work-related social security. To its nature it is instrumental and value neutral. The second category of work can be characterised as meaningful for the one doing the work and it often reflects the new thinking that is required from changed societal circumstances, of which green work is an essential part. Yet, work performed in this sector lacks legal protection, support or proper compensation.

A welcomed reassessment of work and its regulation is the Supiot Report. On the invitation of the European Commission, a group of lawyers and economists looked at the needs for reforming labour law. The report of the committee, led by Alain Supiot, has by Marsden and Stephenson been characterized as "one of the most original contributions to thinking on the reform of the employment relationship and employment law."[151]

Meaningful work

The Stiglitz commission points to the challenges we face in perceiving the value of work particularly in activities such as medical services, educational services, information and communication technologies, research activities and financial services (Stiglitz commission, 2008: 11). The employment-based perception of work is incapable of capturing substantive aspects; value considerations do not fit the paradigm. Be work environmentally harmful or green jobs, be the products things we need or don't need, be the work something we are passionate about or something we

---

[151] Marsden, D and Stephenson H, Labour Law and Social Insurance in the New Economy: A Debate on the Supiot Report, 2001: 1.

do for our livelihood, anything goes as long as focus is placed on work performed in an employment relationship, a salary is paid and the economic transactions are registered as part of the gross domestic product, GDP. This is the dominant perception of work.

"The exchange of cash is the key", Marilyn Waring observes about how we measure GDP (2000: 53) and gives an African perspective on this phenomenon: "The transactions can be immoral and illegal and universally condemned, but no one cares. Resources are mined, skies are polluted, forests are devastated, watercourses become open sewers and drains, whole populations are relocated as valleys are flooded and dammed, and labour is exploited in chronically inhumane working conditions. The statistics record economic growth."

The Stiglitz commission's response to this state of affairs is to broaden income measures to non-market activities (Recommendation 5). Household work is not recognized in official statistics, yet it constitutes an important aspect of economic activity. The commission notes that the reason for excluding such data is not so much conceptual difficulties as uncertainty about the data. There has been progress in this arena and the commission considers that more systematic work should be undertaken. "This should start with information on how people spend their time that is comparable both over the years and across countries." (2008: 14)

What this boils down to, can hardly be better told than Waring does (2000: 53): "Consider Tendai, a young girl in the Lowveld in Zimbabwe. Her day starts at 4.00 am when, to fetch water, she carries a 30-litre tin to a borehole about 11 kilometres from her home. She walks barefoot and is home by 9.00 am. She eats a little and proceeds to fetch firewood until midday. She cleans the utensils from the family's morning meal and sits preparing a lunch of sadsa for the family. After lunch and the cleaning of the dishes, she walks in the hot sun until early evening, fetching wild vegetables for supper before making the evening trip for water. Her day ends at 9.00 pm after she's prepared supper and put her younger brothers and sisters to sleep. Tendai is considered unproductive, unoccupied and economically inactive. According to the International Economic System, Tendai does not work and is not part of the labour force." (Waring 2000: 53). In the affluent part of the world we have groups of highly educated hard-working persons who contribute greatly to a nation's both material and spiritual wealth – artists. Yet, they don't reap the profit. Artists have made the creative sector one of the fastest growing sectors of the economy.

How things are related

In their book The Spirit Level, Why Equality is better for Everyone, Wilkinson and Pickett (2010: 5) observe that we have got close to the end of an era that has lasted for thousands of years, when economic growth has meant an improvement in people's quality of life. In the rich countries economic growth has largely finished its work. "We are the first generation to have to find new answers to the question of how we can make further improvements to the real quality of human life." (2010: 11) Their answer is equality: "The powerful mechanism which makes people sensitive to inequality cannot be understood in terms either of social structure or individual psychology alone. Individual psychology and societal inequality relate to each other like lock and key. One reason why the effects of inequality have not been properly understood before is because of a failure to understand the relationship between them." (Wilkinson & Pickett 2010: 33)

The question of equality is of great relevance for those working in the intersection between employment and entrepreneurship. Many of them are discriminated against in regard to pay. As they mostly lack the support structures that a work place, labour legislation or collective agreements accord, the conditions under which they work can be quite burdensome. Insecurity is often a constant companion. A Canadian study, *Impact of Arts-Related Activities on the Perceived Quality of Life*, revealed that there was no connection between 66 different art genres and the artist's reported sense of psychological well-being. The researchers, A. C. Michalos and P. M. Kahlke, (2008) were surprised, as it is generally recognized that art contributes to people's well-being. They were probably unaware of the hardship that is often associated with artistic work. So, a basic income would be a compensation for society's lacking ability to compensate artists for their work. So much so, as artistic work is an ideal means of improving prosperity without growth.

To be renegotiated

The constant call for economic growth is a major reason for both social and economic ills, but something that is not easily questioned. "Questioning growth is deemed to be the act of lunatics, idealists and revolutionaries", Tim Jackson observes in the Foreword to his report Prosperity without growth? (2009: 7). But this myth about growth has failed us, T. Jackson notes: "It has failed the two billion people who still live on less than $2 a day. It has failed the fragile ecological systems on which we depend for survival. It has failed, spectacularly, in its own terms, to provide economic stability and secure people's livelihoods." (Foreword 2009) Therefore it needs to be questioned. T. Jackson's primary recipe is a new macroeconomics for sustainability. The presumption of growth in material consumption can no longer be the basis for economic stability. The folly of separating economy from society and environment must be substituted by ecological and social sustainability (T. Jackson 2009: 10). Structural change, Jackson observes, must lie at the heart of any strategy to address the social logic of consumerism. "It must consist in two main avenues. The first is to dismantle the perverse incentives for unproductive status competition. The second must be to establish new structures that provide capabilities for people to flourish – and in particular to participate meaningfully and creatively in the life of society – in less materialistic ways." (2009: 11)

The effects of economic security

A number of preconceived ideas had to be done away with when a cash transfer system was tried out in South Africa. One of them was the generally held view in conventional economic theory that a basic income might "undermine labour force participation by reducing the opportunity costs of not working". When empirically tested against the cash transfer systems in South Africa the researchers found that:

- Social grants provide potential labour market participants with the resources and economic security necessary to invest in high-risk/high- reward job search.
- Living in a household receiving grants is correlated with a higher success rate in finding employment.
- Workers in households receiving social grants are better able to improve their productivity and as a result earn higher wages (Samson et al., 2004 in Kameeta et al., 2007: 22).

In regard to the Namibian model for a basic income "The Basic Income Grant", BIG, Kameeta et al. maintain that it is more than an income support programme. "It provides security that reinforces human dignity and empowerment. It has the capacity to be the most significant poverty-reducing programme in Namibia, while supporting household development, economic growth and job creation. The cost is ranging from 2.2% to 3.8% of national income." Over time, Namibia's economy will benefit from the long-term growth impact of the Basic Income Grant (Kameeta et al. 2007: 23). This report was presented in 2007, thus before they tried out a Basic Income Grant in 2008, with the unambiguously positive results we have seen above.

Post script: Many basic income pilot projects have been conducted and there are also on-going ones that will not be accounted here. A glimpse of a Canadian pilot project will be given at the end of this chapter from Evelyn Forget's visit to Finland in 2014.

A good source for following the basic income global scene is the Basic Income Earth Network's Bien News https://basicincome.org/news/.

Basic income – a way of promoting prosperity

The prosperity T. Jackson is in search of is a less materialistic society that will enhance life satisfaction. It is a more equal society that will lower the importance of status goods. It is a less growth-driven economy that will improve people's work-life balance. Enhanced investment in public goods will provide lasting returns to the nation's prosperity (T. Jackson, 2009: 11). A basic income would give people the opportunity to opt out of activities that burden the environment, in which they are engaged solely for the sake of their livelihood. Those who are involved in ownwork, again, do to a great extent contribute to social prosperity through culture, caring functions and other voluntary work rather than environmentally harmful activities. A lot of human energy goes into work in the intersection between employment and entrepreneurship that might or might not be business one day. Whether one is successful or not, should not be an issue as great leaps in development often originate in somebody's failure or mistake. It is work 'outside the structures' rather than employment that drives development. It is here that much green jobs see the light. The one size fits all view of work as employment and economic profit needs to be substituted with a 'both and' approach. Old and new work formats should be seen as complementary.

The notion of meaningful work cuts across formal divisions of work categories such as private and public employment. This is important because outsourcing has blurred the borderline between public and private. Making meaning a part of the equation will give leeway for work in civil society as complementary to work for profit, allowing them to be pursued parallel without internal competition. Or as Robertson says: "We will do what we see to be our own good, useful and rewarding work — for ourselves, other people and society as a whole" (Robertson, 2006: ii). This will bring changes to national economies in the kinds of work people do, the ways they work, and the way society organises work (Robertson, 2006: iii).

Making people part of the equation

As noted above, the Stiglitz commission advocates a shift of emphasis from a "production-oriented" measurement to one focused on the well-being of current and future generations, i.e. toward broader measures of social progress (Stiglitz, 2009:10). Here Wilkinson and Pickett's book The Spirit Level Why Equality is better for Everyone, fills a void. They see that the extraordinarily positive reception their book has received is a sign that there is a "widespread appetite for change and a desire to find positive solutions to our problems." They point to the social failings that has led to pessimism, and on top of that, the economic recession and its aftermath of high unemployment. "But the knowledge that we cannot carry on as we have, that change is necessary, is perhaps grounds for optimism: maybe we do, at last, have the chance to make a better world." (Wilkinson & Pickett, 2010: xi)

In their book Wilkinson and Pickett show that "the quality of social relations in a society is built on material foundations. The scale of income differences has a powerful effect on how we relate to each other. Rather than blaming parents, religion, values, education or the penal system, we will show that the scale of inequality provides a powerful policy lever on the psychological wellbeing of all of us." (2010: 5)

What next?

The Stiglitz commission regards its report as opening a discussion rather than closing it. The report points to issues that ought to be addressed, such as societal values, what we, as a society, care about, and whether we are really striving for what is important. At the moment of writing (28.10.2011) 795,486 persons around the globe have signed Avaaz' petition The World vs. Wall Street in support of the thousands of Americans who have non-violently occupied Wall Street – "an epicentre of global financial power and corruption". The occupants call for real democracy, social justice and anti-corruption.[152] This adds a 'western' dimension to the Arab spring where ordinary citizens began claiming their right against oppressive or undemocratic regimes starting in Tunisia, followed by Egypt, Libya, Yemen, Syria, Morocco. In the Avaaz posting on the internet on 5 October 2011 launching the Wall Street petition, they note that 2011 could be our century's 1968.

In the 1980s Anna Christensen pointed to the failures raised in this paper, in the form of tensions inherent in the wage-labour society. Writing in the context of future studies, she notes that changes have to emerge from the cracks and paradoxes inherent in a society built on wage labour. This change will come about among groups that refuse to adapt themselves to the value order of society, among women, part-time workers, among young people outside the wage labour system that refuse to be miserable and to accept the oppression and humiliation of 'employment enhancing measures'. What the new order will look like, nobody knows, it can only grow through practice, Christensen asserts (1983: 23). And here

[152] http://www.avaaz.org/en/the_world_vs_wall_st

we have a parallel with the project economy and the control embedded in it. The message of my contribution is to allow things to grow without external interference. The central question therefore is to give space for a sound development of today's potentials. A basic income would allow for this. And the Arab spring, as well as the Occupy movement, show that people want change - social justice.

Video

Evelyn Forget presents the Canadian basic income pilote project in the Finnish Parliament in 2014[153]

[153] https://www.youtube.com/watch?v=_bKiRee--ds&t=8s

CHAPTER 13

BASIC INCOME AND THE VALUE OF WORK

2012 - Basic Income Earth Network (BIEN) Congress, Munich, Germany[154]

"[T]he introduction of the GBI (Guaranteed Basic Income) will be a historical milestone of the first importance. By officially disconnecting subsistence from paid employment it will mark the transition to the post-employment age, as surely as the repeal of the Corn Laws in 1846 marked the transition from an agricultural to an industrial society." With this observation James Robertson hits the core of today's challenges in his book Future Work: Jobs, self-employment and leisure after the industrial age. A basic income is central for the adjustments that need to be made to restore a balance in the transitory stage in which we are now. Robertson notes that a basic income "will start reversing the process that began several hundred years ago, when the common people were deprived of access to land and the wherewithal to provide their own subsistence, and so became dependent on paid labour." (Robertson 1986 / 2006: 173)

---

[154] 14-16 September 2012 Pathways to a Basic Income. HOW: The Big Picture – Social and Political Dimensions. This paper rounds up earlier research where I have mapped out changes in working life and contemplated remedies, among which a basic income is crucial.

154

New jigsaw puzzle pieces needed

Hardly any piece of the jigsaw puzzle that the industrial society was made of fits today's reality. New bits and pieces need to be gathered to display the bigger picture of today's information and communication society - its challenges as well as the opportunities it offers. A basic income should be part of this new picture as it could play a pivotal role in unleashing knots in present day perceptions, structures and practices. In short a basic income could

- counterbalance injustices and undo knots in institutional structures that have passed their best before date;
- reduce the price people have had to pay for reckless behaviour in the financial and business world;
- favour entrepreneurial activities that are more focussed on people's needs than big business does;
- favour artistic work, contributing thereby to a greatly expanding sector that do people good and does not burden mother earth;
- reduce our ecological footprints;
- generate a virtuous circle with spin off effects for people as well as local and national economies.

By now, we do not lack information about the changes that have occurred during the past decades. Neither do we lack visions or ideas, but as Mark Newton puts it "the only problem with ... ideas is that it needs people to implement them for it to become more than just a dream". This he says when commenting on Jeremy Rifkin's book *The Third Industrial Revolution.*[155]

---

[155] https://theecologist.org/2012/feb/02/third-industrial-revolution-how-lateral-power-transforming-energy-economy-and-world

Changing mindsets

The bits and pieces of the jigsaw puzzle that make up today's reality form new constellations and we need to be attentive to how they interact. To assist in this, I will here call to mind the ideas of some researchers who have been forerunners in pointing out social change and its directions, of which practical conclusions should be drawn. Jeremy Rifkin was one of the forerunners when he in 1995 drew our attention to the changing role of work in his book The End of Work. He notes that jobs are disappearing, never to come back. Blue collar workers and clerical workers, among many others, are destined for virtual extinction. The new jobs that will be created are, for the most part, low paid and generally temporary. Rifkin foresaw a fast polarization into two potentially irreconcilable forces: partly an information elite that controls and manages the high-tech global economy; and on the other side, a growing number of permanently displaced workers with few prospects and little hope for meaningful employment in an increasingly automated world. By 1995, more than 15 per cent of the American population were living below the poverty line.

Also Richard Florida points to this development in his book *The Creative Class*. He warns of a social divide because of the detrimental effects the decline in industry has had on a large part of the population. He assigns the Creative Class three fundamental tasks:

- to invest in creativity to ensure long-run economic growth;
- to overcome the class-divide that weakens our social fabric and threatens economic well-being, as well as;
- to build new forms of social cohesion in a world defined by increasing diversity and beset by growing fragmentation.

Florida considers that we can meet these challenges only by ensuring that the creativity of the many is tapped and that the benefits of the creative age are extended to everyone (Florida 2002: 318). This gives the members of the creative class an economic interest as well as a moral obligation to ensure that all are integrated into the creative economy. The motive of human dignity is thereby aligned with economic motives (Florida 2002: 321).

Rifkin has taken an increasingly global perspective on the changes facing us, from how it affects working life to its effects on societies and the environment as well as its impact on us as humans. He points to how the global environmental crisis is forcing a profound shift in human consciousness. We have a historic transition from the geopolitics of the 20th century to the biosphere politics of the 21st century. "For the first time in the long history of our species, we are beginning to think as a human race, with responsibilities to each other, future generations, our fellow creatures, and the planet we jointly inhabit." Rifkin points out that renewable energy and Internet-like technology can create an entirely new blueprint for the world economy. (*The Global Environmental Crisis, The Path to Sustainable Development* and *The Third Industrial Revolution: How Lateral Power is Transforming Energy, the Economy, and the World*).[156]

The broader human mobilisation that Rifkin points to has been going on for some time. Manuel Castells drew our attention to this in his analysis of the changes that have led to the Network Society (1996). He observes that identity has become a primary organising principle. Identity is for Castells the process through which a social player primarily perceives oneself and how meaning is formed out of given cultural attributes (Castells 1999: 35,). Richard Florida was on to something similar when working on his book *The Creative Class* (2002). He became convinced that the truly fundamental changes of our time had to do with subtle alterations in the way we live and work. He sees the emerging creative economy as a

156 http://www.theecologist.org/reviews/books/1222135/the_third_industrial_revolution_how_lateral_power_is_transforming_energy_the_economy_and_the_world.htmlhttp://www.foet.org/books/end-work.html)http://www.foet.org/lectures/lecture-global-environmental-crisis.htm

dynamic and turbulent system - exciting and liberating in some ways, divisive and stressful in others." (Florida 2002: x-xi) Florida's conclusion is that "[a] new social class, in short, has risen to a position of dominance in the last two decades, and this shift has fundamentally transformed our economy and society - and continues to do so." (Florida 2002: 82)

All in all, we are faced with a profound paradigmatic shift that requires participation on a large scale if we want to seize the potentials today's conditions offer. As always, in a transition we face a number of challenges. Calderon and Lasegna have caught the present ones in a nutshell when asking how we, in a world simultaneously characterised by globalisation and fragmentation should combine new technology and collective memory, universal knowledge and a culture of community, passion and reason (cited by Castells1999: 35). These are central ingredients when we seek new venues for our lives, to adapt to changing circumstances.

A new approach to work

The good news is that there is today abundant space for activities involving identity, creativity and community. This is because industrial work is no longer available on a large scale. And what is equally important, the creative sector has substituted industry as a driving force in the economy. This is a scenario full of potentials. The ecological footprint of art and culture is vastly smaller than that of industry. Ecology is therefore another strong argument for supporting the cultural sector, in addition to the role it plays for our well-being and identity. It is also to this sector we should look when striving for de-growth, as we here can combine activities that do people good with a minimal ecological footprint. Another important arena is civil society, where identity and community are central ingredients. In addition, activities in civil society are often sparing and caring of nature. So, instead of clinging to the chimera of the old industrial rationale, where people are often submitted to command and control, we should give recognition to activities that are already there, as well as facilitate activities that people are striving to do. Such activities are often done as unpaid work that should be compensated through a basic income. Unpaid work is a fundament both for society and the formal economy, locally as well as globally. It represents largely half of all economic activity. The value of this 'hidden half' is estimated to be roughly equal to the world gross domestic product of the formal economy.[174]

According to German statistics from 2001 unpaid work accounted for a good bit more than half the economic activities, 96 billion € as compared to paid employment 56 billion. If unpaid work were properly valued and facilitated through a basic income, financial equations would greatly differ from present-day economic measurements. An illustration: According to its gross domestic product, GDP, Vanuatu is one of the least developed countries in the world. Yet the quality of life for most people is remarkably high. Vanuatu scored among the best in 2006, when the Happy Planet Index was used for the first time. This index is the first to combine environmental efficiency with well-being, that is, how long and happy lives people live. The Happy Planet Index has been developed by the New Economics Foundation, nef.[157]

The bad news, if it is any news, is that we are stuck with old perceptions that act as a drag on desired change. There is therefore an urgent need to reconsider the notion of work and its value. The Joseph Stiglitz Commission (2008) on the measurement of economic performance and social progress made some constructive recommendations in this regard:
- look at income and consumption rather than production;
- take a household perspective, and;
- look at how people spend their time working. This is comparable both over the years and across countries. Stiglitz considers that the commission's report and its implementation may have a significant impact on the

[157] http://www.neweconomics.org/projects/happy-planet-index

way in which our societies look at themselves and, therefore, on the way in which policies are designed, implemented and assessed (Stiglitz 2008: 9).

A welcomed reassessment of work and its regulation has also been made in the Supiot Report around the turn of the millennium. On the invitation of the EU Commission, a group of lawyers and economists led by Alain Supiot looked at the needs for reforming labour law. Their report has by Marsden and Stephenson been characterised as "one of the most original contributions to thinking on the reform of the employment relationship and employment law." (Marsden & Stephenson 2001: 1)

Three fundamental observations are made in the Supiot report:
- the employment relationship in its existing form has reached its limits as many firms need more flexible relationships with their employees than it can currently provide;
- tinkering at the edges with special types of employment contract for different categories of workers has diluted protection without increasing new jobs; and
- reform of the employment relationship poses severe problems for labour law, collective bargaining and social insurance, because they have all based themselves on the standard employment relationship. (Marsden & Stephenson 2001: 3)

There is a promise of something new in the experts' observations. The fundamental redesign of employment that Supiot and his colleagues proposed included the idea of an equivalent to citizenship rights in the field of work. A person would have an 'occupational status' that establishes a citizen's right involving access to markets and trade. It would also cover the transition between different kinds of activity, market and non-market work, training, re-training, and so on. The right to an income and other advantages would also apply in regard to socially recognised non-market activities. By making workers' employment rights less dependent on their current jobs, such changes would spread the risks of short term and uncertain employment more widely, encouraging thereby different kinds of activities (Marsden, Stephenson 2001: 6). Unfortunately, politicians have not yet been ready to act on these proposals (see Supiot 2009). Nevertheless, the report is a step in the right direction and hopefully its proposals could pave the way for a basic income.

And now finally back to James Robertson who already in 1985 drew attention to the changed nature of work in his book *Future work*. He there points to how work has become individualised and he coined the term ownwork, which he sees as the future mode of work (1985 / 2006). He then questioned the idea of full employment, a concern that he reiterates, now with focus on money in his book *Future Money, Breakdown or Breakthrough?* (2012). "Does it make sense to manage the money system to drive as many of us as possible into paid jobs working for other people and organisations richer and more powerful than ourselves? Might it not make better sense if the money system were managed to allow and enable more of us who wish to work, paid or unpaid, for ourselves and one another, on useful and valuable 'ownwork', to do so?" (Robertson 2012: 88). He illustrates this view with the opinion expressed by James Lovelock who, with his "Gaia" theory, is a central thinker for the environmental movement. "There are very few scientists who have the chances I've had of working entirely independently, and not being constrained by the need to do work that will bring my next grant in. I would never have been allowed to develop Gaia at a university or a government department or an industrial one. You could only do it alone." (Financial Times, 27 April 2007)

Robertson himself shares this experience, as he was able to change to a more independent way of work in the 1970s. "[I]t heightened my awareness of how much a society loses, when greater numbers of experienced and open-minded people do not see similar changes as possible for them."

(Robertson 2012: 15) We are here faced with one of the greatest challenges of our time. Because of the narrow and instrumental focus on work as an employment, many highly qualified persons are either unemployed or the work they are doing is invisible because it is not done in the form of employment. This is a typical scenario for artistic work and also for unfunded research. It is equally true for work in civil society and households. This is the kind of work that the Stiglitz commission, along with many others, want to have included in the measurement of how we fare (GDP). So instead of the idea that as many people as possible should be encouraged, and if necessary compelled, to work for others, Robertson's alternative is a basic income that would make people's independence a reality. A basic income would enable them to decide how more of their rightful share in the value of common resources should be spent (Robertson 2012: 23).

Rifkin, for his part, considers that redefining the role of the individual in a near workerless society is likely to be the most pressing issue in the decades to come. He suggests that we should move beyond the delusion of retraining for non-existent jobs and urges us to begin to ponder the unthinkable; to prepare ourselves and our institutions for a world that is phasing out mass employment in the production and marketing of goods and services.[158] To recognise work that is factually done is a first step. Since some time back unpaid work is being quantified through different kinds of time accounts.[159] This data may offer valuable counter-arguments to the commonly held view that people would not work if they received money for free. According to a German survey, on the question whether you yourself would continue working if you receive a basic income 60 per cent said yes, 30 per cent yes but, whereas 10 per cent said they would

---

[158] http://www.foet.org/books/end-work.html

[159] See for example http://www.levyinstitute.org/undp-levy-conference/ *Unpaid Work and the Economy: Gender, Poverty, and the Millennium Development Goals* Annandale-on-Hudson, NYOctober 1-3, 2005 Bureau for Development Policy, UNDP in partnership with The Levy Economics Institute of Bard College

sleep out. On the question whether they thought that others would continue working 80 per cent considered that they would not!

From the assembly line to design

During the past three decades or so there has been a sea change in the way we work and gain our living. Since the flexibilisation of labour legislation set in, in the 1970s and 1980s working life has undergone profound transformations. It is a very diversified picture, out of which I will here recollect some general trends. In advanced economies the main features have been the dismantling of industrial work, along with a diversification of work formats in part kindled by new technology and in part by an explosion in the creative sector. Income-wise there has been a widening gap between high- and low-income earners, resulting in a growing number of working poor. Another distinct feature is that there is no longer a promise that a high educational level will lead to a job and high income. This represents a new rationale in working life that requires a change of perception regarding work. The instrumental way of viewing work as employment needs to be diversified to bring forth also human, social and environmental attributes to work on a par with economic ones.

Along with this, the traditional attributes of work, supervision and subordination need to be questioned. Furthermore, a diversified approach to work reveals that a simple call for increasing employment as an economic cure is no longer a sound alternative. Instead, we should explore the potentials of a basic income that would facilitate activities of a human, social and ecological nature. A basic income would in different ways compensate for the growing economic inequalities caused by changes in working life. At the same time, it would offer flexibility to working people on a par with employers' call for it. A basic income would offer autonomy instead of the control and constraints inherent in the structures that were tailored for the industrial society.

Tour d'horizon

According to German (DGB) Statistics from 2005, 12 per cent of Germans perceived their work as good, 54 per cent of them were indifferent about their work (Mittelmässig), whereas 34 per cent considered their work to be bad. Not a very flattering picture of how work is perceived. And do we need all the work we're doing? In Rifkin's analysis from 1995 of how working life will develop, he estimated that in 2050 perhaps merely some 5 per cent of the adult population would be needed to manage traditional industrial work. In contrast, Florida reports in 2002 in his book The Creative Class that more than 30 per cent of the American working population worked in occupations that involve creativity. Florida tells us that the Creative Class "has shaped and will continue to shape deep and profound shifts in the ways we work, in our values and desires, and in the very fabric of our everyday lives." (Florida, 2002: ix)

By 2006 the European cultural sector had been mapped out through a comprehensive study, *The Economy of Culture in Europe*, which showed that the creative sector exceeded most other sectors in economic growth, added value and human input (Study prepared for the European Commission 2006 by KEA European Affairs) This transition from an industry-dominated working life to one that reflects features of the information and communication society requires new regulative approaches to work that are still wanting. And it is here that a basic income would have a compensatory and corrective function to the changes that have occurred, of which here some illustrations.

Flexibilisation: Two studies made by the International Labour Organisation, ILO, on part-time work, 1993, and homework, 1995, revealed that while both employers and the national economy had profited from flexibilisation in the form of homework and part-time work, it was an exception rather than a rule that those working in these work formats would have profited. Here we see a major venue toward a growing number of working poor. For a long time, deviations from the 'standard' of fulltime work of unlimited duration was simply labelled 'atypical', despite the increasing reliance on it. Not only is it a contradiction in terms to talk about atypical in such a situation, involved are also deteriorating labour standards that may be ignored because of the convenient label 'atypical' (see Storlund 2002: 165–174). Thanks to the Precariat movement greater attention has become directed to the lowering labour standards involved.

Project work

Parallel with the waning of industrial work, project work made headway. What had earlier been a work format typical for the academic world did now become a panacea not only for employment enhancing measures to compensate for disappearing industrial jobs, but for many other purposes as well. Projects were a convenient way of releasing blocked energies in outmoded institutions, particularly in the public sector. For the fast expanding creative sector project work became something of an ordinary form of work. Project work has much potential if administered properly. But here an opportunity has largely been lost. The potential of paving ways for new forms of work and income has been frustrated by a formidable apparatus of selection and control associated with project work, not least by EU-funded projects. Along with project work also predictability has been lost.

The waning of industrial work coupled by an explosion in creative work gave rise to quite a bewildered picture. New venues for work were needed but of what kind? Innovation became the catchword. There were many projects geared toward finding new jobs and it is from this setting that James Robertson developed his idea of 'ownwork' as the future mode of work. Good examples became another catchword. But here it appears that policy makers and project administrators became hostages of their own aspirations. If innovation is what you look for, how can you make use of experiences gained even if they work well?! Another basic problem is the limited duration of a project. A basic income would do away with all the frustrating aspects of the project economy, starting with the selection process. It would allow for the use of good examples when they are seen as important and activities could go on for as long as they are meaningful.

Robertson points out that in the age of ownwork it will be accepted as normal that most people will work independently for themselves and one another. Institutions will enable them to do so instead of depending on employers for jobs. Such a scenario would do away with public spending on perverse subsidies as well as some of the dependency-reinforcing services now provided directly by big government. Also, expensive contracts to big business and big finance could be dispensed of. Instead that money would be transferred to the distribution of a citizen's income directly to all citizens (Robertson 2012: 23).

The changes in the way work is done and perceived requires an alternative approach to the employment-centred one. Reinhold Fahlbeck proposes value as a determining criterion. He considers "value provider - value receiver" to be more appropriate terms. Those who work provide / create / give / sell new and additional values, whereas their opposite party receives /buys / takes these newly created values. Fahlbeck (2000: 328). Fahlbeck observes that in ICT society knowledge is the commodity that is primarily held by the many and knowledge is never completely standardised. So even independently of personal preferences and choices, the structure of the ICT society in itself represents decentralisation and flexibilisation (Fahlbeck 2000: 333–334).

Roberson may close this *tour d'horison* of changes in the world of work. "The real problem is the false perception of the realities of work and incomes in the late industrial society as it has developed over the last 40 years.... The out-of-date prescription that the normal way for most people to get an income is to earn it in a job." So, in other words, Robertson asserts " it is time to introduce an unconditional Guaranteed Basic Income

(GBI) under which all citizens, rich and poor, men and women, old and young, will automatically receive a weekly basic income from the state." (Robertson, 1985 / 2006: 166)

Drags on change

What is at stake is both the need for a change of perception and the willingness to make changes. One or both of these lacking and we are stuck with business as usual. As noted, we do not lack information about changes that have occurred and the new possibilities they offer. The problem is drags on change, to use Fernand Braudel's pertinent expression in his book The Wheels of Commerce (Braudel,1982: 461). One contemporary illustration of this is that it took almost 20 years for the European Union to arrive at a major regulation of atypical work. Since 1982, the Commission had put forward nine drafts, before a directive was adopted in 1991, extending existing health and safety regulations to temporary workers. Not until 1997 was there a first major breakthrough in the form of a directive concerning the regulation of part-time work (see Storlund 2002: 168).

The way the EU failed to act on the Supiot report that would have adapted the regulation of working life to changed circumstances is a good illustration of this drag on change. In his book *The Future of Money*, Robertson proposes a comprehensive set of reforms in the economic field that would help to avoid a forthcoming catastrophe. "But", he notes "because established financial and economic thinking is so limited and out of date, most practising professional and academic experts in economics, finance and banking may dismiss the book's proposals as outside the boundaries of their concern." This also concerns the politicians and government officials responsible for managing the money system. And not only them. "Even those few who see the need for the proposed reforms will find it impossible to put them into practice without strong support and pressure from outsiders, including active citizens and NGOs." (Robertson, 2012: 12.) In other words, we are all part of this exercise.

How to go about it?

Robertson's message with his book Future Money, Breakdown or Breakthrough? is that we need a Copernican revolution in human understanding of how the money system works and how it ought to work. He considers this revolution to be more and more urgently overdue. Robinson notes that this revolution will not only be intellectual and scientific. It will also be a revolution in practice (Robertson, 2012: 11). This is an interesting aspect of the ways the thinkers looked at here, look at our time. They directly refer to the degree of engagement of all of us. So, the question is, what role will human interests and concerns play in this new setting where people are the organising factor? Will it be possible, through this change of focus, to ensure an autonomous sphere for ordinary people thwarting thereby the dominance of the economy? This is how Rifkin looks at today's challenges: Old industrial giants such as General Motors, Sears, USX, Boeing, and Texaco, are giving way to the new giants of cultural capitalism, Viacom, AOL Time Warner, Disney, Sony, and News Corporation. These transnational companies, with communications networks spanning the globe, are mining cultural resources in every part of the world, repacking them in the form of commodities and entertainments. The top one-fifth of the world's population now spends as much money accessing cultural experiences as buying manufactured goods and basic services.[160]

Rifkin warns that when culture itself is absorbed into the economy, only commercial bonds will be left to hold society together. In his book *The Age of Access* he poses the central question whether civilisation can

---

160 http://www.foet.org/books/end-work.html

survive when only the commercial sphere remains as the primary arbiter of human life. Will there be any time left for relationships of a non-commercial nature? Here a basic income comes into the picture as an important countervailing power. A basic income would create a reserved sphere that would secure the autonomy of persons as a barrier against the commercial sphere. An intriguing part of this scenario is that we might not be aware of how these changed circumstances impact on all of us. Florida noted on this score: "it struck me that the members of the Creative Class do not see themselves as a class - a coherent group of people with common traits and concerns." According to Florida we find ourselves in the puzzling situation of having the dominant class virtually unaware of its own existence and thus unable to consciously influence the course of the society it largely leads. (2002: xi). It is time for the creative class to grow up and take responsibility (2002: xii).

Critical mass

Both Rifkin and Robertson emphasise civil society as an important motor for change, "I still see this shift of emphasis towards local and personal co-operative self-reliance as a vitally necessary response to the future that human societies now face", Robertson says, but he notes that in today's global village there are obviously crucial matters to be dealt with at national and international levels as well. But how will the people running those big systems let go of the power they have over us now? "It is wishing for the moon to hope that they will voluntarily get off our backs without being encouraged or compelled to do so. Smooth and peaceful liberation will only be achieved when it is matched by deliberate, planned giving up of power – decolonisation." (Robertson 2012: 16)

But on the other hand we have the developing capacity of the internet to provide people-to-people instantaneous mass communication. This may speed up the pre-political process that Robertson calls for. And we have, indeed, seen impressive popular responses in the past two years through social media and above all through Avaaz. Avaaz, which means "voice" in several European, Middle Eastern and Asian languages, is a great illustration of today's potentials of grassroots mobilisation. It is a movement that was launched in 2007 with the democratic mission "to organize citizens of all nations to close the gap between the world we have and the world most people everywhere want". With a small core team and thousands of volunteers the Avaaz community campaigns in 15 languages on six continents backed up by more than 15 million members. They take action such as signing petitions, funding media campaigns and direct actions, emailing, calling and lobbying governments, and organizing "offline" protests and events, to ensure that the views and values of the world's people inform the decisions that affect us all. Of this we have got encouraging experience with the Arab spring, the Occupy movement and many more campaigns.[161]

Avaaz' mission is to empower people from all walks of life to take action on pressing global, regional and national issues, from corruption and poverty to conflict and climate change. Their model of internet organising allows thousands of individual efforts, however small, to be rapidly combined into a powerful collective force. In *The Third Industrial Revolution* Rifkin also emphasises bottom-up, collaborative effort rather than large political structures. Top-down structures can easily be targeted by corporate lobbyists aiming to prevent change. The challenge thus is to get past industry lobbyists who are concerned with further entrenching the status quo. If Rifkin's opus can do this, it could genuinely have the power to change the world for the better, Newton says.[180]

Rifkin has been an advisor to the European Union since 2002. In that capacity, he is the principle architect of the Third Industrial Revolution

[161] See Highlights page at http://www.avaaz.org/en/)

long-term economic sustainability plan that addresses the triple challenge of the global economic crisis, energy security, and climate change. The Third Industrial Revolution was formally endorsed by the European Parliament in 2007 and is now being implemented by various agencies within the European Commission as well as in the 27 member-states.181 There is thus no lack of civic involvement. What is required is enough enlightenment among people in power positions to take people's voice seriously and to promote the liberating potentials of information and communication technology. Along with this we need to identify and remove obstacles as well as devise structures and practices that will facilitate creative environmentally friendly activities throughout society. A basic income is ideal for this task.

CHAPTER 14

HUMAN RIGHTS UPDATE –FROM SOVEREIGNTY TO COEXISTENCE

2015 - in Pax[162]

Abstract

Peace and human rights are intimately associated. "If human rights are to be taken seriously ... the international control of the way states carry out their duties of protection and promotion in this field will become the big problem..." So Salvo Andò notes in an article The welfare state as a legal obligation (1999). This requires a change of perception and changed practices at many levels that will be mapped out here in a tour d'horizon from colonial times to contemporary deliberations of how to promote a culture of peace. A number of western-centred notions need to be updated that now stand in the way of making the new human rights culture an international reality and a promoter of peace.

The challenge

If we take the human rights culture seriously, we must start by recognizing the kind of challenges we face. Here UNDP's status report about the Millennium Development Goals in 2003: More than a billion people still struggle to survive on less than a dollar a day. Most of them also lack access to basic health services and safe drinking water. Globally, one child

---

162 Hartama-Heinonen, Ritva & Kukkonen, Pirjo (eds), AHTActa translatologica Helsingiensia, Vol. 3

out of five does not complete primary school. More than 14 million children lost one or both parents to HIV/AIDS in 2001. Nearly 800 million people, or 15 per cent of the world's population, suffer from chronic hunger. Half a million women die in pregnancy or childbirth each year. The Human Development Report (2003) contends that these negative trends can be reversed through political will in the developing world and new financial commitments and trade policies in the wealthiest nations.

If we look at hunger, Paul Streeten (1997) observes that hunger and malnutrition are not due to global shortages of food. It has been estimated that 2 per cent of the world's grain output would be sufficient to eliminate hunger and malnutrition among the world's under- and malnourished. Streeten (1997: 154–155) notes that because hunger today is unnecessary, this makes its continued existence so shocking. There are many reasons for this state of affairs. Among them, Streeten points to the reduced role of governments in grain markets and trade liberalisation, signalling the end of an era when governments controlled large grain surpluses. As a consequence, future food emergencies in developing countries will lead to substantial increases in grain prices (Streeten 1997: 155). This is one of many fundamental problems facing humankind that need to be approached in new ways, testing our commitment to the human rights culture.

In 2013, the Human Development Report identifies policies rooted in the new global reality that could promote greater progress. A far better representation of the South in global governance systems is called for, and new sources of financing public goods are pointed to. Also, specific drivers of development transformation are brought to the fore that could make a significant contribution to development thinking.

Sovereignty under the magnifier

Salvo Andò (1999) notes that it is clear that the theory of national sovereignty is an inadequate test of the legitimacy of international behaviour when the interests at stake (as in the situations referred to above) transcend national boundaries and are not territorially confined. Indeed, the political categories which found expression in the concept of sovereignty have themselves been superseded by modernist transformations which have simultaneously altered both the fundamental definition of a human person, as well as the nature of potential threats to fundamental human freedoms (Andò 1999: 59).

The traditional view of sovereignty stressed the rights of those who governed, whose interest lay in affirming their *jus imperii*. The governed were primarily considered as the subjects to whom obligations were attributed, obedience to the law being one such central obligation (Andò 1999: 63). Old perceptions of sovereignty, and the administrative practices through which sovereignty was sustained, are perhaps more easily perceived if we look at former colonies (although I maintain that they survive all around us, in all countries, in many shapes and forms). I shall use the example of Malta to illustrate this. As a colony, Malta was a 'special case' in the sense that it was the Maltese themselves who invited British rule in order to obtain protection against Napoleon. But this was not considered a ground for granting the Maltese any special rights and privileges in the early 19th century.[163]

The process, through which Malta became a British colony, was an outdrawn one involving Napoleon's seizure of the Maltese islands from the Order of the Knights of St. John. Contempt for the way the French ruled caused the Maltese to revolt, and it was in order to bring this revolt to a

---

[163] For an account of the process through which Malta became a British colony, see Joseph Attard, *Britain and Malta. The Story of an Era.* 1988: 1–25.

successful end that they invited Britain. Ironically enough the British had encouraged the development of a system of self-government, a popular council, the Consiglio Popolare, in 1802, when it still seemed that the Maltese islands would be back under the rule of the Order of St. John. When eventually Britain became the formal colonial master, such democratic aspirations were put in suspense (Attard 1988: 25). And whatever degree of Maltese influence there would be in the subsequent succession of constitutions,[164] the mother country reserved the power of disallowance to the Crown and the power of veto to the Governor (Cremona [1994] 1997: 7). The 1849 Constitution may illustrate this. A Council of Government of 18 members was introduced with Maltese representation. The Council had the power of making laws for the peace, order and good government of the Island, provided such laws were not repugnant to the law of England (Cremona [1994] 1997: 7–8).

A central feature of the colonial system was that the backbone of government was bureaucracy, not politics. And this applied equally to the metropolis and the colonies. Thus politics played a minimal role in colonial affairs.[165] This has had repercussions at two levels, at least, as D.K. Fieldhouse observes. There was a clash of cultures that was most clearly seen in tropical areas, where a European culture was superimposed on a very different social organisation. The populations did not have any tradition of a western style parliamentary government and few conceived of public administration, as the west understood it. Anything resembling democracy was therefore out of the question until and unless a colony had undergone basic restructuring (Fieldhouse 1981: 25). In this respect, the Maltese situation differed. The Maltese certainly had had experience of western bureaucracies, having been ruled by the Order of the Knights of

[164] J.J. Cremona [1994] 1997: 2. During the British rule constitutions followed each other in rapid succession: 1813, 1835, 1849, 1903, 1921, 1936, 1939, 1947, 1959 and 1961.

[165] Fieldhouse, Colonialism 1870–1945. An Introduction, 1981: 26.

St. John for almost 270 years, with grandmasters representing distinguished aristocracies from different European countries.

Role models

The conceptual shift that has occurred in constitutional history from jus imperii to democratic rule calls for changed attitudes not only to sovereignty, as an attribute of a governing power, but also toward those who have given government its mandate, the people. Here it is important to be aware of the way old role models may still exercise an influence. What role models were the Maltese exposed to by all the external powers that had ruled the Maltese islands? The social history of Malta could be read as one such long narrative. But to cut a long story short, this is how the first British Civil Commissioner of Malta, Sir Thomas Maitland is pictured. 'King Tom', as Maitland came to be called, was a dour but benevolent autocrat. His was a one-man rule; indeed he could take anything but opposition. His system was aptly described as driving and kicking mankind onto obedience; but he was a capable statesman and administrator and was able to effect many important and beneficial changes in both the administrative and the judicial systems of the Island. Thus J.J. Cremona ([1994] 1997: 2) describes how British rule in Malta was opened, as a complete autocracy. This caused much resentment among the Maltese. They pressed for a representative Council, relying on their ancient rights and privileges, on their Consiglio Popolare and on a Declaration of Rights of the Inhabitants of the Islands of Malta and Gozo that the leaders of the people had drawn up in 1802. Further they drew on the voluntary association of Malta with Britain (Cremona [1994] 1997: 3). But their arguments were of no avail.

Another example of how imperial powers treated the populations they dominated is the view of censorship prevailing during colonial times. The Maltese were told that censorship was exercised by the Government in pursuance of a *jus gentium* or a rule of law common to European nations (Cremona [1994] 1997: 5). Malta's association with Britain has by Joseph Attard (1988) been described as "wrought with trials and triumphs, hardship and benevolence, anguish and heroism." This period was characterised by continuous efforts by the Maltese to extricate themselves from their longstanding domination by external powers and a feudal form of government (1988: vii). A remark made by Samuel Taylor Coleridge of the Maltese colonial scene, that he experienced first hand, may sum up the experience of many a colony. "[W]hat wonder, if the opinion becomes general, that alike to England as to France, the fates and fortunes of other nations are but the counters, with which the bloody game of war is played".[166]

The rule of law in social welfare and its roots

Many literary works, such as Victor Hugo's Les miserables could be read as a text-book on the rule of law in operation. This social epos illustrates the use of public power in an oppressive way, resulting in force and a deprivation of human dignity. The narrative displays a formalistic view of authority that leaves no room for proportionality or fairness. Peter Englund (1991) illuminates this phenomenon in an account of poverty. When poor laws were enacted all over Europe in the 16th century they were enacted not for the poor but against them. They signalled the replacement of traditional charity by a collection of oppressive instruments that were applied with increasing severity as time went by. Gradually people were locked up in the emerging spinning and weaving 'work- houses', and En-

[166] Samuel Taylor Coleridge, *The Friend. The Third landing-Place*, Essay VI, cited in Ganado & Sammut, Malta in British and French Caricature 1789–1815, 1989: vii. This book is based on caricatures in British and French papers with historical notes, giving an 'illustrated' historical account of the war scenes at the time.

glund remarks that this was a clever way of getting labour for the emerging industries. And with this came the modern notion of poverty entailing low social status, lack of power and exclusion (Englund 1991: 169).

This development is not just another illustration of the sad nuisances of the past, Englund notes. It is important in European history, because it was in this war against the threatening poor that the repressive machinery of the modern state took form. It was to a great extent out of the closed spinning and weaving houses that the modern factory emerged as a system (1991: 169). Behind this development we have the consolidation of royal power at the domestic level, with the ambition of total control, of exploiting its citizens to the full (Duby 1988: xi). One can still see legacies of this in the way social welfare is legally regulated and administered in industrialised countries. This is one explanation why economic, social and cultural rights have not been able to provide the protection they were intended to give. Their impact is further undermined by the way classical rights and liberties have been perceived and implemented.

Classical rights and liberties

One of the cornerstones in the 19th century liberal scheme was freedom of contract. This was accompanied by a requirement of strict adherence to contractual obligations, leaving no room for social equity aspects. This is perhaps best illustrated in the relation between employers and workers. Originally, labour contracts were treated under the same conditions as contracts between merchants or manufacturers and any protective legislation would have been seen as a violation of this freedom of contract. The US Supreme Court was faced with a number of cases involving an assessment of the constitutionality of protective statutes, which were seen as an arbitrary interference with the liberty of contract, which no government can legally justify in a free land.[167] This was the new setting of the industrial era, which to a considerable extent rearranged human constellations, as well as attitudes. Anna Christensen (1988) has pointed to this in her analysis of the normative structures operating in society, as representing either conflict or harmony. The conflict-prone relationship is associated with contract, and social practices associated with contractual relationships. The relationship reflecting harmony, again, represent groups of people, who assemble around "a joint venture", where the normative relationships are determined by the aim of this venture. In this setting, individual interests are subordinate to joint aims.

Historically, Christensen (1988: 39) notes, the contractual relationship emerged as a normative relationship between strangers, even enemies, between different families or competing groups. Within these groups again, the joint endeavour determined the normative relationships between its individual members. The outlook and composition of these constellations varies with time reflecting their social environment. Christensen points to how, in the patriarchal system, the notion of a joint venture was dominating, whereas rights played no essential part. The subordination of the worker in a patriarchal system was balanced with care functions. In their time, old mill societies were in their kind rather phenomenal social welfare societies with housing, health care in the work place, midwives and own schools, Christensen (1988: 40–41) observes. This aspect has often been forgotten because we have tended to see subordination without a notion of what went with it. With industrialisation, capitalism and trade unions, the patriarchal system was torn apart. The potential harmony in a status relationship was, thereby, replaced by conflict in a contractual relationship (Christensen 1988: 41). Now, my right as against

[167] Justice Harlan, in Adair v. United States, 208 UL 161, 1908, cited in Robert Hale 1952: 390.

others' became the predominant focus. And, as noted, the singular focus on freedom of contract left out any other considerations, such as, whether there was any substance to this freedom or not. In the world of work trade unions became the joint venture, through which efforts could be made to give some substance to this 'freedom' for individual workers.

The universal declaration of human rights – a new departure

The Universal Declaration of Human Rights completely inverted the old picture of sovereignty, Andò notes. Attention was shifted away from the right of the sovereign to impose his law on his subjects to a focus on the citizen's right to the recognition and respect of his / her fundamental human rights vis-à-vis the sovereign (1999: 63). As the expansion of human rights imposes ever increasing restriction on the sovereignty of states, international relations will come to be governed by principles aimed at guaranteeing an ever more dignified human existence. This is how the right to development should be understood (Andò 1999: 60).

The recognition of human rights involves a need to acknowledge that the human person is an essential point of reference both of social organisation and of public powers, as is also confirmed in many national constitutions.[168] Analysing the constitutions of different European countries, Andò points out that above all constitutional law provides the individual institutional guarantees against the abuse of power. The public status of the individual and the constitutional control of the state's powers are two keywords in a legal system, which is based on the absolute value of the individual and his / her links of solidarity with other persons. This 'personalist' character is expressed among others in the Italian, German and French constitutions (1999: 77).

[168] For an account of constitutional provisions concerning human rights in different European countries, see Andò 1999: 67–76.

The justice quality of legal regulation

I here approach law in its widest sense as the justice quality of the regulation of relations and transaction in which people are engaged.[169] The justice quality of legal arrangements can only be properly revealed if we pay attention to human beings in their real life context and to the relationships in which people stand to one another. This relational aspect is central to theories of social justice. Concepts devised by such theories can therefore assist in remedying shortcomings in the way societal matters are today legally perceived and regulated. A decisive aspect here is to make the human being a starting point, instead of laws and regulations that constitute the starting point in a legal positivist paradigm, which caters for hidden paradigms and agendas that are remnants of past orders and practices. Taking human beings as a starting point, I propose that we focus on how a person's autonomy is affected by the particular setting in which this person lives and acts. This approach also allows us to distinguish what Francis Bacon (1858, Aphorism 1, V, p. 88) has termed three fountains of injustice: mere force, a malicious ensnarement under the colour of law and harshness of the law itself (see Storlund 2002: 77). When focus is placed on a person whose autonomy is jeopardised, it will be possible to distinguish at what level we need to look for remedies. It will allow us to contrast factual situations to the constitutional provisions that today are intended to accord the human being a fundamental value around which the entire juridical system should rotate (Andò 1999: 81).

A contextual assessment of different settings and states of affairs, by which people's autonomy are affected, will also assist in doing away with the hidden paradigm of individuals as social atoms; instead it will reveal communities of interest and inter-dependencies. Some new constitutions also recognise that rights do not concern a person in isolation, but also the

[169] Galanter, Marc, Justice in many rooms, 1981: 161.

social rights of the community by means of which the person finds fulfilment. This was stressed in the Italian Constituent Assembly when the new constitution was drawn up. Andò observes that they wanted to affirm a different concept of the democratic state that ratifies the "sacred, natural, inalienable rights of the citizens in opposition to the fascist state which, by upholding reflected rights, i.e. the theory that the state is the exclusive source of rights, denied and violated human rights at their foundations."[170]

On paper we have rights – how to make them a reality?

Rights and social justice stand in a close relationship to one another. An important part of social justice consists in respecting the positive rights which people have. The most powerful instrument for achieving this end is of course the law, David Miller notes in his book Social Justice. Any socially just society must therefore include a public mechanism for specifying and protecting people's rights. It will, however, be a matter of argument how far the existing legal system, in protecting the rights that it protects, realises justice, Miller remarks. He ([1976] 1979: 77) points to the need to strike a balance between 'conservative' and 'prosthetic' justice – between the justice which preserves established rights and the justice which modifies these rights in terms of an ideal standard – a principle of desert or need.

Work to be done on many fronts

As long as legislation and practices have not been adapted to the rationale that a human rights culture represents, we operate with both hidden paradigms and agendas that I have attempted to spell out in a book To each

---

[170] Andò 1999: 83, citing La Pira, La Costituzione della Repubblica Nei Lavori Preparatori dell' Assemblea.

one's due at the borderline of work (Storlund 2002). In addition to the remnants of old orders that operate in public administrations, business and working life, we also need to pay attention to the perception of us as humans, to which Andò (1999) refers in regard to the new European constitutions, because we still to a great extent operate with an instrumental and atomised view of a human being. In order to remedy this, we need to be aware of human nature, recognising that we are not always neutral agents. We are very much the product of a cultural upbringing, which changes over time.

The following observation made by Stephen D. Hudson may summarise this. Our choices of criteria or standards themselves, are not products of pure, disinterested rational consideration, as is demanded by theory. On the contrary, they are very much products of our traditions and social experience. Built into the very patterns of our thought, there are our indices of value. Evaluation exists and changes with our cultural learning and interpersonal identification. It is this process of identification that gives us a clear sense of what constitutes 'rational human behaviour', Hudson notes.[171] In the culture that human rights has brought about 'rational human behaviour' differs from the culture deriving from sovereignty and classical rights and liberties. We are thus all involved in the process of making human rights a reality for all humans through our own perceptions, thoughts and behaviour.

Education is, of course, primordial in influencing the way we perceive things. One occasion that I will rely on for the further development of traditions, social experience and values is a seminar Ways of promoting a culture of peace held in 2003 that offered professionals from different cultures and disciplines an opportunity to critically assess traditions and social experience. The co-organiser of this seminar, Johanna Lasonen

---

[171] Cited in Thompson, Kirill, How to rejuvenate ethics 1991: 497.

(2004), (then) holder of the UNESCO chair at the University of Jyväskylä, Finland, points out that education can be considered an ethical activity, where certain values are inherently present. She relates this to the goals of internationalisation where focus seems to be on the economy and on promoting mobility rather than on human growth and values. Teachers and students live in the midst of discussions about the consequences of a global economy such as changes in working life, wars, offences against humanity, racism and environmental problems. Although internationalisation is often a goal of official educational policy, Lasonen (2004) notes that it may vary to what extent these issues are discussed and problematised in teaching – learning situations. Promoting a culture of peace is perhaps the widest possible topic allowing a multitude of aspects to be raised and contrasted. There is space for different voices reflecting particular political settings and cultures. Here are some voices that illuminate different aspects of the theme:

Emmanuel Ohene Afoakwa (2004) notes that peace is not only the absence of armed conflict, but also a dynamic set of relationships of co-existence and co-operation among and within peoples. It involves respect for the human values and a concern to provide the greatest possible well-being for all. This is threatened by armament, the great economic and social inequalities that divide humankind, and by the contempt for basic human rights and the dignity of the individual. It is only possible to achieve peace in a world where the observance of international law replaces violence, fear and injustice (2004: 69).

Thus, Afoakwa states: My concept of Culture of Peace should have the form of a broad socio-political and cultural movement that implies a global effort to change how people think and act in order to promote peace. It means transforming conflict, preventing potentially violent conflict and rebuilding peace and confidence among peoples emerging from war. It also requires specific measures and the mobilization and participation of all people and involves a profound transformation of institutional structures as well as the values, attitudes and behaviours of individuals and groups in order to address the cultural roots of violent conflicts and wars. Afoakwa stresses that the key word here is trans-disciplinarily, since peace can be threatened in many ways, from cultural to political, by people of all races, genders, ages, types of jobs and scientific disciplines. "A Culture of Peace will only succeed if based on mutual understanding and an open active attitude towards diversity." (2004: 69)

Kwasi Agyman (2004) offers another approach to the question of peace. He makes a distinction between a causal and a purposeful angle of peace. From the causal angle Agyman puts the question: What are the conditions that are inimical to having, seeking and pursuing peace?, whereas the purposeful angle is brought forth by the question: What good is it in having, seeking and pursuing peace? What are the benefits of having, seeking and pursuing peace? From these questions, Agyman notes, follows the next obvious question: What is peace? And his answer is: If there is any one word that defines peace, I dare say, it is freedom. It is freedom to be morally responsible to live a productive, happy life. Thus, it makes no difference whatsoever whether it be ignorance, arrogance or oppression; inequality, poverty or insecurity; wars, hunger, diseases or lawlessness; barbarism, tribalism, strive or colonialism; fear, lies, slavery or immorality; the definition of peace, as being free to live a morally responsible and productive life, remains the same in any of the above-cited instances, or wherever there is a lack of human dignity and moral living (2004: 23). These are causal factors that are necessary but not sufficient for peace, says Agyman. He insists that humankind must be obligated by its own interest to choose to seek and keep peace, that peace must be proactively pursued for the good of all.

As one possible way of fostering peace among peoples Agyman proposes inter- dependency. If I depend upon you, and you depend upon me for your life and welfare, it would be in each other's interest to seek and respect our respective, yet mutual, welfare. Thus, if mankind can find a way to create inter-dependency between nations, cultures, in short, between all the peoples of mankind, then such alone would obligate everyone to be each other's keeper for the mutual good of all as well as in respect of one another. Let's try this for peace-sake, it might work for mankind (2004: 23–24).

Mark Mason (2004) addresses the question of fostering a culture of peace through ethics and values in an open society. He sees justice as being prior to peace, for peace without justice is likely to be only an apparent peace that is brittle, temporary and unfair to, perhaps even oppressive of, some. Mason offers the concept of 'ethics of integrity', implying respect for the dignity of each other's. This notion requires at least that we arrange our institutions and practices to maximize the life chances of all, both in terms of the basic wherewithal for human flourishing, and in terms of opportunities for a meaningful and fulfilled life, whether this is sought in autonomy or in community (2004: 25– 26).

Mason (2004) pledges for an open society because in a closed society power is abused and corruption rots. It is in a closed society that moral responsibility, liberty, life chances, the truth, justice, respect for human rights and dignity – for life itself, are trampled on as human lives are crushed. Thus, Mason notes, we must work in whatever ways we can to develop respect for and the implementation of the Universal Declaration of Human Rights. This may involve challenging the sovereignty of the nation-state, and working at both the supra- and the sub-national level. The Universal Declaration of Human Rights needs to be justified to those who do not yet accept it as having transcultural normative reach (2004: 25–26).

In line with the above illustrations of what a culture of peace implies and requires, Andò notes that all in all the recognition of human rights is an open recognition of social transformation and of the unavoidable new human needs which it brings along. He observes that the recognition of rights must be continually updated and increased, under the pressure of the logic that started it (1999: 93–94). And this, needless to say, is an on-going process and one that defies definitions. On this score, Andò also notes that to bring about social justice and to know how to adapt the legal welfare state to such a task is an objective that cannot be defined once and for all. How social rights are to be determined, that is, how acts of distribution are to be performed, necessitates a continual rewriting of fundamental rights, which are in constant development. And, notes Andò, the wider the area covered by human rights becomes, and the more human rights and citizen's rights coincide with one another, the more indispensable the welfare state becomes, since it becomes the essential instrument to guarantee human rights (1999: 94).

The new agenda – a we paradigm

In this paper we have now travelled centuries in time and made a 180 degree change of perception, from an undifferentiated notion of sovereignty, illustrated by Malta as a colony, and the view of the equality of rights in the classical rights tradition as expressed in labour relations in the early 20th century, to the human being as a point of departure, as a logical consequence of the new human rights culture. The classical rights tradition is one expression of the economic rationale on which western legal traditions are based, viewing man as an economic individual, a homo economicus, as a subject principally involved in economic transactions. This view of a person is also reflected in all declarations of rights since the French Revolution, up till the constitutions of the post world-war II period, whereby man was seen as an individual and his freedoms as individual freedoms. In the constitutions of the post-war period, focus has changed to persons who find their fulfilment in interacting and co-operating with other people (see Andò 1999: 98).

Also, the role of the researcher has changed from an allegedly disinterested neutral observer of facts that can be scientifically verified, to a participatory one in what I call a 'we paradigm'. Because as Hudson notes, our moral practices are human ones, which could also be expressed as our human practices being moral ones. Hudson (1986: 108–109) observes that "[o]ur moral theories are about human justice, kindness, honesty, and friendship. Facts about us, and our place in nature – that for instance, we are creatures tied to and constrained by our social and evolutionary history – bear on such theories. For that very reason, our theories do not apply to God or angels. [...] any passable view of our nature will reveal the labyrinthine, knotty structure of our emotions, sentiments, needs, and feelings: what creatures like us are like and about. ... And the facts about us, as revealed through the lessons of history, and the investigations of economists, biologists, psychologists, anthropologists, sociologists, and ethnologists, support just such a view."

Furthermore, we need to pay attention to how people relate to each other, and what expectations people place on each other's conduct. Here Christensen's (1988) considerations of the normative structures, referred to above, can assist us. In the status relationship the worker enjoyed some personal autonomy in the knowledge that the employer, if he lived up to his responsibilities, provided for the necessities of life during employment. When this relationship was transformed into a contract between 'formally equal partners', this autonomy was lost, as the obligations weigh heavy on a contractual partner who is in a subordinate position, in a relationship, which easily is interpreted from a perspective of distrust.

The combination of workers into trade unions came to provide a remedy for this position of factual inequality, and now the trust was located in the collective body of workers. The collective defence and promotion of workers' interests now seemed to offer some security and thereby some autonomy for a worker, which had been lost when the care function of the employer was removed. But this collective of workers was at odds with the atomistic world-view, which the contractual approach represented, and here we have two distinct 'worlds', that are still with us, that Ferdinand Tönnies (1955) has described as *Gemeinschaft* (community) and *Gesellschaft* (association).

Hudson (1986: 110) notes that if we, like Hume and Aristotle, take the good person living the good life as the Alpha and Omega of serious moral inquiry, we need to assess the manner and extent to which the ideal can be implemented, or as Hume used to put it 'be reduced to practice'. It is only in practice that we can make sense of ethics. And this also involves the researcher. A research tradition that borrows its research methods from natural sciences assumes a status similar to that of *Gesellschaft*, an outsider. In the paradigm I suggest the researcher is as much a part of the social venture as everybody else and endowed with the same dispositions. This entails a we paradigm, where the researcher becomes a mediator between *Gesellschaft* and *Gemeinschaft*, in line with Lasonen's (2004: 11) observation about teaching being an ethical activity. A we paradigm will also reveal the factual inter-dependencies there are in different settings, to which Agyman referred.

The Dalai Lama has formulated this problem in a lucid way in his book *Ethics for the New Millennium* (2001). He notes that the sharp distinction we make between the self and others is largely something we have learned to see in that way. It is possible, he says, to enlarge our perception of ourselves in such a way that we define our interests in relation to others. As a person's interests can only be defined in relation to the interests of others, we can see that our own interest and that of others are intimately combined, and at a deeper level they will converge. And as our interests are linked, we are confined to ethics as the unavoidable meeting point between my wish for happiness and yours (Dalai Lama 2002: 54–55). Contrary to natural catastrophes, those caused by human beings, such as wars, crime, violence of different kinds, corruption, poverty, failure in one's duty, betrayal and social, political and economic injustices are all consequences of negative human behaviour. Who are responsible, The Dalai Lama asks and he answers that there is not a single social group or other that does not contribute to the daily harvest of bad news. And contrary to natural catastrophes, we can solve the problems we cause, as they are all basically ethical problems (Dalai Lama 2002: 34).

Conclusion

If we were able to live up to The Dalai Lama's view of interdependence, the distinction between Gemeinschaft and Gesellschaft, as pictured by Tönnies, would dissolve. Also, the inter-dependency Agyman advocated for would become visible, because it is there. Consequently, in the same vein as public power needs to adapt to the new culture of human rights, so should also the ethical aspects that this new culture involves, require a new kind of behaviour by the business community. This calls, above all, for a differentiated view of property and transactions that is by no means a new phenomenon. So back again to Aristotle who drew attention to the need for a differentiation between two kinds of property, one that is needed for the household economy, to enable a good life, and the other that is accumulated for its own sake. (Aristotle [1981] 1987: 81).

One big challenge, therefore, is to restrain the accumulation of property for its own sake, in favour of household economies that will allow people to live a better life, allowing them to act as morally responsible agents. The 2013 Human Development Report also calls for a critical look at global governance institutions to promote a fairer, more equal world. It points to out-dated structures, which do not reflect the new economic and geopolitical reality. A new era of partnership is called for with greater transparency and accountability. The report highlights the role of global civil society in advocating for this and for greater decision-making power for those most directly affected by global challenges, who are often the poorest and most vulnerable.

Video from the opening of the seminar Ways of promoting a culture of peace[172]

[172] https://www.youtube.com/watch?v=bPeDEzgXghc&list=PLIYhW8k82efvzVw14l-TVzx2+GSGGj9v

BIBLIOGRAPHY

Acton, H.B. (ed.). *Mill, John Stuart, Utilitarianism, On Liberty and Considerations of Representative Government.* London: Everyman's Library, 1984.

Adams, James Tuslow. *Our Business Civilization, Some Aspects of American Culture.* Boni Books, 1929.

Agyman, Kwasi. *The Causal and Purposeful Angles of Peace, (abstract) Working papers.* Lasonen, Johanna and Horiuchi, Tokiko , (eds.). Espoo, Finland, 13-14 June 2003.

Andreski, Stanislav (ed.). *Max Weber, Protestantism and the Spirit of Capitalism.* London, New York: Routledge, 1983.

Andò, Salvo. "The welfare state as a legal obligation." *Mediterranean Journal of Human Rights* (1999): Vol. 3 No. 1. 77–120.

Antonopolous, Andreas. *The Internet of Money Volume Two.* Merkle Bloom LLC, Kindle Edition, n.d.

Aristotle. *[1981] 1987. The Politics.* Trans. ., revised and re-presented by Trevor J. SAUNDERS. T.A SINCLAIR. Harmondsworth: Penguin Classics, n.d.

Asplund, Johan. *Essä om Gemeinschaft och Gesellschaft.* Göteborg: Bokförlaget Korpen, 1991.

Attard, Joseph. *Britain and Malta. The Story of an Era.* Malta: Publishers Enterprises Group (PEG) Ltd., 1988.

Avaaz.org, The world in action, . n.d. <http://www.avaaz.org/en/ >.

Ball, Philip. *Critical mass, how one thing leads to another.* UK : Arrow Books, 2005.

Barnes, Jonathan. *Aristotle, Past Masters,* . Oxford, UK : Oxford University Press, 1982 / 1985.

Bauman, Zygmunt. *Det individualiserade samhället* . Göteborg: Daidalos, 2002.

Benjamin, Paul. "Who Needs Labour Law? Defining the Scope of Labour Protection, in Labour Law in an Era of Globalisation." Conaghan, Joanne, Fischl, Richard Michael, Klare, Karl (eds.). *Labour law in an Era of Globalization, Transformative Practices & Possibilities.* Oxford: Oxford University Press, 2004.

Birnbaum, Simon. "Universell grundinkomst och den svenska välfärdsstaten: Mot en ny generation av inkomsträttigheter?" *Statsvetenskaplig tidskrift* 4 (2005): 323 - 350.

Boothman, Catherine. " The Experiences of the Culture 2000 Programme as a tool for Unifying Europe - Expectations for the Future, in." *ECA, Artists sharing without Frontiers.* 2003.

Braudel, Ferdnand. *The Wheels of Commerce* . London: Collins, 1982.

Capaldi, Nicholas. *John Stuart Mill. A Biography.* Cambridge: Cambridge University Press, 2004.

Castells, Manuel and Yuko Aoyama. "Paths Towards the Informational Society: Employment Structure in G-7 Countries. 1920-1990." ." *International Labour Review , 1: 5-33.* 1994: 5-33.

Castells, Manuel. *Nätverkssamhällets framväxt, Informationsåldern, Ekonomi, samhälle och kultur, Band 1.* Uddevalla: Daidalos, 1999.

—. *The Information Age, Economy, Society and Culture, volume II.* UK, USA: Wiley-Blackwell, 1997 / 2010, 2nd edition.

—. *The Rise of the Network Society.* UK, USA: Wiley-Blackwell , 1996 / 2010 2nd edition.

Castells, Manuel, Aoyama, Yuko. "An empirical assessment of the informational society: Employment and occupational structures of G- 7 countries, 1920–2000,." *International Labour Review, Vol. 141* 2002.

Champagne, Phil. *Bitcoin. The Book Of Satoshi: The Collected Writings of Bitcoin Creator Satoshi Nakamoto.* e53 Publishing, LLC. Kindle Edition, 2014.

Chopra, Deepak and Mlodinow, Leonard. *War of the Worldviews: Where*

Science and Spirituality Meet - and Do Not. New York: Three Rivers Press, 2012.

Christensen, Anna. "Konflikt eller harmoni. Två normativa strukturer, Politisk filosofi. Rättigheter." filosofi, Sällskapet för politisk. *Politisk filosofi. Rättigheter.* Stehag: Symposion Bokförlag, 1988. 37–70.

Christensen, Anna. "Wage Labour as Social Order and Ideology." *Shifts in Values within Swedish Society.* The Secretariat for Future Studies, 1984.

Cliché, Danielle, Mitchell, Ritva, Wiesand, Andreas Joh., Eds. *Pyramid or Pillars, Unveiling the Status of Women in Arts and Media Professions in Europe.* Bonn: ARCult Media, 2000.

Committee on Economic, Social and Cultural Rights. "Thirty-sixth session, Geneva Item 5 of the provisional agenda General Comment No. 20." The Right to Social Security (article 9) Rapporteurs: Ms. Maria Virginia Bras Gomes & Eibe Riedel, E/C. 12/GC/20/CRP. 1. 1– 19 May 2006.

Conaghan, Joanne, Fischl, Richard Michael, Klare, Karl (eds.). *Labour law in an Era of Globalization, Transformative Practices & Possibilities.* Oxford: Oxford University Press, 2004.

Cooper, David E. "Beauty and the Excercise of Virtue." Buttigieg, Jean, De Lucca, Jean-Paul, Mangion, Claude, eds. *A Philosoper at Large, Essays Commemorating Peter Serracino Inglott.* Paola: BDL Publishing, 2013.

Cooper, David E. Ed. *Aestehetics: The Classic Readings.* Ed. Crispin Sartwell Advisory Editors: Peter Lamarque. Great Britain: Blackwell Publishers, 1997 / 2000.

Council of Europe, Steering Committee for Culture. "National Cultural Policy in Malta, 2002 ." *CDCULT (2002) 14A-résumé* . 20 September 2002.

Cremona, J.J. *The Maltese Constitution and Constitutional History since*

1813. Malta: Publishers Enterprises Group (PEG) Ltd., [1994] 1997.

De Bono, Edward. "Foreword Malta A Second Collection of Tales and Narratives ." Attard, Robert. Gutenberg Press, Malta,. Edward de Bono Foundation, 2001.

De Swaan, A. *In Care of the Stat, Health Care, Education and Welfare in Europe and the USA in the Modern Era*. London: Polity Press, 1998.

Dean, Kathryn. *Capitalism and Citizenship, The Impossible Partnership*. 2003.

Dediu, Dan. "The Influence of Financing Strategies on Contemporary Arts." 2003.

Demarco, Richard. "Kunst = Kapital, Art = Wealth." *Adam Smith Lecture 1995*. 1995. Fife College of Further and Higher Education.

Dracodaidis, Philip D. "Building Cultural Strategies for the Enlargement Countries - Myth or Reality." *Report from a conference in Bucharest, Romania, September, 2003*. Europeam Council of Artists, 2003.

Duby, Georges. "Preface." Ariès, Philippe & Duby, Georges. *A History of Private Life II, Revelations of the Medieval World*. Cambridge, Massachusetts: Harvard University Press., 1988. ix–xiii.

Elisa P. Reis, Moore, Mick. *Elite Perceptions of Poverty and Inequality, National Studies in Poverty Research*. Series: International Studies in Poverty Research. Zed Books, 2005.

Encyclopaedia Britannica. 1997.

Englund, Peter. "Förflutenhetens landskap. Historiska essäer." Stockholm: Atlantis, 1991.

Eräsaari, Leena. "New Public Management on julkisen sektorin vääryyksien isä." Heine, Tuula & Lahti, Markku (Eds.). *Vääryyskirja*. Vammala: Vammalan kirjapaino, 2006.

ERICart. *Creative Europe*. n.d. <http://www.creativeurope.info>.

Eriksson, Lars D. "Socialrätten - I kris eller utveckling?" *Kritik, moral och rätt.* Helsinki, 1992.

Eriksson, Lars D. "Mina metoder, ." Häyhä, Juha (ed). *Minun metodini.* Porvoo: Werner Söderström, lakitieto, 1997.

European Commission. *Culture, the Cultural Industries and Employment.* Staff Working Paper, SEC (98) 837. Brussels, 14 May 1998. working paper.

European Council of Artists. "Artists Sharing Without Frontiers, Networking in the Enlargement Process." *Report from a conference in Bucharest, Romania.* 2003.

Fahlbeck, Reinhold. "Ett revolutionerat arbetsliv? Informationssamhället och arbetslivets omvandling ." *Juridisk tidskrift,* NR 4 (1997 - 98).

—. "Flexibility - Potentials and Pitfalls for Labour Law." *General Report presented at the International Academy of Comparative Law, in Bristol, England.* Juristförlaget i Lund, 1998.

—. *Informationssamhället och arbetslivets omvandling.* Vol. 4. Juridisk Tidskrift, 1997-98.

Fahlbeck, Reinhold. "Towards a Revolutionised Working Life." *Liber Amicorum, Tatashi Hanami.* 2000.

Fieldhouse, D.K. "Colonialism 1870–1945. An Introduction." London: Weidenfeld and Nicolson, 1981.

Finnish Citizen Participation Policy Programme (Prime Minister's Office) . Helsinki, 2003-2007.

Florida, Richard. *The Rise of the Creative Class And How It's transforming Work, Leisure, Community and Everyday Life.* USA: Basic Books, 2002.

Gadamer, Hans-Georg. "The Relevance of the Beautiful and other essays." Bernasconi, Robert (ed.). Cambridge University Press, (1986) 1995.

Galanter, Marc. "Justice in many rooms." Cappelletti, M. (ed.). *Access to justice in the welfare state.* Alphen aan den Rijn: Sijthoff; Stuttgart: Klett-Cotta; Bruxelles: Bruylant; Firenze: Le Monnier, 1981. 147–

181.

Ganado, Albert & Sammut, Joseph C. *Malta in British and French Caricature 1789–1815*. Valletta: Said International Ltd., 1989.

Gould, Carol V. *Rethinking democracy*. Cambridge: Cambridge University Press, 1988.

"Guidelines for Member States employment policies for the year 2001." EU Council Decision, 19 January 2001 .

Hagfors, Robert and Kajanoja, Jouko. *The Welfare State, Inequality and Social Capital*. Paper presented at the ESRC Social Contexts and Responses to Risk Network (SCARR) Conference on "Risk & Rationalities" . Queens' College, Cambridge, 29–31 March 2007.

Hale, Robert. *Freedom through Law. Public Control of Private Governing*. New York:: Fower, 1952.

Hall, Stephen. "Wisdom, From Philosophy to Neuroscience." New York: Vintage Books, 2011.

Harauer, Robert, Mayerhofer, Elisabeth, Mokre, Monika. "'Thanks for Playing Anyway'." *Pyramids and Pillars*. 2002.

Harju, Aaro. - *Järjestötyö on vaativaa ammattityötä,(Organisiational work is demanding professional work), Editorial, 31.05.2006* . Kansalaisfoorumi Verkkolehti, 2006.

—. - *Kansalalisyhteiskunta ja markkinat, Editorial 7.11.2005.* Kansalaisfoorumi, Verkkolehti, 2005.

Harju, Aaro and Backberg-Edvards, Kristiina. *New Work project - Enhancing employment. A research and development project, in , Towards new work, 2001* . Helsinki, 2001.

Harju, Aaro. "Editorial, Järjestötyö on vaativaa ammattityötä (Organisiational work is demanding professional work) ." *Kansalaisfoorumi, Verkkolehti* (31.05.2006).

—. *Yhteisellä asialla - Kansalaistoiminta ja sen haasteet (Joint venture, civil activities and their challenges) 2003* . Vantaa: Kansanvalistusseura, n.d.

Heikka, Mikko,. "Jäähyväiset täystyöllisyydelle." *Suomen kuvalehti 37* 2000.

Heiner, Michel. "Global Basic Income and its Contribution to Human Development and Fair Terms of Global Economic Co-Operation: A Political-Economic Outlook." *Congress of the Basic Income Earth Network*. University College, Dublin, Ireland, June 20- 21, 2008.

Hellman, Gunilla. "Kulturindustrin som investeringsområde." *Nya roller på upplysta platser, Finlandssvensk kulturpolitisk översikt*. Svenska kulturfonden, 2001.

Herle, Anita. *Thinking about other cultures, Philosopher's Zone, Radio Australia* . 11 September 2010. <http://www.abc.net.au/rn/philosopherszone/stories/2010/3004751.htm#transcript>.

Hudson, Stephen D. *Human Character and Morality. Reflections from the History of Ideas*. Boston: Routledge & Kegan Paul, 1986.

"Hyvä elämä – vastavoima kvartaalitaloudelle , , , ." Harju, Aaro (ed.). *Kansalaistoimintaan kätketty aare*. Espoo: Sivistysliitto Kansalaisfoorumi, Painotalo Casper, 2007.

ILO. *Homework, Report V (1)*. International Labour Conference, 82nd Session, . Geneva, 1995.

—. *Part-time work, Report V(1)*. Report V(1), International Labour Conference 80th Session . Geneve, 1993.

Jackson, Ross. *Occupy World Street, A global roadmap for radical economic and political reform*. Totnes, Devon: Green Books, 2012.

Jackson, Tim. *Prosperity without growth? The transition to a sustainable economy*. 2009. the Sustainable Development Commission. <http://www.sd-commission.org.uk/>.

Jeffery, Mark. "Part-Time Work, 'Atypical Work' and attempts to Regulate it." *Industrial Law Journal* September 1998.

Kameeta, Z, Haartmann, C. Hartmann, D. Jauch, H. "Promoting employment and decent conditions of work for all – Towards a good practice model in Namibia." United Nations Commission for Social Development, 45th session, 7–16 February 2007. n.d.

Karhunen, Paula. *Statistics on the number of Finnish Artists.* Facts and Figures , 1/2002.

Kari, Matti, Markwort, Jari. *Kolmas sektori EU:ssa ja eräissä euroopan maissa* . RAY:n avustustoiminnan raportteja 14 . Helsinki: Painotalo Miktor , 2004.

Kauhanen, Anna-Liina. "Luova luokka palaa loppuun." *Helsingin Sanomat, Talous* (4.9.2005).

KEA European Affairs. *The Economy of Culture in Europe, Study prepared for the European Commission, (Directorate-General for Education and Culture).* 2006.

Kennet, M. "An Introduction to Progressive Economics." *Harvard College Economics Review* 2008.

Keynes, John Maynard. "Economic Possibilities for our Grandchildren." *Essays in Persuasion.* New York: W. W. Norton & Co., 1930.

"Konst är möjligheter, (Swedish Summary) Finnish cultural policy program ." Helsinki, 2002. www.minedu.fi .

Korver, Ton. "Reflexive labour law and adaptability." Unpublished, December 2001.

Kukkonen, Pirjo. *Från konst till vetenskap, Begreppet vetenskap och dess sråkliga uttryck i svenskan under 400 år.* Helsingfors: Meddelanden från institutionen för nordiska språk vid Helsingfors universitet, 1989.

"Kunstenaarswijzer ." herfst 2000.

Laan, Medy C. van der. "More than the sum, Cultural Policy Letter 2004-2007." *presented by the Dutch State Secretary of Education, Culture and Science* . 3 November 2003. ACB/2003/51730.

Lama, Dalai. *Ethics for the New Millennium.* New York: Riverhead Books: Richters, 2001.

—. *Etik för ett nytt millennium.* Trans. Översättare Alf Galvensjö. Avesta:

Richters, 2001.

Lång, Fredrik. *Mitt liv som Pythagoras* . Pieksämäki: Schildts, RT-Print Oy, 2005.

—. *Bild och tanke, Om det kategoriala seendets genesis.* Esbo: Förlaget Draken, 1999.

Lasonen, Johanna (ed.). "Cultures of Peace. From Words to Deeds. The Espoo Seminar Proceedings 13–14 June 2003. 23–24." *[Ways of Promoting a Culture of Peace.* . n.d.

Lasonen, Johanna. "Educating People in a Culture of Peace. [Abstract.]. June 2003. 11–13. [Ways of Promoting a Culture of Peace. Joint Seminar, 13–14 June 2003, Espoo, Finland.]." *Cultures of Peace. From Words to Deeds, Seminar Proceedings.* Ed. Johanna , ed, Lasonen. Espoo, 2004 /2004.

Lee, Eddy. "Globalization and employment: Is anxiety justified?" *International Labour Review, vol 135, No 5* 1996.

MacIntyre, Alasdair. *After Virtue, a study in moral theory.* London : Duckwotrth, (1981) 1982.

Maria Virginia Bras Gomes & Eibe Riedel, Rapporteurs. 1– 19 May. Committee on Economic, Social and Cultural Rights, Thirty-sixth session May 2006. Item 5 of the provisional agenda General Comment No. 20 The Right to Social Security (article 9). Geneva, 2006.

Marklund, Staffan, Svallfors, Stefan. *Dual Welfare - Segmentation and Work Enforcement in the Swedish Welfare System.* Umeå: Research Reports from the Department of Sociology, University of Umeå, No 94, 1987.

Marsden D. and Stephenson H., (Eds.). *Labour Law and Social Insurance in the New Economy: A Debate on the Supiot Report.* London, UK: Centre for Economic Performance, London School of Economics and Political Science, 2001.

Maslow, A. H. "A Theory of Human Motivation." *Psychological Review,*

50(4) (1943): 370-396.

Mason, Mark. "Ethics and Values in an Open Society: Fostering a Culture of Peace. [Abstract]." Ed. Johanna (ed.), Cultures of Peace. From Words to Deeds. The Espoo Seminar ProceedingsWays of Promoting a Culture of Peace. Joint Seminar Lasonen. Espoo, Joint Seminar, 13–14 June 2003, Espoo, Finland.

Michalos, A. C. and Kahlke, P. M. "Impact of Arts-Related Activities on the Perceived Quality of Life." *Social Indicators Research* November 2008.

"Millennium Development Goals: A Status Report. UNDP. Human Development Report . ." 2013. Press release.

Miller, David. *Social Justice*. Oxford: Clarendon Press, [1976] 1979.

Molnár, Ferenc. "The Arts and the State." *The New Hungarian Quarterly,* 1979.

Monbiot, George. "The Age of Consent: A Manifesto for a New World Order ." 2003, E-Book 2010.

"National Cultural Policy in Malta, 2002." Council of Europe, Steering Committee for Culture, CDCULT (2002) 14A-résumé 20 September, 2002.

Ohene, Afoakwa Emmanuel. "Peace – well-being for all. [Abstract.] In:." *From Words to Deeds The Espoo Seminar Proceedings 13–14 June 2003. 69. Ways of Promoting a Culture of Peace. Joint Seminar*. Ed. Lasonen Johanna (ed.) Cultures of Peace. Espoo, Finland, 2004. Print.

Putman, Robert D. *Bowling Alone, The Collapse and Revival of American Community*. New York,: Simon & Schuster, , 2000.

Raiskio, Teuvo. "Oppressive evaluation at the borderline of work in post-war Finland,." Harju, Aaro and Backberg-Edvards, Kristiina (eds.). *Towards new work*. Helsinki, 2001.

Rawls, John. *A Theory of Justice*. Oxford: Oxford University Press, (1972), 1978.

"Reflexive Potentials in Industrial Relations and the Law - Collective dismissal: An Illustration ." Rogowski, Ralf, Wilthagen, Ton (eds.). *Reflexive Labour Law.* Deventer: Kluwer , 1994.

Reinikainen, Jouni. "Social rättvisa per medborgarlön? Den egalitära liberalismen i miljöpartiets distributiva ideal,." *Statsvetenskaplig tidskrift 2005 / 4* 2005: 351 - 376.

Reis, Elisa P. "Poverty and Inequality in the Eyes of the Elites." *United Nations University, UNU Wider, World Institute for Development Economics Research.* 12-13 June 2009.

Reis, Elisa P., Moore, Mick. *Elite Perceptions of Poverty and Inequality National Studies in Poverty Research.* Zed Books, 2005.

Rensujeff, Kaija. *Taiteilijan asema. Raportti työstä ja tulonmuodostuksesta eri taiteenaloilla.* Helsinki: Taiteen keskustoimikunnan julkaisuja no 27, 2003.

Rifkin, Jeremy. "The Empathic Civilization: The Race to Global Consciousness in a World in Crisis." *http://www.huffingtonpost.com/jeremy-rifkin, accessed 18.6.20* (n.d.).

—. *The End of Work, The Decline of the Global Labor Force and the Dawn of the Post-Market Era.* New York, USA: G.P. Putman's Sons, 1995.

—. *The Global Environmental Crisis, The Path to Sustainable Development* . (http://www.foet.org/lectures/lecture-global-environmental-crisis.htm accessed 4.6.12. n.d.

—. *The Third Industrial Revolution: How Lateral Power is Transforming Energy, the Economy, and the World,* . Palgrave Macmillan, 2011.

—. *The Zero Marginal Cost Society, The Internet of Things, The Collaborative Commons, and the Eclipse of Capitalism* . New York, USA: Palgrave Macmillan, 2014.

Robertson, James. *Future Money, Breakdown or Breakthrough?* . Green Books, 2012.

—. *Future work. Jobs, self-employment and leisure after the industrial age.*

http://www.jamesrobertson.com/books.htm, 1985 / 2006.

—. "Sharing the Value of Common Resources, Citizen's Income in a Wider Context, www.jamesrobertson.com." 2009.

Romppainen, Esko. ", Järjestöt yleishyödyllisiä yhteisöjä vain tulosvastuisia palvelujen tuottajia ja valtion/kuntien renkejä. ." *Kansalaisyhteiskuntafoorumi 25.5.2005.* . n.d.

Rowson, Jonathan & McGilchrist , Iain. "Divivded Brain, Divided World. Why the best Part of us Struggles to be Heard." 2013. 2016. <www.thersa.org>.

Sadurski, Wojciech. *Giving Desert Its Due, Social Justice and Legal Theory.* Dordrecht: D Reidel Publishing Co, 1985.

Schane, Scott. *The Costly Myths That Entrepreneurs, Investors and Policy Makers Live By* . New Heaven & London: Yale University Press/, 2008 .

Segers, Leon J.J. "Basic Income and the perverted Global Labour Market." *Basic Income Earth Network Congress.* Munich, Germany, 2012.

Shrinivasan, Rukmini. *Social insurance is not for the Indian open economy of the 21st century, https://basicincome.org/news/2012/01/interview-social-insurance-is-not-for-the-indian-open-economy-of-the-21st-century/.* January 30 2012. 2011.

Southgate, Beverly. *Postmodernism in History. Fear or Freedom?* . 2003.

Standing, Guy. *A Precariat Charter, From denizens to citizens.* London, UK, New York, USA: Bloomsbury Academic, 2014.

—. *The Corruption of Capitalism: Why Rentiers Thrive and Work Does Not Pay.* Biteback publishing, 2016.

—. *The Precariat: The New Dangerous Class.* London, UK, New York, USA: Bloomsbury Academic, 2011.

—. *Work after Globalisation, Building Occupational Citizenship* . UK, Northampton, USA: Edward Elgar Cheltenham, 2009.

Stiglitz, J. E., Sen, A, Fitoussi, J-P. *Measurement of Economic Performance and Social Progress.* 2008.

Stiglitz, Joseph. "The global crisis, social protection and jobs." *International Labour Review* 2009.

—. "The global crisis, social protection and jobs (2009),." *International Labour Review* 2009.

Storlund, Vivan. "A global basic income - compensation and investment." *unpublished* (2009).

Storlund, Vivan. "Art the key to a transition from HR to HB - from human resources to human beings." Pogacnik, Miha - Schatz, Roland (Eds.). *A journey of Exploration: Composing Europe.* Bonn: InnoVatio Verlag, 2004. 180-195.

Storlund, Vivan. "Artistic Work - A Precursor of Work in IT Society." Nyström, Birgitta, Westregård, Annamaria, Vogel, Hans-Heinrich (Eds.). *Liber Amicorum Reinhold Fahlbeck.* Ed. Westergard, Annamaria, Vogel, Hansheinrich Nyström Birgitta. Lund: Juristförlaget I Lund, 2005. 543-572.

—. *Basic income and the value of work.* 2012. <http://www.bien2012.org/sites/default/files/paper_150_en.pdf>.

Storlund, Vivan. "Basic Income: How it Fits the Policy Framework for Green Jobs." Rizzo, Saviour (ed). *Green Jobs from a Small State Perspective. Case studies from Malta.* Brlgium: Green European Foundation, 2011.

—. *Civil society – Conditions for an active citizenship.* Espoo, Finland: A conceptual study for the project Conditions for an active citizenship, Experiences of civil activities at Pappilantie, Espoo, 2006.

Storlund, Vivan. "Human rights update - from sovereignty to coexistence (2003 /2015)." Hartama-Heinonen, Ritva & Kukkonen, Pirjo. *Pax.* Helsinki, 2015. 107-121.

Storlund, Vivan. "Hyvä elämä – vastavoima kvartaalitaloudelle." Aaro

Harju, (ed.). *Kansalaistoimintaan kätketty aare* . Espoo: Sivistysliitto Kansalaisfoorumi Painotalo Casper, 2007. 26-33.

—. *Kansalaisvaikuttaminen totta vai tarua. Ruohonjuuritason arviointi Espoon Pappilantiellä.* Helsinki : Kirja kerrallaan, 2007.

—. "Konsten har mycket att ge näringslivet ." *Forum för ekonomi och teknik* (2000): Nr 6.

—. *Public power versus industrial democracy - the case of public employees.* Turku: Licentiate thesis, University of Turku, Finland, 1992.

Storlund, Vivan. "Reflexive Potentials in Industrial Relations and the Law - Collective dismissal: An Illustration." Ralf Rogowski, Ton Wilthagen (eds.). *Reflexive Labour Law*, , . Kluwer, 1994.

Storlund, Vivan. "Time to giva Artists their Due - A Matter of Perception." Mercieca, Simon (Ed.). *Mediterranean Seacapes, Proceedings of an international Conference, Navigation du Savoir Project 2004.* Valletta, Malta: Malta University Publishers Ltd., 2006. 309-318.

—. *To each one's due at the borderline of work - Toward a theoretical framework for economic, social and cultural right.* Helsinki: Yliopistopaino, 2002.

—. "To each one's due at the borderline of work. Toward a theoretical framework for economic, social and cultural rights, disputation lektio." *JFT, Tidskrift utgiven av Juridiska Föreningen i Finland* 2003.

—. "Trade union rights – what are they?" Turku, 1992. Licentiate thesis, University of Turku.

Streeten, Paul. "Hunger." Friggieri, Joe & Busuttil, Salvino (eds.). *Interfaces. Essays in philosophy and bordering areas in honour of Peter Serracino Inglott.* Malta: University of Malta., 1997. 153–164.

Supiot, Alain. "Law and Labour, A World Market of Norms? ." *New Left Review 39* May June 2006: 109-121.

—. "Possible Europes, Interview by Padis, Marc-Oliver." *New Left Review* (May - June 2009): 57-65.

Tönnies, Ferdinand. *Community and Association (Gemeinshaft und Gesellschaft)*. London: Routledge & Kegan Paul LTD, 1955.

Tarasti, Eero. *Existential Semiotics*. Indiana University Press, 2000.

Taylor, Charles. "Identitet, frihet och gemenskap." Grimen, Harald. *Politisk-filosofiska texter i urval*. Göteborg: Daidalos, 1995.

The Ecovaproject . n.d. <http://www.ecovaproject.org/ >.

The New Economic Foundation, nef. *The Happy Planet Index* . n.d. 11 November 2012. <http://www.neweconomics.org/projects/happy-planet-index >.

The Renaissance project . n.d. <http://therenaissanceproject.com/ >.

Theodorescu, Razvan. "European Identity, Regional /National Identities and the Arts." ECA, Artists sharing without Frontiers, 2003.

Thompson, Kirill Ole. "How to rejuvenate ethics." *Philosophy of East & West* 4 October 1991: 493–513.

Tuslow, Adams, James. *Our Business Civilization, Some Aspects of American Culture*. Boni Books, 1929.

Tuula Helne & Markku Lahti, toim. *Vääryyskirja*. 2006.

"UNDP. Human Development Report." 2003.

Van Parijs, Philippe. "A Basic Income for All. If you really care about freedom, give people an unconditional income, net version of an article published in the (2000) ." 2000.

Varoufakis, Yanis. *And The Weak Suffer What They Must?, Europe, Austerity and the Threat to Global Stability*. 2016.

Waring, M. "Towards a Gender Perspective of the National Budget ." *Introductory statement, African Regional Seminar on the National Budget, 22 - 24 May* 2000.

Weisbrod, Burton A. "The Nonprofit Economy ." 1991.

Wellman, Carl. "Legal Rights ." *Uppsala skolan och efter, Filosofiskt symposium*. Uppsala , 1978.

"Wet Inkomensvoorziening Kunstenaars (Wik)." n.d.

Widerquist, Karl. *Property and the Power to Say No: A Freedom-Based Argument for Basic Income.* Oxford, UK: Doctoral thesis: the University of Oxford, 2006.

Wilkinson, R., Pickett, K. "The Spirit Level, Why Equality is Better for Everyone." 2010.

Williams, Lucy A. "Beyond Labour Law's Parochialism: A Re-envisioning of the Discourse of Redistribution Labour law in an Era of Globalization, Transformative Practices & Possibilities,." Conaghan Johanna, Fischl, Richard Michael, Klare, Karl, (Eds.)). Oxford: Oxford University Press, 2002.

Wilthagen, Ton,. *'Flexicurity' reflexivity in national and European systems of labour law and industrial relations* . n.d.

Wolgast, Elizabeth H. *The Ethics of an Artificial Person: lost responsibility in professions and organisations.* Stanford: Stanford University Press, 1992.

Zetterman, J. *De får lön - för att vara medborgare, 21.11.2008,* . 21 11 2008. <http://www.dagen.se/dagen/Article.aspx?ID=160382>.

INDEX